Muslim Women in Kerala

Muslim Women in Kerala
Tradition vs. Modernity

K.K.N. Kurup
E. Ismail

Maulana Abul Kalam Azad Institute of Asian Studies, Kolkata

SHIPRA

Price: Rs. 750; US$ 37.50

ISBN: 978-81-7541-755-7

First Published in India in 2014

Muslim Women in Kerala: Tradition vs. Modernity

Published by:
SHIPRA PUBLICATIONS
H.O.: LG 18-19, Pankaj Central Market, Patparganj,
I.P. Ext., Delhi-110092, Tel: 91-11-2223 5152, 2223 6152
Br.Off.: 4617/18, Ansari Road, Darya Ganj,
New Delhi-110002, Tel: 9650028065, 9810522367
E-mail: info@shiprapublications.com
www.shiprapublications.com

Preface

Muslim women suffer discrimination, not only in our country, but throughout the world due to several socio-economic and political factors beyond their reach. The issue becomes all the more grave that it is intertwined with women's human rights and the Shariah, that over powers everything. The quest for Muslim women's rights has become a theme in the Conference in Washington in 1994, followed by the UN World Conference on women at Beijing in 1995, particularly giving thrust to the condition of Muslim Women and to identify their problems. The general argument often comes in connection with the rights of Muslim women is that they do not want rights based on western concepts which are used as weapons of cultural imperialism and that which may possibly injure the rights that which they already have. It is believed that Islam provides some basic elements of human rights to be required for a gender-just society.

Being a part of the Indian sub-continent, Muslim women in Kerala formed a heterogeneous cultural group having their own vertical and horizontal division by way of following the traditional Islamic law in the premise of traditional and customary cultural traits. Inspite of these dichotomous divisions found in the life of Muslim women in Kerala, an additional element of a Pan-Islamic core also could be seen added in recent years. In an academic dialogue, all such factors concerning women have to be addressed in the light of human rights and their negation to a segment of them in the background of resource sharing and capacity building.

This study, while aims to understand the dynamics of Shariah on Muslim women, examines the various mechanisms through which they could be integrated to the socio-economic ethos of a multi-cultural and pluralistic society as that of Kerala. The study further proposes to a re-evaluation of the existing law prevalent among the Muslims and a re-reading of whatever tenets available in the Quran and Sunnah to avoid the miserable plight of their women. It also demands the urgent attention of intellectuals, religious scholars and activists to a review and rearrangement of the laws in accordance with the human rights and privileges possible in a democratic system, still believing that the proper implementation of religious laws could not in any way contradict with the laws of the land. This will also be an answer to the oft-repeated question why the people all over the world debate only Muslim women and their issues.

The theme, the Muslim women in the post independent era in Kerala, is a matter of pivotal importance for they are the worst sufferers, not on account on any external intervention, but due to the socio-religious compulsions, from within, which make them marginalized. Moreover, these issues of women have been evoked up on by the revivalists as a religious problem rather than a socio-economic and cultural problem. Therefore, the study exclusively focuses to such a dimension where ethno-social constructs are allowed to preponderate over faith to the cause of liberalism and human rights.

In evaluating and presenting a topic like this, what prompted us most is the pitiable condition of Muslim women in Kerala who are marginalized and oppressed by forces both internal and external. To make them aware and empower, great efforts have to be made by social workers, intellectuals and reformers, specially identifying girl children and women who are educationally and socially backward. In spite of the socio-economic progress being made in the country, why the issues regarding Muslim women are still not properly addressed or solved is a question to be answered. While pondering on this aspect, we could realise that this is not merely a question of gender discrimination in a class of women, but of matters related to socio-religious dimensions.

Our earnest desire to work upon such a lively theme has been materialised when we could get a fellowship from Maulana Abul Kalam Azad Institute of Asian Studies, Kolkata, to carry out the project. We are indebted to the academics and administrators of the institute who have taken great concern and curiosity to bringout this volume in the present mould.

We thank profusely Prof. R. Devamalini, Managing Director, Malabar Institute for Research and Development, Vatakara (Calicut), for her bountiful support in the pursuit of the project. We also thank Mrs. A.N. Rejani, Vismaya Computers, Puduppanam, Vatakara, for the completion of the DTP work on time.

Since the theme is contemporaneous, our effort is to collect the material by interviews, field work and partially with the help of providing questionnaire. We are thankful to all who have generously extended their support and spending their valuable time for response and making themselves available for our demands and disturbances. Importantly we should register our grateful thoughts and remembrances to those women, though mute and voiceless, who expressed their feelings and emotions through their faces and eyes, which are more meaningful rather than words.

Dr. K.K.N. Kurup
Prof. E. Ismail

Contents

Introduction

The position of women in Islam has always been the subject of controversy among scholars and laymen alike especially in the context of its responses with the contact of western ideologies. It is still a live issue capable of generating great passion and heated discussion for those who seek gender equality with an objective and democratic approach. Recent investigation on society and gender analysis often leads to new dimensions of cultural diversifications of the World. Scholars on women studies mostly rely on traditionally known factors and rarely on contemporary premises of kinship for their arguments. But there are some who give due weightage to the role of women in the whole process of social formation with a bearing on generation of resources, distribution and consumption. Muslim women constitute more than half of the human resource of the Islamic world. Therefore their role to the over all growth of the Muslim world is very significant as an academic and pragmatic research.

Being seen as structurally and attitudinally different from the rest of societies, women in the Islamic society of Kerala also is to be analysed and studied, in this context with a rational approach. Religion still persists on that society as a canon and a canopy. This singularity, apart from its structural distinctness, also provides an impeccable source for the mobilisation of its identity with its gender disparities. At the same time, to see women in such a society as the "victims of an oppressive ideology" or simply as the forceful agents of positive constructs is also the two extremes which possibly may lead only to the simplification of the issue in a traditional society as that of Kerala Muslims.

Muslim Women in Kerala Society

As in other parts of the country, the condition of Muslim women in Kerala society is not so hopeful as expected. This may be due to several socio-economic forces that embedded in their own society and to some extent in the general Indian situations. It is also true that no study on Muslim women in Kerala could be materialised only with a structural theorisation. What poses most as the lacuna to the study is the paucity of sufficient source material except some religious injunctions and traditions of the past. Moreover, as in all societies, the old concept of "a model and virtuous woman is pious or religious" still continues in the Islamic society also without any test of change particularly when it confronts with the contemporary social realities. Religion, belief system and tradition are often brought forth to the rescue of those ideologies which embark on the culture gender matrix alone. Hence various constraints have brought the investigator more to depend on field studies with credible and balanced data rather than historical and archival documents.

Most of the scholars, whoever examine the problem, certainly admit the need of change but only within the framework of rigid and fundamental Islamic values unaffected by the varying conditions of social progress. Sociologists and experts on womens' studies often argue that an evaluation of any matured society could better be made by reading the barometer of women's condition in that society and its approach to liberalism and enlightenment. Islam as a religion has imposed manifold gender restrictions on its fair sex as revealed through the Quranic tenets and traditions. Islam presented the ideal of sex equality almost nearer than ever in an Arabian society though primitive and reverse looking. They stood on the same stand for centuries, on issues like polygamy, inheritance and legal status. This situtaion perhaps is because of the reluctancy to utilise the Islamic allowances like the *Ijma* (consensus) and *Ijthihad*, (Reasonable/Scientific interpretation) where the Quranic tenets and traditions are silent.

Studies on contemporary Muslim women in Kerala particularly after Independence, are almost nil, except some stray references found in some surveys and statistical directories. Apart from the male bias and response, there are some socio-cultural reasons for not getting proper information from females. This perhaps may be partly due to the inherent reluctance that the women folk showed to such attempts and partly due to the system of *Purdah* they observed. As women in other traditional communities in other parts of the country have different parameters to decide the status and role of the women in the Islamic community also had certain dictums. Their segregation and rarely experienced synthesis are regulated by religious dogmas, social taboos, cultural traits and traditional entanglements.

It is true that Islam imposes a radically different gender based view on women than any other religion or ideology and it is always maintained uninterruptedly by tenets, traditions and male-authored texts. In such a social situation any breach is explained as crucial and highly dogmatic which finally becomes an excuse for transforming the negative into something positive and powerful. While Islam entered into Kerala, their women folk relatively enjoyed more freedom due to the peculiar socio-cultural circumstances of the time. As a trading community, the Arabs and others extensively married local women from coastal areas and this created the matri-local residential system as social scientists like Katheline Gough and others have articulated. Moreover, the women-dominated matrilineal system widely prevalent in Kerala, also was accepted and followed by the Mappila Muslim community as a cultural continuation from the Hindu community. Such local constraints might have been reasons for not imposing purdah (veil) as a cultural restraint among the Mappila Muslims of Malabar for such a long period.

Medievalism with its traditional approach practically worsened the situation of women in general due to several socio-economic factors triggered by feudalism. The segregation and oppressive constructions imposed over women continued even after the decline of feudalism atleast in the case of Muslim women who were only aspiring to have the much required 'protection and security' as a legacy of the feudal world. Even the system of purdah became a positive option to the privileged classes in the urge to create an identity. Many ascribe patriarchy as an important reason to the gender inequalities and subordination of women in the Islamic society of Kerala. It means male-domination, making the father's sole authority over the girls before their marriage and its continuity by the husbands after the marriage. It acts from various dimensions from family to the work place in different forms like discrimination, disregard, exploitation, oppression and violence. Religions like Islam also play an important role for perpetuation of the patriarchal ideology. The superiority of men in the social structure is mainly on account of this control of the economic resources and socio-political institutions. In all socieities, such previleges are often denied to women.

No doubt that the plight of the Muslim women in the post independence era in Kerala begins, in addition to various other factors, with the result of the denial of modern secular education to them. This made them more negative, passive and powerless in the socio-political scenario of Kerala, easily becoming the victims of their own destiny. In a traditional society, gender plays a central role in determining the status and position of a person. Even human rights are denied to women because of their gender inferiority. This is one of the main reasons for women protest and struggle for their rights in different parts of the world. But such attempts are almost nil in such situations in Kerala where Muslim women suffer the worst compared to others. Though the new revivalists have given some space for their growth and freedom, the strict stipulations never allow them to cross beyond the orbit of religion and its ideology. This made them more reverse looking and backward. The challenge that faces the Muslim women in Kerala today is that how to be free from such entanglements and to go forward with others in accordance with the social change already set in.

Moreover, since religion dominates the life style of Kerala Muslims, they should be first made aware of the constraints and pressures that put over them. This must be achieved through a re-reading of the religious texts which have been interpreted from an androcentric point of view for centuries. It requires both diachronic as well as synchronic notices to avoid a 'literalist' approach one could often make. Islamic religious literature, particularly the *Hadith* texts follow the patriarchal attitudes as they came into being in a maledominated society. Hence social issues concerning women, especially in a closed society as that of Kerala Muslims, seriously affect the interaction with surrounding social structures. Again, since Islamic social system is more often considered as 'divine' and '*shariah* - based', both academics and researchers rarely touch upon it, and if any, with much caution.

Contemporary Studies

Though there are very few religion-based works on women in Islamic society of Kerala, there is still a dearth of serious and indepth studies on Muslim women treating it in a wider socio-economic perspective. Those limited numbers are the sectarian contributions of the revivalist groups mainly from the *Jama'atis* and the *Mujahids*, that too in Malayalam. Apart from dealing contemporary socio-economic problems, focus also is given to the issues concerning marriage, divorce, polygamy, etc. as a part of the general survey of Islam among its followers. Compared with the early reformers like Makthi Tangal and Vakkom Moulavi, modern revivalist writers like C.N. Ahmed Moulavi, Shaikh Mohammed Karakkunnu, M.N. Karasseri and rarely some Sunni scholars have made very little contributions in this regard. In Malayalam some women writers like V.P. Zuhara through her publication *Nisa,* Shamsad Hussain (*Between Minority and Gender Status*), Khadija Mumtaz (through her Novel *Barsa*) have made meagre attempts to project the Muslim womens' issues in Kerala. But in the work of Zoya Hassan and Ritu Menon (*Educating Muslim Girls - A Comparison of Five Indian Cities, 2005*), a statistical account of Calicut city in Kerala is given in detail. Burning issues including secular-education, Purdah system, the pressure of the *Ulemas* with the imposition of Muslim Personal Law to make Muslim women 'unequal citizens' are all to be discussed in detail with a liberal and human approach to the requirement of modern social situations in the world context.

The works of Western based Arab Feminist writers like Fatima Mernissi who won over the issue of "cultural loyalty and betrayal" with double identities (See Mernissi's *Beyond the Veil, Male-Female Dynamics in Muslim Society* (1975) and *The Veil and the Male Elite, A Feminist Interpretation of Women's Rights in Islam* (1991), by Amina Wadud-Muhsin, a representative of an Africań - American who argue that Islamic injunctions must be interpreted in relation to specific historical circumstances, have extensively utilised to pose the problems faced by the Muslim women in the Kerala context. The Lebanon-born Nazira Zei-ed-Din who did research on the subject of *Hijab* (Veil) argues that veiling was anachronistic and that Islam, if properly understood, treated women as equals of men. Wadud's provocative work, *Inside the Gender Jihad: Women's Reform in Islam* (2006) is giving a true picture of the gender crisis all over the Islamic world.

A recently published challenging work is *The Caged Virgin* (2006) of Ayaan Hirsi Ali, the Netherlands-based Somalian Feminist, who presents a World wide view of oppressed Muslim women, ofcourse with an "uncomfortable truth" to the traditionalists. *Women in Islam* (2001) by Annie Sofie Roald, a converted Muslim of Norwegian origin, is also a much debated work on the subject. Nawal el Saadawi's, *The Hidden Face of Eve* (1980), Leila Ahmed's *Women and Gender in Islam* (1992), Mahnaz Afkhami's (ed.), *Faith and Freedom,* Y.Y. Haddad and John, L. Esposito (ed.) *Islam, Gender and Social Change* are some of the other works consulted to have a theoretical frame work of the issues faced by the women of Muslim world. What we could see in the present day is the origin of hundreds of such works since Islamic presence is perceived as a homogenous mass, particularly in the context of the "clash of civilizations" as observed by Samuel Huntington.

As in other parts of the world, the conservative Muslims in Kerala argue that women's subordination is divinely ordained, because it is codified in *Shariah*. But *Shariah* is a product of human (male) interpretation of Islamic laws, and there is great diversity between religious laws in different parts of the Muslim world. While giving stress to regional and cultural baggages, Fatou Sow argues that "there is not one type of Muslim women; and they differ according to their countries, culture, language and other influences. (*Dawn*, Special Supplement, Mumbai, Jan; 2004).

Both academics and social activists treated the problem of Muslim women in India with misconceptions of religious ideology that governed the community rather than the analysis of socio-cultural melieu of the community itself. But writers like Zoya Hasan and Ritu Menon have attempted to examine some socio-economic issues in the Indian situations exploring the 'Sociology of Muslims' rather than the 'sociology of Islam, as they themselves claimed. In their study *Unequal Citizens*, the Kerala Muslim women also have been dealt with some data and survey documents. They also widely utilised the observations of writers like Gail Minault and Nasreen Fazalbhoy, who are not completely free from the aforesaid misconceptions, but follow different dimensions in understanding the Muslim women's problem in colonial and post colonial India. Shibani Roy's study on Muslim women, though concentrates on North India (*Status of Muslim Women in North India,* New Delhi, 1979) also emanate some generalisations of Muslim women in the Indian context. Some other works are Azra Asghar Ali (*Indian Muslim Women 1920-47,* 2000), Archana Chathurvedi (*Muslim Women and Development, ed. 2000),* Zakia. A. Siddiqi and Anwar Jahan Zuberi, (ed. *Muslim Women: Problems and Prospects,* New Delhi, 1993) also give some insight to the study of the problem in the general Indian context in their works.

But a dearth of a comprehensive study on Muslim women in Kerala still remains afresh. With all the rights and previleges showered over them, the fact remains that women are one of the most oppressed segment of humanity in the developed as well as in the developing world. No doubt that the status of women in a society is a significant reflexion of the level of social justice in that society. The poverty itself is defined in the form as a woman by sociologists. It is also counted on account of their income, education, employment and the potential power that they have in the family as well as in the society at large. After a comparitive analysis of various indicators like socio-political factors, tradition, religion and belief system of Kerala Muslim women of distinct classes and regions, it has been observed that a major share of them, more than 80 per cent, is deplorably inferior to their sisters of the same classes found in similar regions in the same socio economic structures. Hence a contemporaneous study like this requires more of an investigational analysis more based on field data. Like the women of Muslim societies all over the world, the Muslim women of Kerala too suffer from the same universal handicaps, especially due to the rigid and closed nature of their societies. In the absence of primary source materials except few canonical scriptures and some commited male-authored religious texts, we are constrained to look for oral history, traditions, discourses and the selection of which are also made with much caution. A micro level study on Muslim women in Kerala certainly reiterates the fact that the majority among them are the most disadvantaged and marginalised, while compared to all other sections of Indian societies.

Moreover, to make this study more effective and time-honoured, a detailed questionnaire is prepared and distributed among different classes of women, of different age groups, economic position, marital status, urban-rural classifications, illiterate and educated, etc. (the list of which is appended) a major share of questions are based on Quran and Hadith literature, related to women and their rights. They include matters concerning gender relations, polygamy, inheritance, divorce, legal status, veiling, etc. The questionnaire also contained the present-day social issues of Muslim women related to education employment, family planning, child bearing, home management, domestic violence, sexual harrassment at work place, dowry, sex-selective abortion, etc.

Muslim women fortified with the old practices of polygamy, muttalaq (*Tripple Talaq* - uttering 'I divorce' thrice at a sitting) and the veil in addition to the over all pressures of the Mulsim Personal Law. and Shariah, always became an easy prey to the oppression and marginalisation created by their own community. Moreover, socio-political issues developed in the national level like the Case of Shah Bano (1985) and the issue of Mandir-Masjid (1992) have been utilised by the fundamenalists in Kerala for augmenting communal politics and segregation in all modes of minority deal including gender. Hence all the chapters in the study are prepared insuch a vision by giving a key focus to all the lively issues faced by Muslim women in the contemporary Kerala society. Therefore the work is both anecdotal and analytical rather than the modern feminist perspectives on Muslim women found the world over.

Chapterisation

The first chapter has been arranged in such a way that it would help to legitimise the stand taken upon the women in the right dimension and to substantiate the arguments that follows. Historical record shows that the Prophet often consulted women and gave full weightage to their opinions. Khadija, who later became the wife of the Prophet, was one of the earliest converted to Islam and a woman of enterprise and free will. Aysha, who became the wife of the Prophet after the death of Khadeeja, was a co-ordinator and interpreter of the major section of traditions (*Hadiths*) of the Prophet and who even led a battle against her enemies. Fathima, the daughter of the Prophet, again, was a woman of scholarship and being the wife of Hazrat Ali, who too fought with endurance when the rights of her sons were denied. The same was the case with Nila, the wife of Uthman, the 3rd Caliph. A woman is known to have corrected the authoritative ruling of Caliph Omar on dowry. Women prayed in mosques unsegregated from men. Caliph Omar also is said to have appointed women officials in the market of Madina. In the medieval period, in the Sufi circles, women acted as teachers and spiritual inheritors. Rabiah al-Adawiyah, a female mystic of Basra, symbolises "spiritual excellence over gender and serves as a historical example of female autonomy and freedom from male authority". There were women rulers like Khayzuran, in 8th century itself in the Abbasid Caliphate. Malika Asma bint Shihab al Sulayhiyya and Malika Arwa bint Ahmed al Sulayhiyya, both held power in Yemen in the 11th century. There were also queens among Berbers and Mamluks. Zainab al Nafsawiya was a noted Berber queen. However the status of women considerably decreased in the Islamic world in the pre-modern period itself due to several socio-ideological reasons.

The second Chapter centering on Indian Muslim women is to make the reader aware of the condition of Muslim women in India after the advent of Islam as a socio-cultural entity. Though not with much freedom, Indian womanhood is always honoured. The entry of Islam did not improve the status of women in India substantially. Even Manu, the Hindu law giver who openly denied freedom to women, says, "Women must be honoured and adorned..... Where women are honoured, there the gods are pleased, but where they are not honoured, no sacred rite yields reward" (Manu, III, 55-9, p. 85, Yajnavalkya. I, 82, text, p. 172, V.S. Mandalik, Bombay, 1880). Both in the Sultanate and Mughal periods, the observance of purdah and seclusion became a common practice. Some sections of Hindu women, particularly belonging to upper classes like the Rajputs and Brahmins also lived almost in seclusion. But the poor in the rural areas, who had to work outdoors for their maintenance, could not have afforded to observe purdah, irrespective of their religious taboos.

Chapter third, on Muslim women in Kerala highlights the sociological problems including segregation life, culture and value. Although they did not have much sociological segregation, but continued to live with their traditional and cultural baggage. Mainly being local converts, they could enjoy their age old practices as others in the parallel societies. Even purdah in the strictest form was not insisted. Matriliny as a socio-hierarchical institution, was basically opposed to the tenets of Islam, but continued in Islamic society of Kerala, without the conspicuous hegemony of the women as practised and followed by their Hindu counterparts.

The fourth Chapter on Gender and Reform concentrates on the various attempts at social change by the reformist movements particularly concerning women and their upliftment. Sectarian religious organisations have brought forth several ideological injunctions based on the Quranic tenets and traditions. Theoretical explanations are often given to establish the gender equality among Muslims by extensively quoting the scriptures. Quran even allots a chapter on women, *An Nisa* (Chapter IV), but never one on men, Verse 228 of Surah 2, *Al Baqarah* (the Heifer) clearly emphasises the equality of men and women. Again, verse 35 of Surah 33, *Al-Ahzab* (The Confederates), also stress on the fact that men and women are equal in all respects. The contemporary debate on the liberation of Muslim women depends on the attitude of the Muslim society controlled by the traditional Ulemas. The question of social change among Muslims in Kerala context is not merely linked with religion or education alone, but to its attitudinal velocity to be accepted in the changing situations of modernity.

The fifth Chapter on purdah deals with various aspects regarding the observance of Purdah by Muslim women in Kerala. Traditional Muslim women's head, face or body covering of numerous varieties across time and space, are often referred to as the purdah or the veil. *Hijab* is a symbol of modesty, privacy and morality. The Arab women, especially in urban centres, observed it as a sign of high status and respectability. Originally this was a practice borrowed from Byzantine, Greek and Persian societies. To scholars, starting from Amir Ali to Feminists like Fatima Mernissi and Amina Wadud, the system was a temporary measure instituted by the Prophet. "It was never intended", stated in the holy scriptures, "to be a permanent institution, and it finds no place in the Quran". This was a practice well established in pre Islamic societies of West Asia which naturally became a life style of the Muslims of the region.

In the sixth Chapter on Tradition Vs. Modernity an indepth study has been done to highlight the the contraversies and conflicts that face the women of the Islamic community of Kerala after Independance. With all the ideological and revivalistic advancements made in the Muslim society of Kerala in the 20th century, it is the women folk of that society that suffered the most in the conflict between tradition and modernity. It is true that several movements have enlivened among the Muslim masses in general but consciously or unconsciously the major share of its women were either marginalised or segregated on the issue of *Shariah* and Seclusion. This reverse looking attitude of the Muslims towards their women in Kerala has to be analysed in a wider historical canvas since it is linked with several aspects like religion, secular education and social seclusion. The Islamic society in Kerala in the 20th century was totally controlled by the religious functionaries like the *Mullas, Musaliars* and *Tangals* and the so -called inside reformers who are mere literalist Quranic readers and who have no other perception than religion and its paraphernalia. Such an attitude towards women, instead of growth and development, further pushes them back to centuries behind, compared to others, and make them to be a section of the community unfit to face the fresh challenges of modernity and democracy.

Aspiration

Can we aspire to have a gender-just society in the near future in the Islamic Society of Kerala? The answer to this question is affirmative and that will decide the course of the conclusion. A problem often confronts to a researcher who works upon a thematic problem like this is the perception that Islamic Society is a homogeneous or monolithic mass. But our experience globally and naturally is that it is highly heterogenous with extensive variations in terms of class, language, culture, ideology and ethno-history. The recent western approach to evaluate Islamic society projecting a bi-polar model with two cultural patterns, is also found unscientific not only in the light of the developments at the Arabic-speaking heartland of Islam, but also with the recent emergence of the new ethnic and cultural groups in the wide Muslim diaspora as explained in the European imperialist theory of the 'West and the Rest'. Whether East or West, gender disparity over powered all socio-economic issues in a patriarchal system which dominated any society from the ancient to the modern times. An egalitarian gender -free social system could not be achieved without the complete emancipation of women and freedom from all sorts of oppressive inhibitions. Therefore, the present study on women in the Islamic Society of Kerala after independance is an investigation into the new challenges that emerge in a pluralistic society as that of Kerala which is still striving to be modern. Such an earnest attempt has a didactic aspiration to revitalise the retrogressive social system and to regenerate the progressive historical forces. It is expected that an action-oriented research programme could contribute to social mobility, gender equality, resource-sharing and proper empowerment. These qualities are essential for growth of democracy, social justice, economic progress and liberalism.

1

Women in Islam

A Conceptual Analysis

> For men and women who are devoted to God-believing men and women, obedient men and women, truthful men and women, steadfast men and women, humble men and women, charitable men and women, fasting men and women, chaste men and women, men and women who remember God often - God has prepared forgiveness and a rich reward. (Surah 33:35)

This particular verse of the Quran in the chapter "The Clan" believed to have been revealed as a direct response to the Prophet's wife Umm Salmah who asked him why the Quranic revelations never specifically mentioned women[1]. The common term used in the Quran addressing the people is *Bani Adam* or *Insan*. '*Bani Adam*' means 'children of Adam' or 'people'. *'Insan'* means a human being or 'person' indicating both 'male and female' without a particular gender identification. Hence every instruction given to believers in the Quran refers to both male and female alike. They have been given the same religious duties and will be judged accordingly. The Quran further reaffirms this concept when it says:

> O humanity! Have reverence for your Lord, the One who created you from a single soul and from that soul He created its mate, and through them He spread countless men and women far and wide, be mindful of God, in whose name you make requests of one another. Beware of severing that ties of kinship. (Surah 4: 1)

This holds that women are not in any way inferior to men, and were created from the same single soul. In Islam women are given equal rights and responsibilities doctrinally. But some contextual variations could be seen when it faces practical application as evident from several verses revealed in particular situations. Hence it is true that Islam possesses a radically gender based view on women than any other religion or ideology watchfully maintained by tenets, traditions and male-authored texts.

Emergence of Islamic Legal System

In Islamic law a woman is equal to her male counterpart and liable for her actions as a male. She has the same right as a man to be educated and to become an effective member in the community. Men and women are moral equals in the sight of God and are expected to fulfill all the obligations as a Muslim with regard to prayers, fasting, alms giving and Haj pilgrimage. Islam generally improved the condition of women compared to the early Arabs, particularly prohibiting female infanticide rampant in Arabian society. It emphasised the contractual nature of marriage insisting that the bride-price be given to the bride alone instead of giving the same to the father or her family[2]. Women were granted the right of inheritance and maintenance including the period of 'idda' (the waiting period following death of her husband or divorce). During the time of the Prophet, giving a woman any inheritance was a great departure from the Arab practice. Till the Quranic injunctions, women not only did not inherit from their relatives, but they themselves were bequeathed as property to be distributed. The Quran lays down that a son would inherit double the share of a daughter showing an inbalance in their rights. But the then Arab society was tribal and patriarchal where women generally have no financial security other than that received from men. She has no financial obligation in keeping the household whereas men have to attend the entire household, that too without any claim over the woman's share. Again, the law that a male receives a share equal to that of two females applies only to the inheritance of children from their parents. But in the case of the property of a deceased offspring, the parents (both male and female) will get the shares equally. Moreover, a woman's share is for the use of the woman alone. The addition one-third (Sura 4 verse 11) a man gets is to provide provision for his wife and children, an obligation on the man alone. The wife is not responsible for care taking her husband nor is she responsible for the welfare of the children. Even the suckling of a baby is not the wife's concern as per the Islamic injunctions.

In the issue of legal testimony also women's status in Islam is half of her counterpart, the man. This aspect also, has been highlighted to illustrate women's degraded position in Islamic society by almost all writers and sociologists. This is based on the Quranic verse 282 of Chapter 2, *Al-Baqara* (The Cow). Since the verse is comparatively very lengthy only the relevant part of the verse fit to the context is quoted.

> .... If the debtor is feeble-minded, weak, or unable to dictate, then let his guardian dictate justly. Call in two men as witnesses. If two men are not there, then call one man and two women out of those you approve as witnesses, so that if one of the two women should forget the other can remind her[3].

No doubt that it reveals the commercial morality of its highest order giving due importance to evidence, witnesses, and to avoid doubts in all deals. The first part of the verse deals with transactions involving future payment and hence a written document is recommended. Moreover, cash payment and delivery on the spot require no evidence in writing, but to such transactions oral witnesses are recommended. To many Islamists, this verse is an exception to the general rule that the testimony of a woman is equal to that of a man. The Shariah generally accepts that two female witnesses are advisable in cases where women have little knowledge and no expertise of the subject. In modern society, where both women and men are well versed in business and financial matters, there is no special danger of a woman forgetting or misunderstanding a transaction[4]. Again, there is no reason to believe that such a verse is exclusively on account of a woman's deficiency in intelligence or faith. Through so many verses in the Quran, it has been ascertained that women possess a great deal of goodness and spiritual righteousness. Prophet himself said: "One good woman is better than a thousand improper men". Moreover, the first witness to Islam was a woman, Khadijah (wife of Prophet), and the only witness to the martyrdom of the 3rd Caliph Uthman was his wife, Nila. So when women themselves have been accepted in early Islam as sole witnesses, then what right do those people have who come much later, to declare that women are worthy only half of a man's evidence and that if they are killed, their compensation should be half[5]. This may be due to the changing social relations to a male dominant social system all over the world.

Another issue regarding women in Islam is centred around the seclusion of women, which has nothing to do with the religion of Islam. The centrality of the problem is again after the verses in Chapter 33 in the Quran which were revealed totally contextual. It reads:

> 'O, consorts of the prophet, you are not like ordinary women. If you are truly mindful of God, do not speak too softly in case the sick at heart should lust after you, but speak in an appropriate manner; stay at home, and do not flaunt your finery as they used to in the pagan past; keep up the prayer, give the prescribed alms, and obey God and His Messenger. God wishes to keep uncleanness away from you, people of the [Prophet's] House, and to purify you thoroughly: (Surah 33: 32-33)

Devout women who wanted to follow the Prophet's wives and their practices may accept it. But it is not at all binding to the common people living in different circumstances. The wives of the Prophet mostly lived in urban quarters in Madina where only a public life could be possible. The privilege of seclusion in such situations indicates distinct and superior rank in societies where much of the life was found 'on the street'. A retreat from such a life for women like the Prophet's wives is appreciable. It is not a compulsion for all to stay indoors.

This issue of seclusion is mainly cultural and not religious. The separation between public and private space is the massive distinction between the society of the East and the West. In the East nearly half of the population is confined to private space and the public space is meant for men only. In a village, the women can have considerable freedom, since most of the villagers will be either their own relatives or working partners in community life.

Moreover, in the pre-Islamic society of Arabia, women including slaves were extensively owned and enjoyed by nobles and wealthy men. Like property or cattle they were inherited as a part of an estate. In such a situation, the question arises that, how can they all be set free from men's ownership and made equal to him? Such reprehensive custom could be eliminated only gradually as evident from the Quranic Verse,

> If we had ordered, 'Lay down your lives' or 'Leave your homes'; they would not have done so, except for a few (4:66)

Such ordainments expose the Quranic view of the seclusion of women and equality and their gradual but cautious deliverance from the Period of Ignorance to fit into the socio-economic conditions of Islam.

In this connection, it is relevant to examine the injunctions and practices of Prophet Mohammed in his dealings with the fair sex. There were several instances of the Prophet, consulting women other than his wives, and giving due weightage to their opinions. He even appointed Umm Waraqah as the Imam (who leads the prayer) of her household[6]. Some Hadiths (Sayings of the Prophet) stress the high standard of conduct which a man is meant to maintain in his relations with women. For example,

> Only a man of noble character will honour women, and only a man of base intentions will dishonour them[7].
>
> No believing man should hate a believing woman, for if there is any habit of hers that displeases him, there will be some other habit of hers which pleases him[8].
>
> The best among you is he who gives the best treatment to his women folk[9].

The Prophet once explained the best way of charity in the following manner:

> Shall I not tell you what the best object of your charity? It is your own daughter who has returned to you as a widow, or a divorcee, and who has no one to earn for her except you[10].

This clearly means that to spend on a daughter in need is the best form of charity. Women including Aysha, the wife of the Prophet, significantly contributed to the interpretation of both Quran and traditions. A woman is known to have corrected the ruling of Caliph Omar on dowry. It was a common practice in Madina during the period of Prophet itself, women praying in mosques unsegregated from men as now experienced during the Haj pilgrimage. This practice of women going to the mosques is still continuing in most of the Islamic countries. Anne Sofie Roald, a converted Muslim of Norwegian origin and an author, cites several examples of Muslim women going to mosques. An Imam who belongs to the Salafi movement in Sweden explained that "according to Islam nothing prevents a woman from visiting a mosque[11]. She also refers to the *fatwa* (religious decree) of a Jordanian cleric Sheikh Nasr ad-Din al-Albani (d. 1999) proclaiming women meeting in the mosque as a *bid'a* (innovation)[12]. In the early Islamic period, women freely engaged in commercial transactions (Khadijah, the wife of Mohammed, the Prophet, was a business magnate of Mecca) and practiced as religious instructors. Aisha, the second wife of the Prophet after the death of Khadijah, was a well-known authority in medicine, history and rhetoric, apart from Quran and Hadith. Caliph Omer appointed distinguished women as officials in keyposts and even in shopping malls of Madina. Some women are said to have converted to Islam before their husbands, a clear indication of their independence in decision making.

No woman could be seen in the helm of religious affairs or acting as Caliphs. But several of them are found handling as political leaders in different parts of the world. In the 8th century under the Abbasid Caliphs, Khayzuran governed the Muslim Empire. In the 11th century Malika Asma bint Shihab Sulaihiyya and Malika Arwa bint Ahmed Sulaihiyya held power in Yemen. Sittal Mulk, the Fatimid queen of Egypt (11th century), the Berber Queen Nafzawiyah (11th century), Shajar al Durr in Cairo and Sultana Razia in Delhi are other noted examples. There were several Muslim queens in Mangolia, Indonesia, Spain and Morocco in the early modern period. In the enlightened period of the Abbasids in Baghdad and Damascus, and in the glorious period of the Khedivs in Egypt, several women writers, poets, achievers in fine arts with great intellectual attainments could be seen. Rabiah al-Adawiyah was a noted mystic from Basra lived in the early medieval period. Although Islam does not discourage women to discharge their civic duties and social and political commitments without much curtailment to individual freedom, a sudden decline in their status generally could be visualised in the modern period, particularly with the dominance of the West and its culture. However, in the modern period also several Muslim rulers came to power through ballot in countries like Pakistan, Bangladesh, Turkey and Indonesia.

Purdah (viel) and Muslim women have become a central theme, particularly after the U.S. incident of September Eleven globally. Purdah implies complete segregation of men and women. The traditional Muslim womens' head, face or body covering of numerous varieties across time and space are often referred to as the purdah or the viel. It is often treated as a symbol of modesty, privacy and morality. The Arab women, especially in Arab quarters, observed it as a sign of high status and respectability. Burqa is not a religious invention, but rather one with roots in the pre-Islamic cultures of Persia and India[13]. In fact scholars note that middle class Muslim women in the 7th century began covering their heads because it was the tradition of Christian Byzantines, who wanted to distinguish themselves from the masses[14].

Virtually the Quran does not contain anytime concerning Hijab of Muslim women as it is practiced today. Neither the text of the Quran nor the hadith require Muslim women to wear Hijab[15]. The verses in the Quaran concerning hijab are four, two of them addressed to the wives of the Prophet and two to Muslim women in general. The first verse related to the wives of the Prophet has been referred to earlier. (Surah 33:32-33) and the next reads as below:

> Believers, do not enter the Prophet's apartments for a meal unless you are given permission to do so; do not linger until [a meal] is ready. When you are invited you go in; then, when you have taken your meal, leave... When you ask his wives for something, do so from behind a screen: this is purer both for your hearts and for theirs...[16]

The other two verses which are usually taken to justify the imposition of Hijab on Muslim women are the verse 31 from Chapter *Al-Nur* (Light) and Verse 59 from the Chapter *Al-Ahzab* (The Joint Forces).

The first one reads:

> And tell believing women that they should lower their glances, guard their private parts, and not display their charms beyond what (it is acceptable) to reveal; they should let their head scarves fall to cover their necklines and not reveal their charms except to their husbands, their fathers, their husband's father, their sons their husband's sons, their brothers, their brothers' sons, their sisters' sons, their women folk, their slaves, such men as attend them who have no sexual desire, or children who are not yet aware of women's nakedness; they should not stamp their feet so as to draw attention to any hidden charms... [17].

The second verse often quoted in favour of Hijab (Chapter 33:59) reads:

> Prophet, Tell your wives and daughters, And the believing women, that they should cast their outer garments over their persons (when outside): that is most convenient, that they should be known (As such) and not molested.

Various interpretations have been given to these verses by scholars like Imam -al Din al Sufi, commonly known as Al-Khazin, Imam Abdullah Al Nasafi, Imam Al Tabari, Ibn Masud and Ibn Abbas, who had exposed their contradictions. But all of them agreed that women should not veil their faces and their hands and any one who advocated that women should cover all their bodies including their faces could not base his argument on any religious text.[18]

Dress Code

Across much of the world today, Muslim women of all ages are increasingly turning to veiling. Is this trend a sign of piety or a way of asserting Muslim pride? Certainly not, because the veil is not included in the five pillars of Islam. Two relevant questions often come from liberal Islamists. One is, whether piety justifies veiling? And the other is, does the veil really provide women freedom from sexual harassment? Both have negative answers in our experiences of living spaces of all Muslim women throughout the world. Marnia Lazreg, Professor of Sociology, Hunter College, University of New York, also explores the adverse, psychological affects of the practice on the wearer and those around her and pays special attention to the negative impact of veiling for young girls[19]. Moreover, if women were to be covered completely, there would have been no need of the Verse 30 as found in Chapter *al-Nur.* It reveals, "Say to the believing men that they should lower their gaze and guard their modesty" (24:30). The verse unequivocally asks both men and women to observe modesty. But, as Ziauddin Sardar observes, it has been given a patriarchal spin that puts the entire burden on women. Modesty has been interpreted to mean that women should cover themselves from head to toe[20].

Veiling was a custom of rich families as a symbol of status both in the pre-Islamic and Islamic ages. Most of the Quranic interpreters like Sheikh Abdul Quadir al Maghribi refused the concept of total veiling and considered it as an aristocratic habit to distinguish the women of rich and prestigious families from other women. Islamic scholars like Sheikh Mohammed Ghazali does not find any harm in the women assuming any power other than the Caliph, that too with some reservation since it is political in nature. He believes that this approach towards women is passed on from the *Jahiliyya* (pre-Islamic) period to the present day society and Muslim women on any account need not have to cover totally, leaving their identity especially by covering faces and heads[21]. If total veiling has been made compulsory, Muslim women would have covered their faces in the course of the Haj and routine prayers, the two fundamental observances of Islam. But Islam insists that the women should not cover their faces in such occasions. Moreover none of the four Imams has said that seeing a woman's face is unIslamic or objectionable.

Islam sees men and women as one in humanity and in discharging their responsibilities as revealed through Verse One of Chapter Four which has been referred to earlier. During the time of the Prophet Women were equals at home, in the mosques, in public life and even in the battlefield. Abu Halim Shiqa, a noted modern Islamic scholar, also finds out differences in the status of women during the time of the Prophet and the present day, only because the Islamists rely on some weak traditions of the Prophet made in some special contexts to establish their argument.[22] With all such "inside" dogmas the situation becomes more aggravating as a result of the rise of fundamentalism globally, particularly when religious teachings are manipulated politically. This has put even the advocates of women's rights all over the world in a defensive strategy. Most of them resort to religious discourses to oppose conservative and fundamentalist forces, showing that texts such as Quran can be interpreted in support of women's human rights. It is only a part of doing justice to them. Quran reveals,

> You who believe, be steadfast in your devotion to God and bear witness impartially: do not let hatred of others lead you away from justice, but adhere to justice, for that is closer to awareness of God[23].

Such injunctions are very many not only in the Quran but even in the traditions of the Prophet highlighting the importance of justice to all irrespective of gender.

The incidents since 11th September in the US, the Madrid bombings of 2004 and London bombings of 2005, the words 'Islamic' and 'fundamentalist' have been coupled together in the headlines of the West. They have, created a stereotype that may a secularist Muslim find it alarming and insulting and charge it as a part of western racism or a 'clash of civilization', [24]. The Taliban's approach to women in Afghanistan is too notorious that they ban women seeking employment and even from being seen in public places. This is more terrible for a section of people who have lost their husbands, sons and other male relatives in the civil war there. Here comes again the question, 'Does Islam treat women as second class citizens?' Even when we get an idealised picture of women in Islam citing and highlighting the role of Khadijah, Aisha (Wives of the Prophet) Fatimah (daughter of the Prophet) Rabia (the lady mystic), Sukaina or Razia (rulers), the pathetic situation of them in the present day world is not at all encouraging or above criticism. Writers like Akbar. S.

Ahmed links this new trend of the seclusion of women with the colonisation of the west. To him colonisation caused to the loss of confidence finally leading to a loss of tolerance. Muslim men-folk reciprocated to this "loss" by segregating their women pushing them to the walls of homes in the name of 'protection' putting tent-like Burkhas over them. Such a perception often poses an argument that when Muslim society is confident and in a state of balance, it treats women with fairness and respect, and when Muslim society is threatened, it treats their women with indifference and harshness[25]. This theory webbed on East-West contest finds erroneous because the present day Islamic pressures found in several protected and walled Islamic countries both in the heartland of Islam in West Asia (Egypt, Syria, Saudi Arabia and Gulf region) and in the whole Asian sub continent (Pakistan, Bangladesh, Indonesia) neither substantiating nor corroborating with such a contention. Islamisation and a special brand of fundamentalism are taking shape in recent years centred around women in Islamic societies. In fact Islam is counter acting with modernity. But for many, Islam itself is an artefact of modern living. This is how Islamists argue that it is sublime and error-free.

Islam provides equal opportunity for both men and women as evident from several verses of the Quran. For example, Surah Yasin [Repentance] reveals:

> And we produce therein orchids with date palms And vines, and We cause springs to gush forth therein; that they may enjoy the fruits of it. It was not their own hands that made all this. How can they not give thanks? (36:34-35).

God does not give fruits of the soil to men alone to enjoy but He gives it to women too. Surah *an-Nisa* (Women) asserts again when it says:

> "To men is alloted what they earn, And to women what they earn" (4:32)

In another verse in Surah *at-Tauba* (Repentance), it is further ascertained that,

> "The Believers, men and women, are protectors, one of another: they enjoin what is just, and forbid what is evil; they observe regular prayers, pay Zakat and obey Allah and his Messenger, On them will Allah pour His mercy. (9:71)

An oft-quoted verse from the Quran with a Mullah-male-oriented interpretation is that of from Chapter on Women, Verse 34. It reads:

Husbands should take good care of their wives, with [the bounties] God has given to some more than others and with what they spend out of their own money. Righteous wives are devout and guard what God would have them guard in their husband's absence. If you fear high-handedness from your wives, remind them (of the teachings of God), then ignore them when you go to bed, then hit them. *If they obey you, you have no right to act against them* (4:34).[Emphasis by the author]

This is an important verse that Ulemas often quote against women, highlighting men as protectors with superiority over women. The term *Qawwamun* also means maintainers. It also means that one who stands firm in his affairs. The traditional Ulemas translate it is as an 'authoritative power'. The good wife is obedient and harmonious in her husband's presence, and in his absence guards his reputation and property and her own virtue. In a case of confrontation some steps in procedural order are to be taken like (1) verbal advice or admonition, If not, (2) suspension of sex relations, If this is not sufficient, (3) some slight physical correction may also be administered. Even this is considered inadvisable by Imam Shafi[26].

Scholars like Fazlur Rahman (1919-88), a liberal thinker from Pakistan, interprets the Sura 4:34, in a distinct manner with a contention that, from the specifics of the Quran "the general has to be embodied in the present concrete socio-historical context" determining priorities in order to implement the Quranic values afresh[27]. Hence, for him, men's superiority over women in 4:34 is not inherent but purely functional. If a woman is economically sound and shares her income with her husband, "the male's superiority would to that extent be reduced, since as a human he has no superiority over his wife"[28]. Barbara F. Stowasser, an authority on Quran and contemporary Arab studies, also shares the arguments of Fazl-ur-Rahman after analysing the traditionalists like Al-Tabari, Ghazzali and conventional modernists like Mohammed Abduh and Rashid Rida and secularist and liberal thinkers like Mohammed Taha, Ahmed Naim and Abu Zaid and Feminists like Fatima Mernissi and Amina Wadud Muhsin. Barbara argues that varied interpretations, conventional and modern, create new paradigms on women's issues providing a pluralistic attitude that characterises contemporary Islamic thought[29].

Several interpretations have come to the Quranic term *Wadribuhunna* derived from the word *daraba*. It has several meanings and 'chastise' or 'beat' is only one of them. This revelation has come in a particular context when a woman in grief came to the Prophet and complained that her husband slapped her unnecessarily and Prophet with sympathy to the woman immediately told the woman to retaliate for it. This is the situation of the revelation of verse 34 of chapter 4. In the same way the Arabic word *qanitatun* is interpreted by the traditionalists as 'obedient to men' or husband. But here also the ultimate or the implied meaning is virtual women are 'obedient' and that too to God. One of the earliest interpreters of the Quran, Abu Ja'far Mohammed al-Tabari (d.

922), the author of *Tarikh al-imam wa'almuluk* (History of Imams and kings), has made a reasonable comment on this controversial verse saying that the Prophet cleared the doubt of the term with a gesture of blowing a kerchief. Fazl-ur-Rahman also advocates a hermeneutical model in such interpretations giving importance to the time and circumstances of the revelation. The reader is expected to go to the intentions and implications of the Quranic expressions. Since it is meant for all time and universal, it must be evaluated with a practical approach. Here comes the value of *Ijthihad* (scientific/reasonable interpretation) and *Ijma* (consensus) as the Prophet himself suggested where the Quran and Sunna (traditions) are silent or ambiguous. But it should be in accordance with the original intention of the revelation manifested in the new environments. Basically this is a search to the "spirit" of the Quran[30].

The duty of men is emphasised wherever the Quran deals the relationship of men and women including husband and wife. Equality of men and women is further highlighted in the Quran through the Verse 228 of Chapter Two, *Al-Baqara* (The Cow). This Verse is something connected with the divorced women. It reads:

> Divorced women shall wait concerning themselves for three monthly periods. And it is not lawful for them to hide what Allah hath created in their wombs; If they have faith in Allah and Last Day. And their husband's have the better right to take them back in that period, if they wish for reconciliation. And women shall have rights similar to the rights Against them, according to what is eqitable; But men have a degree over them. (2:228).

This is a revolutionary declaration of sexual equality at a time when nothing could be expected in favour of women in a patriarchal society as that of the Arabs.

Use and Abuse of Misogyny

A tradition of misogyny is often applied to Islam by some writers, centred around some fake or weak traditions (hadiths) reported to have been made by the Prophet. It says: "Those who entrust their affairs to a woman will never know prosperity"[31]. Since it is found in the collection of Bukhari, usually considered authentic, it is accepted by some without much examination. But modern writers like Fathima Mernissi questions the authenticity and validity of the tradition with a detailed study of the whole situation and the circumstances that one Abu Bakra, a converted slave of the city of Taif, who claims to have heard from the mouth of the prophet[32]. Abu Bakra says that the Prophet had made such a remark, when he heard that the Persians have "named a Woman ruler" in the crisis that prevailed after the Roman invasion. Finding

Bukhari incomplete, Mernissi seeks more in the commentary of al-Asqalani (d. 852 A.H) who have written seventeen volumes on the *Sahih* of Bukhari. He gives the identity of the incidents with a historical background and reliable clarifications. When Ali retook Basra defeating Aisha (the wife of the Prophet) in the Battle of the Camel, Abu Bakra again is reported to have repeatedly reminded her this tradition of the Prophet[33]. Moreover, this Abu Bakra has a notorious pre history of punishment from Umar for acting as a false witness in the case of Zina (fornication) accusing a prominent person[34]. Such *hadiths*, seems to be "authentic", particularly on women and politics, are to be rejected. Scholars like al-Tabari considers them sufficient for depriving women of their power of decision making and for justifying their exclusion from politics.

The same is the case with some of the prophetic traditions associated with his close companion and comrade Abu Huraira (Father of the Little Cat)[35]. One such *hadith* goes like this: "The Prophet has said that three things interrupt the prayer (namaz) of believers, the dog, the ass and the woman, in between the person and the qibla, (direction towards Mecca)[36]. Here, if the hadith claimed to be true, the woman is equated with the dog and ass. Aisha, herself an authority of traditions and the wife of the Prophet, totally refuted such a hadith, because of her own experience, the Prophet used to take prayer while Aisha lying on the bed between himself and the qibla: Again in another occasion, Aisha confronted with Abu Huraira on a reported *hadith*, which claims that the Prophet had said that a woman got hell because she starved a female little cat and did not give anything to drink. She challenges Abu Huraira in all these statements concerning women. This also reveals some kind of contradiction on feminineity between Aisha, the mother of the believers, and Abu Huraira, a companion of the Prophet and an opponent of Aisha. Such "traditions" often quoted by Prophet's companions themselves are often triggered against women and their liberation by later writers of Shariah without much examination and scrutiny. In order to become a source of traditions, the qualification that a person only as a 'contemporary of the Prophet' is not enough. Malik Ibn Anas (710-796AD), one of the Imams and Interpreters of Islamic jurisprudence, suspects and in many cases even rejects the opinions of some transmitters who have neither intellectual capacity nor practical insight. In the words of Malik,

> Knowledge cannot be received from a mentally deficient person, nor from someone who is in the grip of passion and who might incite *bid'a* (innovation), nor from a liar who recounts anything at all to people.—And finally one should not receive knowledge from a Shaykh even a respected and very pious one, if he has not mastered the learning that he is supposed to transmit[37].

Therefore, it is clear that such misogynistic traditions are reverently collected and presented by modern scholars as authentic only with the excuse that they are found in the so-called 'authentic' (Sahih) Collection of Bukhari. The later collections of such traditions, particularly concerning women, are only the work of human endeavour with a possibility of deviation on some points. The copying and reference of such traditions to the issues of the present day may not do good for the making of an egalitarian society we look for where gender has no role.

Now we have to examine that how such a rigid misogyny has crept into Islam. Is it a continuation of the past or is it originated exclusively from the Islamic concepts?, Or the conglomeration of both? Anthropologists, Archaeologists and historians agree that women in the ancient period had a high social status till the beginning of urban societies and city states. The concept of goddesses in the Mediterranean region, especially in Mesopotamia and Egypt, and the Mother goddess of the Indian sub continent are examples to illustrate the elevated status of women in that period of human existence. Mesopotamia (Modern Iraq) which later became the heartland of the Abrahamic religions (Judaism, Christianity and Islam), also finds the rise of earliest urban centres in 3000 BC itself. Experts on women studies have brought to light several theories on the decline of the status of women in the feudal and pre-modern periods. Gerda Lerner considers the high labour power as a result of increased population, the reason to possess more women as a property both for reproduction and for balancing the labour force. Her concept of women as the first valuable property in the primitive period is only an extension of the theory of Engels to whom women is the first "private property" in that period[38].

Consequent on the rise of urban societies, male dominance increased particularly in the light of military competitiveness. In the words of Leila Ahmed, "The Patriarchal family, designed to guarantee the paternity of property - heirs and vesting in men the control of female sexuality, became institutionalised, codified and upheld by the state"[39]. The new economic situations further segregated women from social life facilitating their seclusion. Such a situation continued uninterruptedly in the Judao-Christian societies of the Middle East with more rigidity as a cultural baggage. The Byzantine-Christian societies of early medieval period observed the practice of the very strict seclusion of women including the wearing of the veil. Even before the advent of Islam, the Christian religious and the Greeco-Roman traditions have well established the male dominance causing major loss to the rights of women. Islam merely continued a restrictive trend already established. In one sense Islam accepted the code of the dominant, explicitly of the Christian population without bringing a radical change[40], but with a continuity more ardently.

Such assumptions of modern feminist writers like Leila Ahmed seem to be incomplete. What we could experience is, instead of a mere continuation, ideological transmission to the inherited and existing cultural ethos by imposing and compelling with a religious doctrinairism. Here the age-long socio-cultural milieu has been enveloped in strict religious dogmas within the parameters of Islam. If Islam could legitimise the misogyny, claiming that its foundation is based on the Christian construct of the past, it would appear more simplistic and inaccurate, because the religious laws regulating issues on women later have been constructed on the basis of the interpretations on various Quranic verses alone. It is true that a return to the rigidity of the religion is due to several factors, the dominant of which is foreign domination and their cultural pressures. This is quite evident in the situations after the so called 'Islamic' revolution in Iran. The Iranian Revolution, of course, has led to freedom, a freedom from imperialistic oppression, in the social, economic and cultural life of about forty million people. But it was virtually a return to the paraphernalia of the shell of Islam. It became 'a model' for those who go for an 'Islamic model' in all countries of West Asia and South East Asia where Islamic societies have a majority.

Women and Personal Laws

Hence once again women were condemned to toil, to hide behind the veil, to quiver in the prison of a harem fenced in by high walls, iron bars, window-less rooms and the ever present eunuchs on guard with their swords[41]. In their quest for liberation from the cultural pressures of Western Imperialism, they (the Islamists) could take asylum only in the old social order of Islam, now found in a reformed form by the efforts of Hasanul Banna, Mohammed Abdu, and Jamaludin Afghani. But in most of the countries, a growing conflict being fought out rigorously on the basis of Islam, which gains strength, against the forces of progress and those of western imperialism. But what happens in most of the Islamic or Arabic countries is, instead of western, a neo-imperialism of religion (Islamic) is gradually gaining power with the control of clerics, disturbing the whole secular social fabric of the country. The religious leaders as found in Iran, are acting as the spokemen of religion as if they are 'seen god on earth'. Such religious leaders, either do not understand Islam in its true spirit or have accepted to serve a dubious cause. "A religious leader is not a god, he is human and therefore liable to go wrong and to make mistakes"[42]. Any attempt to force women back into the veil and curtail their liberty is reactionary, inhuman and against civil rights.'

We know that most of such impositions in the name of religion are against the universal Declaration of Human Rights (1948) and the International Covenant on Civil and Political Rights (1976). It offers the right to freedom of conscience and expression. Women and men have equal rights to every thing covered in the international Covenant on Civil and Political Rights.

Again the Convention for the Elimination of Discrimination against Women (1981) outlaws discrimination against women, and requires states that ratify it to take positive steps to end such discrimination[43]. Morever, World Conference on Human Rights at Vienna in 1993, further affirmed that "The Human right of women and of the girl-child are an inalienable, integrate and indivisible part of universal human rights"[44]. Until recently, the human rights movement failed to recognize a whole range of discriminatory and oppressive practices against women as human rights violations particularly in Asian-African countries. Only recently issues like dowry killings in India and female genital mutilation in Africa have been taken as human rights issues. This will come under the purview of Human Rights which says "No one shall be subjected to torture or to cruel, inhuman or degrading treatment or punishment". Do we consider the women of the Islamic world outside the orbit of these international laws and Human rights?

The torture and harassment in most of the West Asian and African countries are mainly centred on the issues of veil and female circumcision (now rarely found in some societies of North Africa). Nawal El Saadawi, a doctor by profession, reveals the violence and injustice which permeated her society through her work, *The Hidden Face of Eve* (1977), originally written in Arabic, partly an autobiography and partly a polemic, which exposes the brutal treatment of women in the Arab World. It explores the hidden realities and the shocking experiences she had in Egypt, witnessing prostitution, honour killings and sexual abuse, including female circumcision. Saadawi argues that the veil, polygamy and legal inequality, three major issues that face modern Islam, are totally incompatible with the essence of Islam or any human faith. She writes:

> In the name of religion thousands of people faced, and are facing a horrible death. And in Egypt, under the guise of religion, the forces of obscurantism, orthodoxy and exploitation are banding together in an attempt to deprive people of their daily bread, of their most vital necessities in order to serve the interest of the few. The very same forces simultaneously proclaim that the place of women is in the home, and seek to establish a more modern version of the harem. It is these forces which stand behind the barbaric circumcision to which girls are subjected in some Arab countries, even today[45].

As mentioned earlier, veil was unIslamic and a product of Judaeo-Christian religions existed long before Islam came into being. This also is a reflection of the patriarchal system where women were compelled to cover their heads when men remained bareheaded with an indication that women are incomplete biologically and she becomes complete only with a man, possibly a husband[46]. Since there is a separate chapter on veil, a detailed discussion is not expected here. But for pushing women backward, in addition to polygamy and divorce, veil plays a dominant role in determining the dynamics of the Muslim World as a whole.

While discussing the curtailment of freedom for Muslim women for centuries, some factors, including customs and rituals, rampant in the Islamic societies like that of Egypt, Sudan and Somalia are often brought forth to illustrate the "gender inequality" and the "biological inferiority" of women in such societies. This is the result of a clash of interests often confronts in a society with religious laws and laws of secular nature. The medieval Muslim historian Ibn Khaldun (1332-1406) ascribes to the dominance of the religious laws over others binding on all Muslim societies[47]. But such religious compulsions are not in line with the already accepted *Ijthihad* and *Ijmah* that often Imams and Islamic jurisprudence permit for the issues This is more so, particularly when a number of social practices and rituals are observed in several multi-cultured Islamic societies with extreme strictness and perseverance. Genital mutilation or circumcision, some forms of marriages like the Mut'a, Polygamy and even the practice of veil are to be taken mostly of a continuation of the social ethos where Islam as a religion has been introduced. They have nothing to do with Islam which is practicing only on the basis of Quran and prophetic traditions. But such practices are often characterised as an inalienable part of Muslim societies not only by the critical West but even by the "true followers" from within.

Traditions Not Tenets

No doubt that these factors are still haunting various Islamic societies from West Africa to South East Asia in different degrees and dimensions necessitating fresh dialogues. Hence all such practices, though unIslamic, observed by several Islamic societies, especially in North Africa, are to be examined and evaluated in the light of the negation of complete freedom to women in those societies. The issue of female circumcision, though not universally accepted, is one that often illustrated to show the subjugation of women in Islamic societies. The Somalian born Netherlands Feminist Ayan Hirsi Ali complains that the Muslim Scholars have never condemned it because in Arab/Muslim societies the importance of virginity at marriage counts so heavily[48]. She also says that female circumcision is neither mentioned in the Quran nor recommended by the Prophet. She cites several examples from her own experience, both from Somalia and from Netherlands, where girls have been deserted and persecuted by their own families on suspicion of their virginity if they haven't undergone circumcision and a follow up stitching of the female genital organs in the customary way to prepare the girls for the marriage. "The tradition of stitching is pre Islamic but was adopted by Islam;

you could compare to what happened with the pre-Christian tradition of the Christmas tree in Christianity", Says Hirsi Ali[49]. Genital mutilation of girls is the most underestimated violation of human rights and as per the report of Amnesty International, between 1 million and 1.4 million girls were robbed off their genitals. Hirsi Ali reveals shocking instances of genital mutilations often done by broken glasses in a country way by illiterate and unskilled country women secretly, resulting into numerous health hazards and complications in the later life of women. She also equates the same with the practices of early Christians and Jews as found in the Bible and Talmud. Such rituals virtually create several psychological problems in the life of young girls whose mental and intellectual development are found retarded in their future life. Such traditional and tribal rituals could not be treated as a part of religion only on the fact that it is practiced by a group of people who follow a particular religion.

Nawal El Saadawi has much to say with regard to the female circumcision, being a physician and a social activist. She firmly believes that this practice has gained popularity due to the importance given to virginity by some societies. "Behind circumcision lies the belief that by removing parts of girls' external organs, sexual desire is minimised. This permits a female who has reached the 'dangerous age' of puberty and adolescence to protect her virginity, and therefore her honour, with greater ease.... Female circumcision is meant to preserve the chastity of young girls by reducing their desire for sexual intercourse," observes Saadawi[50]. But Saadawi could find out in 1974 in her research on the subject in the School of Medicine, Ein Shams University, Cairo, that the percentage of educated women who have undergone this amputation of the genital organ was comparatively low. While the percentage among uneducated is 97.5, it is only 66.2 per cent among the educated, that too for a 'social honour' and for the much acclaimed 'purity' of virgins[51].

The African tradition of female circumcision is further elucidated by authors like John, L. Esposito while examining several issues facing Muslim Women in the present day world situations. He sees female circumcision as a symbol of submission and a universally accepted practice in Sudan and Egypt beyond the religion of Islam. To Esposito, "Female circumcision is neither an Islamic practice nor is it widespread among Muslims. Rather it appears to be an African tradition that remains in pracitce in countries like Sudan and Egypt, *among Muslims and non-Muslims alike*"[52]. (emphasis added).

Fareeda Shaheed, a Sociologist from Pakistan, also ascertains the commonality of female genital mutilation in some parts of North Africa which causes "shocking to the rest of the non-shafi'ite Muslim world"[53]. That means the non-Shafiite world is almost not in favour of such practices, inherited from the non-Muslim societies of the past. The Muslim women of such societies even loses their identity if they won't accept such customs prevalent in that society[54]. While analysing various practices in Arab societies like polygamy and the male right to divorce and female circumcision, Leila Ahmed highlights the contradiction and differences of opinion in Arab countries with regard to the reform laws that some of the countries have introduced. An important issue between Egypt and other Arab countries is the clitoridectomy, practiced by some classes in Egypt. It appears to be geographically confined, among Arab countries, to Egypt, Sudan, and some parts of Arabia. She affirms that "it is not an Islamic custom, and in Egypt, for instance, is as common among Christians as among Muslims"[55]. These aspects highlight that women in Islamic community had been exposed to local cultural ethos. Their customs and practices were determined by the ethno-historical moorings of a region. As such attribution of the monolitithic cultural practice for them is of great difficulty.

It is estimated that there are about half a billion women living in the Muslim World from West Africa to the corridors of South East Asia excluding millions in Europe and American continents. Within the pressures of modernism, a major share of them still live in a purely traditional environment created by the male dictations rather than the Quranic dictums. Contemporary Islamic regimes consider colonialism and its after effects as the major causative factors that disturb the cultural ethos of the Muslim societies as we could experience in Iraq and Afghanistan explicitly and in many other Muslim countries implicitly. Though the 19th century Islamic modernism initiated by reformers like Mohammed Abduh and Jamaludhin Afghani in the Middle East did oppose the Western imperialism and its cultural impositions, it is only in the late 20th century aggressive resistance with fundamentalist advances have begun "to revitalise" Muslim societies. This is partly a cultural encounter rather than religious. For evaluating cultural disparities found in the Orient, western scholars usually rely on the status of women that prevails in such societies[56].

Hence the centrality of the issue consists mainly in the rights of women's, the veil, and the so called "vindictive" Shariah. In some Muslim societies, when the question arises whether democracy or shariah to be followed, a good number of them prepared to have the Shariah, because they often equate democracy with western or European democracy that renders "total freedom" for women and a style of life not acceptable to Islam. The survey amounts to 93 per cent in Iran 90 per cent in Indonesia and 94 per cent in Egypt in favour of Shariah. This is mainly not because that they disagree with the concepts of democracy, but because of the fear of the "cultural aggressions" of the west. While acknowledging and admiring many aspects of western democracy, most of them do not favour wholesale adoption of western models of democracy. Many want their own model of democracy which incorporate Shariah, but not depending on western values[57]. In the West Shariah often evokes an image of a restrictive society where women are oppressed and denied basic human rights. This is evident in the Government sponsored Shariah found in Muslim countries like Pakistan, Saudi Arabia, Sudan, Afghanistan and Iran. It was Iran that set a role model for most of the Muslim countries after the Revolution of 1979, overthrowing the secular Shah by the arch Shiite cleric Ayatollah Khomeini. Though not Shiite, most of the Islamic countries copied the Shariah, as in Iran, the effect of which was far reaching. It created a sudden imbalance in the common life of the people making big cracks in the social fabric, whether Muslim or non-Muslim. In the West Muslim women have been portrayed as victims of a repressive social order so severe that it renders, and most women in Muslim societies being unaware that they even deserve some fundamental rights. To make such a propaganda, the press and other medias in the West also play a major role by bringing out photographs, (often fabricated) and investigative news items sometimes even fanciful. The western press consider Muslim women as passive, silent, submissive and pushed to the domestic sphere. According to a survey in the United States, Muslim women are depicted in passive capacities by 73 per cent, compared to men[58], most of them highlighting as the victims of civil rights. This is often linked with marriage and allied matters in Islamic society.

Compared to the issues of legal testimony, inheritance and the veil, the rights of Muslim women are closely associated with marriage, polygamy, divorce, child custody and maintenance. The importance that Islam gave to marriage is clear from the saying of the prophet that it is "half of faith" The Quran reveals in *Surah,*

The Romans,

> "Another of His signs is that He created spouses from among yourselves for you to live with in tranquility. He ordained love and kindness between you. There truly are signs in this for those who reflect" (30:21).

This verse refers to the wonderful mystery of sex and conjugal life. What importance that the Prophet had given to marriage and married life is quite evident from his farewell address made in his last pilgrimage in Mecca. He reminded his followers: "you have rights over your wives and *your wives have rights over you.* so treat them with kindness" (emphasis added) In the chapter for 'Women' in the Quran, Verse 3 states:

> If you fear that you will not deal fairly with orphan girls, you may marry whichever [other women] seem good to you, two, three, or four. *If you fear that you can not be equitable [to them], then marry only one,* or your slave(s): that is more likely to make you avoid bias. (4:3) (emphasis added)

Here we could notice the conditional clause about orphans while introducing the rules about marriage. This reminds us of the immediate occasion of the promulgation of this verse. It was after the battle of Uhd, when the Muslim community was left with many orphans and widows and some captives of war. Their treatment was to be governed by the principles of the greatest humaneness and equity. The occasion is past, but the principles remain. The injunction is only to marry the orphans if you are quite sure that you will in that way protect their interests and their property, with perfect justice to them and to your own dependants if you have any. If not, make other arrangements for the orphans. The allowance of four also is under strict conditions. By this the unrestricted number of wives of the "Period of Ignorance" was now strictly limited to a maximum of four, provided you could treat them with equality. It reveals that polygamy is permitted in special circumstances but it is strictly conditioned on the basis of possible justice. Though the verse seems to be an allowance in contingency, it leads to a negative connotation for those who understand the will of God. Again in another verse, in Chapter Two, 'The Cow', the Quran compares women (wives) to cultivating fields. It reads:

> Your wives are your fields, so go into your fields whichever way you like, and send [something good] ahead for yourselves. Be mindful of God: remember that you will meet Him [Prophet], give good news to the believers. [2:223]

This Verse has been interpreted variously. One interpretation goes like this:

Sex is not a thing to be ashamed of, or to be treated lightly, or to be indulged to excess. It is as solemn a fact as any in life. It is compared to a husbandman's tilth; It is a srious affair to him; he sows the seed in order to reap the harvest. But he chooses his own time and mode of cultivation. He does not sow out of season nor cultivate in a manner which will injure or exhaust the soil. He is wise and considerate and does not run riot. Coming from the simile to human beings, every kind of mutual consideration is required, but above all, we must remember that even in these matters there is a spiritual aspect. We must never forget our souls, and that we are responsible to Allah.[59]

Feminist writers like Amina Wadud takes it totally male oriented and in favour of their sexuality. To her "it is still directed toward men and men's sexual desires, while women and women's sexuality remains passive". She also substantiate her argument further by quoting verse 20 from Chapter 52; which says,

> "They are comfortably 'seated on couches arranged in rows; we pair them with beautiful eyed maidens,"

> and
> “Dark-eyed, sheltered in pavilions [55:72], and “beautiful companions” (56:22),

All are referring virginal *houris* in the heavens to the enjoyment of men in the life hereafter, nowhere extolling the virtues of their earthly wives[60].

Moreover, in the Chapter on Women, Verse 129 reads:

> you will never be able to treat your wives with equal fairness, however much you may desire to do so, but do not ignore one wife altogether, leaving her suspended [between marriage and divorce].

Benazir Bhutto argues [in the light of verses 4 and 129] that God Himself doubts that you can be equal, I don’t know how any man can turn around and say that ‘God has given me this right to get married more than once’.[61]

Marriage as an Institution and a Contract

Islam was introduced into an Arabian Society where a complexity of sexual unions prevailed. In the pre-Islamic social system some of such unions have been partially institutionalised of which two are very common, the *Sadiqa* and the *Ba’al.* Sadiqa, literally a female courtship, is a matrilineal kinship where the child belongs to the mother. It is initiated by a mutual agreement and it takes place at the house of the woman who also retain the right to dismiss the husband. The Ba’al literally means a ‘lord’ or an ‘owner’, where the husband purchases the woman, and the child being the property of the husband, belongs to him. He, while possessing the authority over the woman, has also the right to divorce her[62]. This purchase nature of women continued in Islam with the marital rights of dominion of the husband over his wife. Women in the *Jahiliyya* (period of ignorance) followed the Sadiqa type of marriage where she is totally free with the right of staying with her own tribe, possessing her children and with the right of dismissing her husband at her will[63].

Al-Bukhari, Muslim traditionalist scholar, refers to different types of sexual unions practiced in the pre-Islamic Arabia. One is the most popular as it is found today: A man giving his daughter or ward to another man who gives bride price or *Mahr* and accepts her as his wife. The second type is not exactly a marriage, because one allows his wife, after purification from menses, to have intercourse with another man only with the intention of getting a pregnancy from him. After the pregnancy is confirmed, both husband and wife continue their life normally. It is known as *Nikah-al Istibda* [the marriage of seeking intercourse]. The third one is a commune union of less than ten men with a single woman. If she becomes pregnant and bore a child, she could send for all of them and out of whom she decides one man as the father of the child and he openly receives the child. In the case of the fourth type, many men visit a woman. She receives all without any reluctancy. Practically they are the prostitutes. When the women get pregnant and delivered, all the visitors assemble to detect the resemblance of the child with the man in the crowd and the child is attached to him. After the advent of Islam in Arabia, the Prophet destroyed all such marriages except the one described first and which people practice today[64].

Another type of marriage that the Arabs and Persians practiced was the *Mut'a* or temporary marriage that both Bukhari and Tarmidi extensively mention in their works. It continued till modern times, particularly by travellers and traders. Such marriages were common among the Arabs who settled at Calicut in their hey day of trade and commerce. (This aspect and its socio-cultural impact will be discussed in the forth coming chapters). This type of marriages lasted for three nights to any stipulated time as per the contract. This marriage consummates when a man and woman agree to live together for a few days or for a few months. This partnership could be extended if they wish, or else they decide to part by giving a fixed amount of money for the "services" rendered. Travellers and tradesmen greatly benefited by this kind of marriage because when they arrive first in a strange town or place, they could marry a woman in exchange of some money in accordance with the period of his stay. Such a woman naturally would take care of him and his belongings till the contract ends. As the term indicates, this was a mere 'marriage of pleasure' and a dignified prostitution. Though it was practiced in the early days of Islam, soon outlawed[65]. But *Mut'a* is still practiced by a section of the Shiites. Mut'a is the last remains of that type of marriage which corresponds to a law of mother-kinship. Hence Islam condemns it and makes it the 'sister of harlotry', because it does not give the husband a legitimate offspring. Mernissi also considers it a system opposed to Islamic ideal because it gives the woman to initiate and terminate the marriage and with a different paternity rule that Islam does not agree with[66]. Shaikh, M. Husayn Al Kashiful-Ghita, a leading Shia Shaikh, believes, that Mut'a Marriage is highly recommendable for travellers especially when they are young to avoid "excessive control and suppressing of sexual desires" and "physical and mental illness". By practicing Mut'a the honour of men and women would be saved, the Muslim community would grow in number, the world would be rid of illegitimate children and moral values would be strengthened[67]. The Sunnis consider it as a "lustful act concealed under a religious cover[68]. That is why during the initial days of Islam itself it was prohibited by Umar, the 2nd Caliph. Though theoretically Shiahs accept *Mut'a*, like the Sunnis, they too do not practice this system of marriage in modern times.

Polygamy is another factor that often attaches as a hindrance to the freedom of Muslim Women in modern times. It is a practice according to which one man may have several wives simultaneously, a controversial issue in modern Islamic societies. Polygamy is a pre-Islamic practice from Mesopotamia and the Mediterranean that continued in Islam. However, the Quran limited the number of wives a man may marry simultaneously to four. Many modern Islamic nations have either outlawed or regulated polygamy, for example, Egypt in 1920, Sudan in 1929, India in 1939, Jordan in 1951, Syria in 1953, Pakistan in 1961, Turkey in 1971, and South Yemen in 1974[69]. This is a major issue that confronts the Muslim societies in different parts of Islamic World. Islamic polygamy is based on the Verses 3 and 129 of Chapter Four, 'The Women', (referred earlier). The context, as said earlier, is also in connection with the treatment of orphans and their property after the Battle of Uhd. The Verse doubts the fair treatment between wives and give emphasis to "marry only one". The context and the intention of God and implied meanings are all revoked by many of them and go for a simple interpretation to have four wives simultaneously. The Prophet never married throughout the life of his first wife, Khadijah. Hazrat Ali, the fourth Caliph and the son-in-law of the Prophet never married more than once during the lifetime of his first wife, Fatimah. Such polygamous marriages were more out of necessity of warfare, widows caring, or for new tribal connections as political strategy which often find in the early modern statesmanship. Mohammed Abduh, the modern Islamist jurist of Egypt, stresses the need for the option of polygamy to remain open in case of necessity, such as for instance, in times of war or when the woman (wife) is infertile. "Polygamy is in contrast to the original nature of marriage. Verily the origin is for a man to have one woman, and he is towards her as she is towards him"[70].

Moreover, a woman in Islam is an identity in her own right. Even after her marriage, she does not take her husband's name. The Polyandrous types of marriages were referred to *Sahih-al-Bukhari* as per the description of Aisha, the wife of the Prophet, prevalent in the Pre-Islamic age. The speciality of the polygamy in Islam or as practiced by Prophet was strictly virilocal, but in a matrilineal context. In this case the husband visits his different wives where they resided with her parents or tribes. The type of marriage that Islam legitimized was deeply consonant with the socio-cultural systems already prevalent in the Middle East. Moreover, it was a transitionary period from Jahilliyya (Ignorance) to Islam. Hence as Leila Ahmed observes, "within Arabia patriarchal, patrilineal, polygenous marriage was by no means starkly innovative. Rather, Islam selectively sanctioned customs already found among some Arabian tribal societies while prohibiting others"[71]. The laws regulating marriage and divorce and the code of conduct for women were all developed in the later phase of Islam based on various interpretations of Quran and

Sunnah, not only of the four traditional canonical Imams, but including others like Ghazzali, Ibn-Taimiyya and a host of others. In this context we should also take into notice of the socio-cultural conditions of Arabia in the pre-Islamic and the nascent Islamic age. Meccan Society is commercial and its property generally is in herds and material goods. But Medina is primarily agricultural with distinct law of inheritance and customs and hence practically immobile. Their attitude toward marriages also was different compared to the Meccans. Medinian women were noticeably more assertive than Meccans. Hence intermarriages between them were almost nil[72]. Umar the Caliph, is reported to have complained that before coming to Medina "we the people of Quraysh [Mecca] used to have the upper hand over our wives, but when we came among the Ansar (Helpers/Medineans), we found that their women had the upper hand over their men, so our women also started learning the ways of the Ansari Women"[73].

Women in the Arab world enjoyed greater amount of freedom both in the *Jahiliyya* and Islamic periods. Though the society was mainly tribal, women played prominent role in the economic, social and cultural life of the period. Their participation in almost all wars of the period as soldiers is specially noted. Naseeba bint Ka'ab fought by the side of Prophet in the Battle of Uhd, and is reported to have wounded more than thirteen times. Hind, the wife of Abou Sufian, fought against the Prophet. The wives of Prophet like Khadijah and Aisha were also noted for their imposing personalities, independence and scholarship. Aisha was well known for her strong will, versatility and eloquence. Once the Prophet also is reported to have said to his companions, 'Draw half of your religion from this red one'[74]. But the Arab society was gradually transforming from matrilineal to patrilineal as a result of the advent of Islam, particularly when men exercised supremacy over economy and religion [75]. In many of the early social formations such transformation had already taken place. Religion and its tenets also played a serious role in such transformation.

Women's identity in the initial days of Islam is quite noticeable due to their involvement not only in scholastic discourses or debates on *Hadiths*, but in the male domains including war. As discussed earlier, a number of women including the wives of Prophet participated in the battles and one eye witness described, "Seeing Aisha and another wife of Muhammed's, their garments tucked up and their anklets showing, carrying water to men on the battlefield"[76]. Moreover, Aisha's active role in politics is well established in the first civil war in Islamic history, the Battle of the Camel, where Muslims shed the Muslim blood for power and supremacy, and that too against a legal heir, Hazrath Ali, the pet and son-in-law of the Prophet and the last of the Orthodox Caliphs (Khulafa-ul-Rashidin). Here also comes the question of veiling. Does a woman could fight on a Camel's back with complete veiling and without the fear of possible exposure? Such instances also give some space to believe that the general assessment about veiling described by the Ulemas that it was 'first observed by the wives of the Prophet' is only relative and contextual.

Hence the incidents and some customary practices found in the initial days of Islam are not truly in-line with the rigid Quranic interpretations of later times. Quran also is not considered as a book of law. At the sametime it provided principles and guidelines incorporated into Islamic law through viable selections and Imamic interpretations. At a time when women were treated as a 'patriarchal property without rights' as found in the early Arab society, Quranic reforms and prophetic discourses greatly enforced the status of women. This is a major deviation from the existing customary laws that prevailed in the Arab tribal society. Though polygyny continued to be permitted, restrictions on the number of wives and equal treatment to them were imposed. When the question of divorce comes, men are warned to stick on his responsibilities including maintenance of the divorced women and child support. In addition to this, women are also given the opportunity to divorce their husbands in various occasions when they are found unfit and irresponsible to their wives, by a custom known as 'fasq', legally accepted by the Islamic jurists. While Quran allocates some religious duties and rewards to women equal to men, and a free access to public places including mosques as experienced during the time of the Prophet, what happened to such position in the later days? Scholars ascribe to the moral degeneration of the society as a whole and the fear of the *fitna* (moral disorder) due to their presence must have been taken into consideration by some Caliphs and Imams for imposing a restriction over them. The increase in numbers of the followers of Islam, social mobility and incessant wars must also have alienated them from the forefront with deep concern of the loss of this "valuable property" of the community.

In all encounters in history, women are attacked, oppressed and harassed being the first object or target to lessen the morale of the enemy. War became the arbiter for all the evils prevailed in society and for deciding socio-political issues of the day. In such a situation of human crisis the seclusion of women was considered most desirable. Then arose several male-oriented interpretations for the selected verses in the Quran revealed in different and distinctive circumstances and social situations. Amina Wadud Muhsin (born in 1952), an interpreter of the Quran, observed: "Interpretation of the Quran can never be final". She also argues that child bearing is not a primary necessity to a woman and no indication is given that mothering is her exclusive duty[77]. The Prophet was suckled by a woman called Haleema for payment as per the custom of Arabia.

From such an elevated situation of women generally and wives specifically, how their status has been decreased to the present day oppression and curtailment of freedom, as the modernists often complain? This debate is centred around some of the verses of the Quran and traditions of the Prophet without much care to their context. The fundamentalist interpretation often attach these verses sometimes revealed in connection with the wives of the Prophet or in some specific situations where the Prophet is entitled to solve issues. Hard core theorists like the Wahabis generalise these verses as if they are applicable to all Muslim women who are supposed to emulate the behaviour of the wives of the Prophet. The Quran itself distinguishes the verses which are universal principles and those related to specific social and cultural contexts subject to interpretation.

In the Chapter, The Family of Imaran, (the father of Mary) emphasising that the Quran confirms earlier scriptures and the central tenet of faith is devotion to God.

It reads: It is He Who has sent this scripture down to you [Prophet].

> Some of its verses are definite in meaning - these are the corner stone of the scripture - and others are ambiguous. The perverse at heart early pursue the ambiguities in their attempt to make trouble and to pin down a specific meaning of their own: only God knows the true meaning. (3:7)

But those who advocate a literal interpretation of the Quranic verses believe that the gender inequality, if any, apply universally with a perception that it is an all time prescription of God on humanity. In this, they stress on two concepts, the biology of women and 'fitna' (temptation) and thereby argue for complete subjugation and seclusion. This attitude towards women were prominent throughout Islamic thought and she always remained a force of danger to man and society on account of her power of attraction or 'fitna'. Though not a new idea, it assumed greater importance in Islamic theology. Therefore the Arabs considered women a menace to man and society and to avoid this, she was compelled to be isolated at home[78]. The Arab attitude towards women and sexual life has been explained in detail by great Islamic jurists like Abou Hamid-al Ghazali who quotes the Prophet with this renowned saying: "Marriage is my law. He who loves my way of life let him therefore follow my law"[79].

Polygyny and Divorce: Dilemmas of Interpretation

An important factor often associated with the freedom of women and polygyny in Islam is the issue of divorce. Marriage and divorce in Arab countries are chiefly based on the Quranic tenets and prophetic traditions. As said earlier, these are not meant for all the people, for all time and for all situations with a universality. Even the canonical Imams – Shafi, Hanafi, Hambali, and Maliki– differ on several fundamental issues of Islamic ideology. Later theologists like Gazzali, Taimiyya of the medieval period and Mohammed Abduh, Rashid, Rida, Abdul Wahab and Jamaludhin Afghani later, have all individualistic attitudes in the interpretations of Quran and traditions, ofcourse in consonance with the permitted *ijthihad* and *ijma* The Quran always insists on compassion and tolerance as well as mediation in all occasions of divorce.

In the Chapter *Al Baqra* (The Calf), the verse 237, insists the much required generosity towards one another. It reads:

> "If you divorce wives before consummating the marriage but after fixing a bride-gift for them, then give them half of what you had previously fixed, unless they waive [their right], or unless the one who holds the marriage tie waives [the right]. Waiving [your right] is nearer to godliness, so do not forget to be generous towards one another; God sees what you do." (2:237)

As per the tenets of Islam, divorce is a last resort, discouraged rather than encouraged. According to a prophetic tradition, "of all the things permitted, divorce is the most abominable with God". But what we could experience in the Modern Islamic world is the complete undermining of this ideal and compromise with the realities of the patriarchal societies. Hence divorce, rather than polygyny, has become a serious social problem among Muslims. This situation has been compounded by the fact that women have been unable to exercise their rights either because they were unaware of them or because of pressures in a male dominated society. Those leaders who are interested in the reform of Islamic legislations never attempted to reform the laws concerning the status of women and their rights. Hence the political leaders and state apparatus in Islamic countries took speedier initiative in other spheres except the cases concerning women, and if at all any problem arises, it is observed only with deep silence.

Mohammed Abduh, the puritan reformer of Egypt, was a pioneer among those who opposed polygamy and he said that if at all it was a necessity in the early days of Islam, it is not at all acceptable in the modern situations. A most horrible practice found formerly in many Muslim societies is the concept of 'Muttalaq' (Tripple Talaq). This simply means divorce one's wife, saying, 'I divorce' three times. This, in Islam, is allowed, that too reluctantly with conditions and time span. Often men misuse it consciously without sticking to the conditions and the length of time required for the same. Divorce three times meant only to give the couple enough time to reach into an agreement or conciliation giving ample opportunities for their union or reunion, if divorced once by word alone. Moreover, the problems of polygamy and divorce in the Islamic societies are now not only the issues of women alone, but of their children, particularly the females who have no scope of a better future. The divorced mothers without any economic standing will be easily driven to prostitution or to any anti-social activities. Most of these women without having proper education could not seek a job except the choices of becoming maid servants or mistresses in households where also they often become victims of sexual aggression. Saadawi comments on the legal system generally prevalent in many of the Arab states including Egypt as the "remnants of feudalism and the patriarchal system where the women become like a piece of land owned by the man, who is permitted to do as he wishes, to exploit her, to beat her, to sell her at any time via divorce or to buy over her head a second, third or fourth wife"[80].

Again, women who are employed, are more free and are not expected to submit to the humiliation and oppression of their husbands when they are threatened of divorce. The complications of the system of polygamy and divorce are also partly due to the rigid social practices and the inhibitions and taboos prevailed in the religious controlled social formations. In Arab-Muslim societies pre-marital relations are strictly forbidden. Even masturbation is considered sinful. Therefore, the only available and possible man-woman relationship comes through marriage alone. She is exposed to all the pressures and punishments of a cruel veritable society. Naturally this causes to the increase of marriages which are more easy to be solemnised, and to consequent increase in the divorces putting a great burden on the already crippled society. Hence women who could not stand on their own, due to the lack of education and employment, are easily taken to the ties of wedding for food, shelter and sex, much to the satisfaction of a patriarchal society, and to avoid the possible social stigmas, that they have to face all along in their life.

Moreover, recently some Islamic countries have introduced reforms favouring women including the abolition of polygamy, severe restrictions on divorce and financial compensation to widows and their children. Some of the countries also issued strict rules regarding the marriageable age for both male and female thereby prohibiting child marriage and allied issues. Although polygamy is allowed on some conditions in some Muslim societies, the vast majority of Muslims today are monogamous. This great change is mainly due to modern education rather than legislations.

Polygamy, licencious and free divorce, sexual segregation and the veil are all intertwined and mutually contributory for lessening the freedom of women in a patriarchal society as that of Islam. These restrictions under the guise of religion also greatly marred the present day living conditions of women in Islamic societies. Public appearance, free drive and employment have become important issues among Muslim women in leading a modern life-style. Saudi Arabia with its rigid religious regulations, compared to other Islamic countries, have even banned women from driving their own cars and to have free employment in several sectors. But most Muslim countries including the Shiite Iran have given up such restrictions on women claiming modernity, but in general, not to be branded as a free society. These restrictions originate not from Islam but from customs, cultural baggages and traditions often wrongly justified under an Islamic banner. The ability to work or drive or dress has little to do with Islam or Quranic laws, but a lot to do with the cultural aspects and interpretations of Islam. The conditions of women in Saudi Arabia, Egypt, Iran, Pakistan and Malaysia are giving varied pictures of the role of Muslim women in a practicing society, but still with the lack of "openess", compared to the west, again as a brand of the Orient.

Some of the modern reformers with conservative rigidity have interpreted and defined the religious tenets within the parameters of the Quran and traditions with an aim of generalising the situations. There are several references on divorce in the Quran which favours women who become victims of it, and also articulating several conditions, inalienable duties and financial commitments to men who are intending for divorce.

For Example, in Chapter two, verse 229 reads:

> Divorce can happen twice, and [each time] wives either be kept on in an acceptable manner or released in a good way. It is not lawful for you to take back anything that you have given [to your wives].

Verse 231 of the same chapter further says:

> When you divorce women.... either keep or release them in a fair manner.

Again, as the Verse from *Al Baqra* reminds,

> Divorced women shall also have such maintenance as is considered fair, this is a duty for those who are mindful of God. (2:241)

In the Chapter on Women, Verse 20 reads:

> If you wish to replace one wife with another, do not take any of her bride-gift back, even if you have given her a great amount of gold.(4:20)

Moreover, Chapter 65 of the Quran is titled as 'Divorce', and verses there stresses the aftercare of such unfortunate women who are divorced.

> When any of you intend to divorce women, do so at a time when their prescribed waiting period can properly start.... Do not drive them out of their homes.. (65:1)

Again,

> House the wives you are divorcing according to your means, wherever you house yourselves, and do not harass them so as to make their

> lives difficult. If they are pregnant, maintain them until they are delivered of their burdens; If they suckle your infants, pay them for it. (65:6)

Are these constraints imposed over men capable enough for restricting both polygyny and divorce made in effect so mechanically, unilaterally and unlawfully? It is a debatable question. No doubt that polygyny is an impediment to progress because it fosters a turbulent home life with discord among wives. But as some others have argued, polygyny rarely become a solace for those women who live in conditions of humiliation, grief and squalor to a noble state of matrimony acting as a catalyst for liberating them. For them, it is "one of the manifestations of the liberation of women, empowering her will, since the man does not marry other wives without her permission"[81]. Hence writers, both men and women, have made interpretations within an Islamic frame work, turning to Quran and traditions of the Prophet, to define women's rights in the modern period.

Now we will pass on to various Muslim states of modern period and how they work upon the *Shariah* or on liberal Islam. It is true that while projecting the tenets found in religious texts in favour of all matters concerning women, some modernists seek the ideals of western provenance linking them to those found in Quran. But even if they manage to assert that all exist in the holy texts, that could not be taken as a part of a liberal and secular milieu, because texts like Quran had been specific on men's authority over women except in the spiritual sphere. This contradition often comes when we analyse the role of women in Muslim societies using an empirical apparatus to formulate a frame work and by applying the sociology of religion in a given politico-economic dynamics. The daily news from the Islamic Republic of Iran on trivial matters like the colour and shape of a woman's scarf or the length of the skirts or thickness of stockings are catching our attention as factors of oppositional reactive energy working in the new political sociability aiming at women in Iran and to enforce the much acclaimed "code of modesty". Writers like Afkhami make some conclusions with regard to the status of women in the post-revolutionary Iran. "The fact is that a modernising state in a traditional society is usually an ally of the women's movement against a majority in the society that, "without the support of the modernising state and its political organs... women's rights are unattainable in an Islamic society"[82]. These conclusions proclaim the effects of the coercive state policy as the only model for Iranian women in a Shiite clerical set up.

The contradictions emerging in a colonial state when it collides with the local culture is quite evident in the case of almost all Islamic societies in the post colonial state formations. As Partha Chatterjee suggested, the colonial state instituted the bases of a modern regime through its institutional system like bureaucracy, law, education, health, police, military and the courts to use social regulation as an aspect of the self-disciplining of individuals and to make power more productive and efficient. These institutions produced a new consciousness, apart from the regional, which is considered inferior and backward[83]. The conditions experienced in the most powerful Islamic States of the post-colonial period like Iran and Egypt clearly manifest this state of affairs, following different ideological modes.

Here we can exclude both Afghanistan and Pakistan for reasons other than the above and could be discussed later classifying in another category. Hence the colonial states with their alien ruling groups which initiated the regimes of modernity, were destined to fail completely standardising its power as part of creating a modern state. The Islamists too have their own interpretation of modernity. But with its political triumph in any state, what we could experience is the colossal end of it. The Liberal feminist, Mernissi's sample study on Moroccan women and their status in the traditional Muslim family system, discloses several facts regarding the male-female relations. In her interviews, she realised two major differences between the lives of traditional and modern women. For the traditional women sexual segregation had been very strict all over their lives, but for the modern women the segregation is not limited to the period of puberty alone. The modern women did not feel that sexual segregation is an important factor in their future lives[84]. The problem in front of many Muslim states is the implementation of Shariah within the purview of human rights. Individual countries like Egypt, Saudi Arabia, Iran, Pakistan and Morocco have introduced their own religious laws based on Shariah as Divine Laws. Since Shariah is a conglomeration of various hermeneutic approaches of Islamic jurists, it also carries some elasticity in its content and application. Our experiences in Egypt, Turkey, Lebanan, Pakistan and Indonesia fully endorse this cultural particularism often leading to cross the borders of *Shariah*. Eleanor Abdella Doumato of the University of Rhode Island has examined the ambiguity of *Shariah* and the politics of women's rights in Saudi Arabia in the context of the grant of refugee status for a Saudi girl in Canada. She complained that her basic human rights to life, liberty and security were threatened due to her refusal to accept the restrictions on women in Saudi Arabia. She could not work, study or dress as she pleased and often had been subjected to violence on numerous occasions simply for walking alone in the streets without a veil[85]. Of course the Saudi Shariah is totally within the contours of Wahabi or Salafi activism that outlaws all Sunniite and liberal views confined within the concept of 'Ijthihad'. An issue on the question of women driving, in November, 1990, alarmed the clerics of the Supreme Religious Council there which ultimately banned such attempts of women branding it 'beyond the bounds of morality'. In all Muslim societies, what we could experience is, the use of same *Shariah* for not allowing the basic human rights of driving or travel or to manage a business, to project the cause of the Islamists. The victims too use the same language of the *Shariah* to protect and legitimise their rights. Human rights clubbed with women's rights are found ambiguous in the language of Islamic rhetoric, and women's rights are allocated in accordance with a different standard as per the prerogatives of men with a ban in the space of men[86].

In the last two decades, the aggression on women has increased alarmingly as a result of the combination of religious authorities and political power in different parts of the world. The worst victims of this politico-ideological vendetta could be seen in the Islamic states of Algeria, Pakistan and Afghanistan. A concerted effort of state-sponsored rape could be seen in the post Benezir era in Pakistan. Most of the rapes on women are targetted against the women who were either supporters of Benezir or followers of her political party, the PPP. While there is a politics in the rapes of these women, the fundamentalists also were silent because they could not tolerate women working in public space as per their conventional notion of Islam. The cases of Rahila Tiwana, a PPP student activist, Veena Hayat, a friend of Benezir, and Khurshid Begum, a poor washer woman whose husband happened to be a supporter of the PPP of Benezir, all reveal the activities of male-dominated feudal society where religion also has been brought to justify their attacks on women in the guise of a "political rape"[87]. Khalid Ahmed, a noted Journalist from Pakistan reveals the shameful situations that prevailed in Pakistani society. He says: "Feuds are settled through rapes, men avenge themselves each other by raping each others' mothers, wives, daughters and sisters. A brave adversary is supposed to break down under the grief and dishonour of the violation of his women folk"[88].

It is estimated that more than 80 per cent of world's total refugee population is Muslim, mostly Afghans, Azerbaijanis, Palestinians, Bosnians, Kurds, Somalis Sudanese and Tajiks, in which 75 per cent is women and children as the victims of forced migration. After becoming free from the Soviet Yoke, the Afghan government under the control of the Mujahidin virtually Taliban, introduced a rigid administrative system with the tribal (usually styled as Islamic) influences. The war conditions in Afghanistan worsely affected its women folk, most of whom still live in refugee camps. Since veiling has been imposed over them, they could not even collect their food rations in public or seek medical help if they have no male relatives. Such a situation forced them to be malnutritious and unhealthy. Moreover, in Afghanistan, the tribal religious leaders, deny education to both women and children, instead they train them to be *Jihadis* at a very early age itself with a special instruction to women to bear maximum children to recruit to the contingent of the *Mujahidin*. Here too the violation of human rights on women under the guise of religion, affect them alarmingly creating life-long psychological effects without any hope of survival in future.

Fundamentalist-sponsored killings are found rampant in Algeria where too women were hunted down, raped and killed by the so-called *Jihadis* usually on the excuse of a veil or for showing freedom to go to a school or for seeking some employment for living. A news report from a woman journalist reveals ".... In Algeria every day women are being kidnapped, raped, mutilated, tortured to death and killed by members of fundamentalist armed groups which the United States government helped to train and with whom it continues to urge the Algerian government to dialogue"[89]. Such crimes and severe atrocities against women are mostly carried out by Islamic *Jihadi* groups like the Armed Islamic Group (GIA) in Algeria. The lists of the unveiled women, mostly students and employed, appear in public as potential military targets, often on the walls of mosques or in public places. One common statement of such type is, "O, you woman who wears the Jilbab (full robes), May you be blessed by God. O, you who wears the *hijab* (head scarf), May God put you on the straight path. O, you expose yourself, the gun is for you"[90]. The pressure of women to wear the Hijab by the fundamentalists in Algiers also indicates the misuse of religion by these criminals to exploit women for rape and revenge so rampant in the whole of Algeria.

The condition of comparatively liberal Islamic states like Jordan also is not much different with regard to the status of women conceptually. Women constitutes above 50 per cent of Jordan's four million population. Since the legal age of marriage for girls is fifteen, 23 per cent of divorcees involve young women under nineteen. The migration of Palestinians in Jordan also marked a transformation in the socio-legal system of the country with Islamist underpinnings. As in other states, women are the worst sufferers in the new rigid religious system in Jordan. Toujan, a well known Jordanian Television talk-show host and a product of the Jordanian University, took the initiative, as a feminist, for forcing a woman's movement inviting great opposition from the government and traditionalists including apostacy and heresy due to her views on Quran and hadith. Though Jordanian women have acquired some political and human rights, it could not become totally free from the grip of the *Shariah,* especially when it is ironically created by the liberal King Husain with his American wife who followed a western style.

Discourses and Whip of Change

Hence, the problem here is whether Muslims should accept the male-made *Shariah* (need not be framed fully in consonance with Quran and Sunnah) or the spirit of the tenets of the Quran and hadith as followed by the Prophet and his successors, and importantly not the interpretations. Again, the so called

Shariah or Islamic law followed in most of the Muslim countries and in various Islamic societies are not uniform. The Muslims with distinct cultural background are not in consensus either in agreeing or in following such laws because in most cases they act as parallel to the civil and criminal laws of the state. Islamic *Shariah* should not be the verdict of a group of scholars or a political dictation, instead, it must wholly be based on the true spirit of the Quran and tradition (hadith). Great Islamic jurists themselves have different versions and interpretations, from the Imams of the early period to those of the modern period. Moreover, Quran emphatically affirms the freedom of thought and action of all believers and no one has authority over another in matters of religion. Even the Prophet is not entitled to look after the deeds of men. In the Chapter on Women in the Quran, verse 80 reads: " He who obeys the Messenger, obeys Allah; But if any turn away, We have not sent thee [The Prophet] to watch over them." (4:80). Nazira Zein-ed-din, one of the earliest of the Muslim feminists (born 1905, Lebanan) argues, that the question of belief or non-belief and the question of carrying out the instructions of Islam are matters between God and the individual. "No one on earth, not even God's apostle, is responsible for those who believe or those who do not, and no measures should be taken against those who refuse to be Muslims" [91]. In the chapter on Cow, Quran Stresses: There is no compulsion in religion: True guidance has become distinct from error..." (2:256).

The recent developments based on human rights issues in many Islamic states, especially in Saudi Arabia, are not at all in accordance with the above tenets found in the holy scriptures. Several instances of gender related inequalities are reported in work places which compells women to seek employment elsewhere. These are the result of "policies instituted and enforced by the state as representing the will of the people, the values of religion, and the common good" [92]. Here the concept of human rights is centred around a particular code of Islam, a Saudi Salafi model, imposed with the sceptre of the sate. In Saudi Arabia, the Basic Law promises significant social and economic rights to its citizens like employment, public education, health care and all the benefits of the social welfare system. But no where it addresses the women's rights. Their access to the employment of their choice is severely restricted by the regulations that they may work only in places that are completely sex-segregated for women. Everything, whether it is education, employment or even mobility, should be within the 'Islamic margins' which are conspicuously becoming narrower in recent years. The question here is only of the imposition of human rights of international value on women who suffer most in such societies, where the politically institutionalised inequality regime prevails, often concealing their ideological rigidities. Though Muslims claim Islam as the total 'way of life', 'a blue print', for the entire spectrum of social life, cultural diversities and social differences make them more identical with individual societies in which they live. Therefore the claim is more rhetorical than real and more an aspiration than a lived reality. From the formative days of Islam onwards, we could experience this diversity of religious interpretations and distinctions in the various schools of thought initiated by the Imams and Islamic jurists. Islamic world, from its initial stage to the modern times, has never been homogeneous culturally or even religiously as the fundamentalists now claim. This is the same thing with other religions like Christianity and Hinduism also.

In the ongoing analysis, what we could hypothesize is that religious fundamentalism revives and asserts itself when it confronts with some reverses or defeat. It was after 1967, with the defeat of Egypt by Israel, that Islamism in the guise of revivalism took hold in the whole Arab world, particularly in Egypt. Instead of seeking a materialistic interpretation of such defeats, the religionists find a general consonance in the abandonment of God and his religion. In such situations the fundamentalist groups take strength and propagate for a retreat from the worldliness and a return to Islamic mode of life including a dress code for keeping their identity. They target both the westerners and the western-led Arabs. While opposing the western culture, these people tactfully condemn and oppose a gender free life which ultimately affect the women folk greatly, who otherwise would have acquired education, employment and an independent life.

But what we could experience in recent years is that as a result of revivalism in different parts of the world, within the opposing secular and regional idioms, Islam has been presented as an ideology and "solution", particularly in the context of combating colonial pressures. Within the purview of a uniform code of conduct (The Shariah) and a code of dress (the Veil), a new concept of 'Muslim Identity' has been visualised which is either not available or not known from West Africa to South East Asia except in some Arab countries of the Middle East. This cultural pressure also has to be taken into account when we complain on the western imperialist trends. Both elements with equal power of dominance do harm the regional ethos in the name of modernity of the West in one side and fundamentalism of the revivalist Islam on the other side.

This is what happened in the case of Kerala also when the Islamic fundamentalists arose out of the issues of the Babri Masjhid which was demolished by the Hindu obscurantists in 1992. The destruction of the disputed Masjid is not a symbol of Islamic defeat, but this has been propagated as a symbol of opposite terrorism and a model action which according to their propaganda, may possibly be continued in future. Thus attempts were made by the hard-core Islamists in Kerala to a "revival" of a religious ideology with an outward identity of imposing an Islamic dress, the *Ziyy al-Islami.* Such a dress code is not known in the past in Kerala. This is the most important and couspicuous element that imposed over women as a token of identity apart from all other restrictions on education, employment and public life. Thus with such a heavy baggage they are projected as a symbol of resistance and rejection. A newly woven role model of Islam is now thrust these poor, innocent and illorganized women who already have been crippled with several restrictions in a male-dominant society as found today. The problem is one of religious dominance over regional ethos which highly necessitates for creating a uniformity by religiosity alone. While striving for an ideological "purity", regional or indigenous cultures and its milieu must be surrendered. This is the greatest value that a society should pay for this artificial and temporal unity as some aspire to, and which also could not be materialised all along, from the beginning of the Islamic society of the Prophetic age to the present day. Any attempt for legitimisation of such an ideology will find its virtual isolation from the liberal and secular premises, of democracy and modern social institutions.

Notes and References

1. Ruqaiyya Waris Maqsood, *Islam,* Hodder Education, London, 2006. p. 137.
2. John, L. Esposito, *The Oxford Dictionary of Islam,* London, 2004, p. 339.
3. *The Quran* 2:282, Trans. M.A.S. Abdel Haleem, Oxford University Press, 2005, p. 32.
4. Ruqaiyya Maqsood, *op. cit.* p. 141.
5. Benazir Bhutto, "The Fight for the Liberation of Women", *Women's Studies Quarterly,* Vol. 24, Nos. 1-2, 1996, pp. 91-97.
6. Esposito, *op. cit.,* p. 339.
7. *Kanz al-'Ummal,* 16/371, in Maulana Wahiduddin Khan, *Women,* Good Word Books, New Delhi, 2002, p. 17.
8. Muslim, *Sahih, Kitab ar-Rada,* 2/109, *Ibid.*
9. At-Tirmidi, *Sahih, Abwab ar-Rada,* 2/1091, *Ibid*
10. Ibn Majah, *Sunan, Kitab al-Adab,* 2/1209-10, Khan, *op. cit.* p. 19.
11. Anne Sofie Roald, *Women in Islam—The Western Experience,* Routledge, London, 2002, p. 53.
12. For more details see Al-Albani, Nasir-ad Din, *Jibab al-mar'a l-muslima* [The Muslim Women's Dress], Dar IbnHazm, Amman, 1994.
13. Mackenzie Carpenter, Staff Reporter, *Pittsburgh Post Gazette News,* Online, 28-10-2001.
14. *Ibid.*
15. *Bouthaina Shaaban,* "The Muted voices of women interpreters", in Mahnaz Afkhami (ed.) *Faith and Freedom, Women's Human Rights in the Muslim World,* IB Tauris, London, 2000, p. 69.
16. Quran 33:53, trans. MAS Abdel Haleem, Oxford, 2005, p. 270.
17. *Ibid.* p. 222.

18. Bouthaina in *Faith and Freedom*, *op. cit.*, p. 71.
19. Marnia Lazreg, *Questioning the Veil, Open letters to Muslim Women,* Princeton University Press, Online Report, 28-10-2001.
20. Ziauddin Sardar, *What do Muslims Believe?*, Granta Books, London, 2006, p. 79.
21. Shaikh Mohammed Ghazali, *Sunna Between Fiqh and Hadith,* Cairo, 1990, p. 52.
22. Abu Shiqa, *Tahir al mara'a fi asr al-risalah* (The Emencipation of Women during the time of the Prophet), Kuwait, 1990, p. 5-6.
23. Surah *Al-Ma'ida* (The Feast) Verse-8.
24. Samuel Huntington, "A Clash of Civilization?" *Foreign Affairs,* 72, 1993.
25. Akbar, S. Ahmed, *Islam Under Siege,* Blackwell, U.K. 2003, pp. 116-117.
26. Interpretation of the term found in the tradition of *The Holy Quran* published by the Presidency of Islamic Researches, IFTA, Mecca, n.d. pp. 219-220.
27. Fazl-ur-Rahman, *Islam and Modernity: Transformation of an Intellectual Tradition,* Chicago University Press, 1982, p. 7.
28. Fazlur Rahman, *Major Themes of the Quran,* Minneapolis, Bibliotheca Islamica, 1980, p. 47.
29. Barbara F. Stowasser, "Gender Issues and Contemporary Quran Interpretation", *Islam, Gender and Social Change* ed. Y.Y. Haddad and John L. Espasito. Oxford University Press, 1988, pp. 30-42.
30. Fzlul Rahman, *op. cit.,* pp. 4-9.
31. Bukhari, *Sahihul Bukhari,* Vol. 4, p. 226.
32. Fathima Mernissi, *The Veil and the Male Elite, A Feminist Interpretation of Women's Rights in Islam,* Basic Book, New York, 1991, pp. 49-61.
33. Asqalani, *Fath-al-bari,* Vol. 13 and 46 in Mernissi Fathima, *op. cit.*, pp. 56-57.
34. Mernissi, *op. cit.,* p. 61.
35. His original name was Abdullah, but the Prophet nicknamed him as Abu Huraira (Father of the Little female Cat) on account of a small cat with which he always went around.
36. Bukhari *Sahih-ul-Bukhari,* Vol. I, p. 99.
37. Ibn-Abd-al-Barr (978-1070), *Al-Intiqa,* Beirut, Lebanon, Darul Kutubal - Ismiyya, n.d., pp. 10-16.
38. Gerda Lerner, *The Creation of Patriarchy,* Oxford University Press, New York, 1986. Lerner divides women as 'respectable' who are under the sole control of men and those who are 'public'. Her analysis denotes the superior role of a patriarchal society. See also, Frederick Engels, *The Origin of the Family; Private Property and the State,* Eleanor Leacock (ed.) New York, 1972.
39. Leila Ahmed, *Women and Gender in Islam*, Yale University Press, NewHaven and London, 1992, p. 12.
40. *Ibid.,* p. 33.
41. Nawal El Saadawi, *The Hidden Face of Eve: Women in the Arab World,* Zed Books, London, 2007, Preface, p. xvii.
42. *Ibid*, p. xxv.
43. Geraldine Terry, *Women's Rights,* Pluto Press, London, 2007, p. 28.
44. Article 18 Vienna Declaration and Programme of Action, World Conference on Human Rights, Vienna, 1993.

45. Nawal El Saadawi, *op. cit.*, p. 7.
46. *Ibid.*, p. 8.
47. Ibn Khaldun, *The Muqaddimah* (An Introduction to History) Franz Rosenthal (Trans.), Princeton, 1969, pp. 154-155.
48. Ayan Hirsi Ali, *The Caged Virgin—A Muslim Women's Cry for Reason,* The Free Press, U.K., 2006, p. 705.
49. *Ibid.*
50. Nawal El Saadawi "Circumcision of Girls", *op. cit.*, p. 50.
51. This study was conducted by Saadawi under the project titled "Women and Neurosis"
52. John, L. Esposito, *What Everyone Needs to Know About Islam,* Oxford University Press, New York, 2002, p. 102.
53. Fareeda Shaheed "Net working for Change: The Role of Women's Groups in initiating Dialogue on Womens Issues" in Mahnaz Afkhami, *op. cit.*, p. 84.
54. *Ibid.*, p. 86.
55. Leila Ahmed, *op. cit.*, pp. 175-76.
56. Edward Said, *Culture and Imperialism,* Vintage Books, London, 1994. p. 39. Said's earlier work *Orientalism* (1978) gives the western version of Islam through his terminologies equalising it with terror, devastation, demonic, hordes of hatred barbarians, as a 'lasting trauma' for Europe etc., (*Orientalism,* Reprint, 2003, pp. 59-61).
57. John, L. Esposito and Dalia Mogahed, *Who Speaks for Islam?* Gallup Press, New York, 2007, pp. 47-48.
58. Kamalipour, Y, *The U.S. Media and the Middle East: Image and Perception.* Connectient, Prayger Publishers; 1995.
59. The *Holy Quran*, Translation and Commentary by IFTA, Mecca, p. 96.
60. Amina Wadud, *Inside the Gender Jihad, Women's Reform in Islam.* Oxford, 2006, p. 193.
61. Benazir Bhutto, "Politics and the Muslim Women", in Charles Kurzman (ed). *Liberal Islam* Oxford University Press, 1998 p. 110.
62. Robertson Smith, *Kinship and Marriage in Early Arabia,* Boston, 1903, p. 92.
63. Fathima Mernissi, *Beyond the Veil, Male-Female Dynamics in Muslim Society,* Saqi Books, London, 2003 (edn) pp. 74-75. To substantiate to her argument, Mernissi widely quotes from Al-Isfahani (Trans. W.R. Smith), *Kinship in Early Arabia.*
64. Al-Bukhari, *The Sahih,* 36-p. 428. M. Watt (Trans.) "Mohammed at Medina", pp. 378-379 in Mernissi Fathima, *Beyond the Veil*, pp. 76, 186 (Notes).
65. Muslim, *Al-Jami' Al-Sahih*, pp. 130-131.
66. Mernissi *op. cit.*, pp. 77-78.
67. Sheikh Ghita *History and Principles of Shiism,* 1985.
68. Akbar, S. Ahmed, *Discovering Islam, Making Sense of Mulsim History and Society,* Routledge, London, 2003 (Reprint), p. 58.
69. John, L. Esposito, *The Oxford Dictionary of Islam, op. cit.,* p. 249.
70. Abduh Muhammed, *Tafsir-al-Manar,* Vol. IV, 350, Dar-al-Fikr, Cairo, n.d.
71. Leila Ahmed, *op. cit.*, p. 45.
72. *Ibid*, p. 52.

73. *Sahih-al-Bukhari,* 7:88. Montgomery Watt, *Mohammed at Medina,* Oxford, 1956, pp. 272-273.
74. Ahmed Kharat, *The Status of Women in Islam,* Egypt, 1975, p. 64. The usage 'red one' is due to the colour of Aisha's face.
75. Nawal El Saadawi, *The Hidden Face of Eve,* Zed Book, New York, 2007, p. 189.
76. Leila Ahmed, *op. cit.,* p. 53.
77. Amina Wadud, "Quran and Woman", in *Liberal Islam, op. cit*., p. 133.
78. Nawal El Saadawi, *op. cit.,* p. 204.
79. Abou Hamid Al Gazzali, *Ihya Uloomudin,* Cairo, 1970, p. 683.
80. Saadawi, *op. cit.,* p. 300.
81. Abbas Mohmud al-Aqqad, *Al Mar'ah fi Al-Quran,* quoted in Y.Y. Haddad and John L. Espisito (ed.), *Islam, Gender and Social Change,* Oxford University Press, 1998, p. 13.
82. Mahnaz Afkhani, "Women in Post Revolutionary Iran; A Feminist Perspective", in In the Eye of the Storm: *Women in Post Revolutionary Iran,* Mahnaz Afkhami and Erika Friedl (ed), London, 1994, pp. 13-15.
83. Partha Chattergee, *The Nation and its Fragments: Colonial and Post Colonial Histories,* Princeton University Press, 1993, p. 17.
84. Mernissi, *Beyond the Veil, op. cit*., p. 91.
85. In the letter of Edward Broadbent, President of International Centre for Human Rights to Bernard Valcourt, Ministry of Employment and Immigration, Canada, dt. 19th August, 1992.
86. Eleanor Abdella Doumato, "The Ambiguity of Shariah and the Politics of Rights in Saudi Arabia" in *Faith and Freedom*, Mahnaz Afkhani, *op. cit.,* pp. 150-51.
87. Zohra Yusuf, 'A Rising Graph'? *Herald,* January, 1992, pp. 47-48.
88. Khalid Ahmed, "The Sociology of Rape", *Slogan,* February, 1992, pp. 36-37.
89. El-Watan, 6 November, 1994, p. 3 Quote by Karima Bennoune, in her article "S.O.S. Algeria: Women's Human Rights Under Siege" *Faith and Freedom, op. cit.,* p. 185.
90. From the Interview conducted by Karima with Professors Fathima and Zohra (Pseudonames) in Amman, Jordan, 5 November, 1994 in Afkhani, *op. cit.,* p. 187.91)
91. Bouthaina Shaaban, "The Muted voices of Women Interpreters" in *Faith and Freedom, op. cit.,* p. 66.
92. Doumato, *op. cit.,* p. 135.

2

Muslim Women in the Indian Context

A Cross Cultural Critique

The entry of Arab Muslims in 712 A.D. in the North West of India marks the beginning of the political Islam in this part of the sub continent. Though the Arabs invaded in Sind, they were not able to establish a powerful state in the region. But their successors, like the Turks and the Central Asians took it as a challenge and won in their attempts. The politics of religion found a new turn in the military conquests of both Arabs and Turks as the Holy Roman Emperors and the Byzantines have done in western Europe in the heyday of Christianity. Within less than a century the Arabs could establish a vast empire extended from the Atlantic Ocean in the West to the banks of the River Indus in the East and from the Caspian Sea in the North to the valley of the River Nile in the South.

Being traders and conquerors, they could not bring their women folk along with them and this necessitated for the large scale conversions particularly of women. The temporary character of the invasions and the overall uncertainty that prevailed did not allow women to accompany their men folk whose lives themselves were at risk. The traditional division of Hindu society as four castes also accentuated the process of proselytisation from the depressed sections increasing the number, but not at all strengthening the unity and cohesion of the community at large. Islamic society still exposed its inherent disunity in accommodating various social groups and nationalities like the Arabs, Turks, Afghans, Abyssinians, Mangols and Persians. This is apart from its canonical differences and contradictions between Sunniites and the Shiites and various schools of Islamic jurisprudence as the Shafiites, Malikites, Hanafiites and Hambalis.

Islam in the Indian Setting

Conversion mainly took place from among the lower classes. Again, with all the high sounding dogmas, even after conversions, the social status of such women does not increase in a considerable way. Though Islam preaches equality, differences continued in the socio-economic sphere without much change. Moreover, Indian Muslims were treated separately from the ruling classes never giving opportunity to enjoy the fruits of governance. They were those Hindus who were either converted to Islam themselves or were descendants of converted Muslims. During the entire Sultanate period very few native Muslims could get some opportunity in services of the state. The caste system prevalent among the Hindus directly influenced those Muslims who embraced the new religion of the rulers. These distinctions based on different nationalities and births continued completely in the Sultanate period and partly in the Mughal period. Slavery was prevalent both among Hindus and Muslims. They were a dear item, especially the women slaves, in the open market, where people selected and owned them without any scruples. Though some of the Sultans of the early period belong to the "Slave dynasty" on account of their early attachment with slavery, the general attitude towards slaves in the Sultanate neither improved nor even approved in society. Moreover, Purdah system practically segregated women of both the communities from all social transactions and mobility. The status of women deteriorated heavily in society as a result of the lack of education and employment which were denied to them as per the dictates of men.

In the medieval period what we could experience is the mingling of the common people of both the communities who followed the same cultural traits for centuries, apart from the new religious believes that were either accepted by them or imposed over them. The rulers and nobles formed a class by themselves and those who have mixed up on occasions became partners in a situation of political opportunism.

No study of a society could be complete without proper understanding of its women folk and it often becomes a mirror for our further evaluation and conclusion. What we would say is that the Muslim women of the present day society are not a separate entity in our social fabric and they have to be read with the other women of India who too suffer from gender inequality with religious and social disabilities. Such predicaments are merely a continuation of the old system that pushed them back for centuries. The Indian womanhood suffered the same ethos of the past till the social reform movements of the 19th century. For generations, the people, whether Muslims or Hindus, wished to lead a peaceful life and they had no political and religious ambitions, or if at all they had, they were incapable to wield and influence over others. The cultural milieu of our country forced both Hindus and Muslims to live in harmony and influence each other in all walks of life. Both the leaders of Bhakti movement and the Sufi mystics have prepared the way for leading such a tolerant and harmonious life to the common people of our country.

This situation of tranquillity and peace has been exploited by the rulers and ulemas finally resulting into conflicts and polemics. A major section of the people still believed in the unity and co-existence of communities to evolve a healthy and pluralistic society. Political and administrative requirements even pressurised the elite of both the communities to reach into mutual contact and respect including paradigm shifts in society and religion. This change from the past is a major shift in the socio-religious life of the people which basically created an Indian ethos irrespective of the rigidity of religion, caste and class differences.

The ongoing analysis on the social and religious conditions in medieval India is to highlight the miserable plight of women in general including Hindus and Muslims of different social strata of society. While the Vedas and Smritis curtailed the freedom of Hindu women, several religious tenets and the man-made Shariah sidelined Muslim women also from the socio-political realms, only to give space for a male-oriented and dominated society. However several instances of highly accomplished and educated ladies belonging to the royal families as well as to the aristocratic classes, are available to illustrate the complete freedom of Muslim women in all spheres of human life including politics, literature and culture. Sultana Razia (1238-40), daughter of Iltutmish, asserted her rights as the ruler defeating her brother and the intriguing slave nobles of the court. But as a woman and a ruler, she confronted with the male aristocracy of the court who characterised her rule "unIslamic". The ulemas and nobles could not tolerate the rule of a woman. *Hadiths* like that of one Abu Bakra, who quoted a bogus *hadith* stating that "if a woman becomes a ruler, it is disaster for that country", still hold good. It is purely a partisan statement to oppose Aisha, the wife of the Prophet, when she fought against Ali, the son-in-law of the Prophet[1]. Moreover, the Seljuk Turks who invaded India had the rare fortune of getting gifted scholars and poetesses in the Sultanate, from Badakshan, Khurazan, Samarkhand, Bukhara and other well known cultural centres of Central Asia. A noted woman scholar of the Sultanate period was Mah Malik, the grand daughter of Alaudin Jahan Sanz about whom reference could be seen in the writings of Minhaj-us-Siraj, who lived in the court of Nazirudin Mahamood of the Slave dynasty. He admires her great scholarship and intellectual achievements in his *Tabakat-i-Naziri.*

Female Scholarship

The inflow of female scholarly luminaries belonging to the royal families and aristocratic classes continued firmly during the time of the Mughal rule. They included Gulbadan Begum, daughter of Babur and the author of '*Humayun Nama*', Salima Sultana, the niece of Humayun and a high proficient in Persian literature. Gulbadan, a great literary luminary of the Mughal period, owned a personal library including thousands of books in Persian language. Maham Angah, the step mother and nurse of Akbar, is noted for her scholarship and patronage to education. Nurjahan, the celebrated wife of Jahangir, was a woman of unique talent and intellectual endowments. Her profound bearing had made her wise and shrewd enough to carry on the administration of the vast realms towards the latter part of her husband's reign. It is stated that,

> "Nature had endowed her with a quick understanding, a piercing intellect, a versatile temper and a sound common sense. Education had developed the gifts of nature in no common degree. She was well versed in Persian literature and composed verses limpid and flowing which assisted her in capturing the heart of her husband".[2]

Mumtaz Mahal, the wife of Shahjahan, and in whose memory Taj Mahal is built, was well known for her literary tastes and highly developed poetical faculties. Both Noor Jahan and Mumtaz Mahal took initiative to Zenana education of the medieval period. Jahanara Begum, the daughter of Shahjahan, is immortal in Mughal History for her vast knowledge and high cultural accomplishments. Her humbleness is quite explicited in the selection of the epitaph to be inscribed on her tomb. It reads: "Nothing except mud and grass should be used to cover my 'Makhbara' [tomb], since they are the best to cover the tomb of the poor." Sati-un-nisa, the teacher of Jahanara, was another widely read woman in Arabic, Persian and Indian languages. Zebinda Begum, another daughter of Shah Jahan, was a great exponent of mystic poetry who finds a place in the historical novel of David Ross, *Land of the Five Rivers and Sind*. Almost all the daughters of Aurangazeb were noted for their scholarship and erudition. Zeib-un-nisa Begum was the most cultured and talented of them all. According to *Ma'asir-i-Alamgiri,* she learnt the Quran by rote, for which she had received a reward of 30,000 gold coins from the emperor. She had a big library of her own[3]. Being a great scholar in Persian and Arabic, she wrote the *Diwan-i-Ma'qfi,* a collection of verses and *Zeb-ul-Mansat,* a prose work of exquisite charm, in Persian language. The first Persian translation of the Quran, Commentary of Fakhrudin Razi, was done by Mullah Safi-ud-din under her supervision. In Deccan Province too, luminaries like Chand Sultana adorned with scholarship and literary talents. This clearly reveals that only Mulsim women of higher classes with aristocratic background got the opportunity of getting educated, that too in a limited degree. Considering, the limitation of the age, it is difficult, however to presume that the education of the girls had been universal or on a mass scale even among the aristocratic classes.

Since the royales and nobles enjoyed life in its fullest extent, the women of such households are often projected as models of the medieval period and of Muslim life. But this is too distant from the truth because the commons living in the periphery and in villages never had such an opportunity of education and to gain intellectual attainments. The Muslim society of the period with a flash of urban elitism could never realise the pitiable condition of the poor masses leading a life of misery, hunger and ignorance. It was still not free from evils like child marriage, slavery and the purdah system. It is true that their sisters in Hindu families also were suffering from similar evils of *Jauhar, Sati* and child marriage. The greatest tragedy of the day was the complete social neglect of such people, whether Hindu or Muslim, who forms the major share of the population, by the upper classes of Hindu-Muslim societies. An 'enlightened' or 'glorious' rule at the top need not be for the people in the bottom even if one follows a particular religion or the other. Both Indian and foreign writers testify to the general propserity of the country, although they also refer to the acute differences prevailing in the standards of living of the rich and the poor. The common people on the whole were hardworking and of sober habits living in an atmosphere of love and harmony ignorant of the creed and indifferent to the rule above.

Moreover, on account of the seclusion of women within the four walls of their homes, the opportunities of Muslim women for receiving education might have been considerably restricted, and most of the accomplished ladies, particularly those belonging to the upper classes, might have perhaps, received their education under private tutors. Contemporary literary works reveal several such examples with regard to the extent of literacy such women acquired in different societies. Again, the educational and literary accomplishments that the Muslim women of the higher classes acquired in those days were used as a decorum and a tool to an intellectual exercise for their daily life of pleasure and easiness. Most of them were present in *Mushairas, Qawali* venues and *Mehfils* where great poets, intellectuals and Sufi saints were congregated. The biographies, verses and philosophical discourses of some of the women writers of the royal household are excellent pieces of the period revealing a superb culture a human mind can attain in those days and in full harmony with vision, nature and imagination. As is found in other Islamic cities of the world, particularly in West and Central Asia like Baghdad, Damascus, Cairo, Cordova, Istambul, Isfahan, Khorazan and Samarkand, the life of Muslim women of aristocratic aptitude in India also was centred around urban quarters like Delhi, Agra, Lucknow, Fatehpur Sikri, Lahore, Multan and Hyderabad. Though women 'lived' in such cities, what we could notice is, that they had a very limited role in the economic and social life of such cities. Most of them, except the members of the royal household, were servants doing domestic works and caring children. Some of them may have helped their husbands in their trades and crafts. A good number of women of lower classes in cities were acting as entertainers, dancers and singers. Hence they do not make the core of the population. In general, they did not take part in the central activities of the great cities, that is, involving in the production, distribution and control of commodities. Those who were openly active in such dimensions were women of poor families. To the extent to which a family was wealthy, powerful and respected, it would seclude its women, in a particular part of the home, the *harem*, and beneath the veil when they ventured from the house into the streets and public places[4]. A Maliki jurist of Egypt, Ibn al-Hajj (b. 1336) said that women should not go out to buy things in the market, because they might be led into improper acts if they contact with shopkeepers. To quote him,

> Some of the pious elders (may God be pleased with them) have said that a woman should leave her home on three occasions only.: when she is conducted to the house of her bridegroom, on the death of her parents, and when she goes to her own grave"[5].

Such an orthodoxy unwarranted by reasoning had destroyed the quality of women's social and cultural life, in Indian Context.

From the Sultanate to the post Mughal periods, Muslim women of upper class breed mostly lived in the seclusion of the Zenana. But they were not excluded from life. Within the women's quarters of large households, intravisits were common, like at the public bath houses which were reserved for women, and at marriage celebrations or at the birth of child and in other festive occasions where family members and friends are met. These are jubilant occasions when, irrespective of their age, mingled, dined, danced and sang in chorus. There were also occasions for ladies of noble families to take part in administering their properties, ofcourse through intermediaries, usually by handmaids. In the medieval period in India cases are also reported of women appearing before Qazis or Shariah courts to demand their rights. Elderly women could acquire great esteem and power in the family particularly when they had male children. But these are all under the dictums and dictates of a patriarchal society in which the social order was always upon the superior power and rights of men. The relations of men and women were deeply rooted in the cultural and customary traits of Islam which never had been uniform even in different Islamic countries. The Ulemas and the other religious functionaries thus arrived at a conclusion to impose a man-made low, the *Shariah* over them for want of a religious uniformity leaving apart all kinds of differences in custom and culture in a given space. Though Quran asserts equality of men and women in clear terms in several verses[6], it is not properly applied in most of their (men's) dealings with women.

The wide continuity of feudalism as a universal phenomenon and the secluded life of a group of people in social or residential units called *Mohallas* in the medieval and early modern period in India, virtually strengthened the concept of a compartmentalised life as in the walled city life found in West Asia and Europe. Such a life also led to some kind of an inertia and lack of mobility in several societies blockading the chances of interpolations particularly of women folk. Even women of the poorer quarters of the neighbourhood or Mohalla were not allowed to mingle with the women of the quarters where women of superior class lived. At the same time, there was a tendency for the inhabitants of a quarter to be linked by common origin, religious, ethnic or by kinship or by intermarriage. Such links created a solidarity which might be strong compared to several other factors. But life in such quarters could not be equalised with the life of the ghettos where Jews and Christians lived in Europe in the medieval period. Whatever may be the nature and constitution of a quarter, women of that particular quarter enjoyed maximum freedom of movement and action. The present day Old Delhi was such a typical city with the Mosque (Juma Masjid), a central *Suq* from where cultural and economic activities radiated. The old dwelling places and shopping centres are now found exinct with the town planning of Delhi metro administration. But a model of such a walled city could be redrawn still from the remains of the old. The same was the case of Lucknow, Lahore and Hyderabad.

With regard to customs and manners, medieval India witnessed many changes as life could not be stable in those days of war and uncertainty. One important factor that attracts us is the similarity between the customs and practices of Hindus and Muslims despite their religious differences. In many important matters connected with the ceremonies of birth, marriage and death, their ceremonial was, broadly speaking similar. This was, no doubt, due to the fact that the majority of Muslims were Hindu converts, who were deeply attached to their old habits of life. Although commonality of faith made the Muslims more homogeneous than the Hindus, social divisions and class concern were no less pronounced among them inhibiting free social intercourse and intermarriage. In the case of the immigrants and their descendants, old time differences and prejudices persisted. But among the converts, there was a perceptible difficulty in getting out of the old caste structure and caste mentality despite the mere change in faith. The Rajput converts retained their caste nomenclature and family surnames. Converts from the higher Hindu castes and the descendants of the immigrant tribes enjoyed a higher social status which they sought to maintain all along. There are several examples like the Meo tribes who still stuck to their former way of life despite conversion into Islam. Further sectarian differences stood in the way of homogeneity. There was a sharp cleavage between the Sunni sects and the Shiites. But intermarriages among them were not uncommon. Humayun's wife was a Shiah and so was Nur Jahan, the wife of Jahangir. So also was Mumtaz Mahal, the wife of ShahJahan. When we talk of the monotheistic ideology of Islam, we ignore the major schism in Islam, the Suniites and the Shiites, and the sub divisional differences found in the four Orthodox Schools of Islamic jurisprudence like the Hanafi, Hambali, Shafi and the Maliki. All of them differ in their view on the role of women in Islam. Besides, there were ecclesiastical attachments to particular religious leaders and their orders like that of mystics, sufis and mendicants. Various *Silsilahs* of the Sufis like the Suharvardi, Qadiriya, Nakshbandi and Chistiya have distinct approaches with regard to the role of the women in society. The tribal differences as we could see in the present day situations in Arabia, Gulf region, Iraq, Afghanistan and Pakistan, fully ascribe to the differences among them which prevented the growth of communal solidarity. Though not with a caste mentality, as in the case of Hindus, a feeling of 'lineage' and categorisation affected Muslim societies also which recognized social distinctions as in the case of the Syeds, Sheikhs and Pathans, besides those of foreign and indigenous Muslims.

From the experiences of the medieval period we know that the consummation of marriages between Muslims of high social status (like the members of royal family, nobles etc.) and Rajput ladies of rank were comparatively easier than one with a Shia woman or of a different Muslim sect. But in this case also the custom of hypergamy was strictly followed and there were not so much instances of a Muslim woman of high rank ordinarily marrying a male even from the Rajput clan.

The Women of Identity

Muslim women of the medieval period distinguished themselves in their dress and ornaments from those of their sisters in Hinduism. A variety of dresses are found among them from North (Kashmir) to South (Kerala) and from the West (Punjab) to the East (Bengal). The quality and shape of the dress vary from the higher classes to the lower. The lower classes of women naturally copied the local practices from their Hindu sisters, but with some distinction of a long cloth covering their head and body as their religion required. The lower garment fully covered the bottom part of the body, till the feet. The most popular dress consisted of a 'Lahanga' (long and loose skirt) and a 'Choli' (a jacket). Abul Fazl refers to 'Lahanga' as a popular dress of Muslim women. He also refers to 'Pyjamas' worn by upper class ladies [7]. The main distinction found among the Muslim women is their wide use of 'Salwars' and 'Kameezes' with full sleeves. A 'Duppatta' or a long scarf was also worn covering the head, the upper parts of the body, the shoulders and bosom. Ornaments with precious stones were worn extensively as bangles, necklaces and anklets. Embroidery and decorative needle work with beautiful designs and colours were done to the dress of the upper class. The aesthetic sense and fashion consciousness of Nurjahan is praised by all writers. She had revolutionised the pattern of dresses and had designed new varieties of brocade and lace, gowns and carpets[8]. Though Muslim women of higher rank observed purdah system, the lower ones usually went out unveiled as their Hindu sister of same status. Women of the medieval period were fond of perfumes and Abul Fazl refers to a variety of perfumes prepared and used by the women of the period. Use of 'Mehandi'(henna) also was inevitable both for the rich and the poor alike in festive occasions.

Analysing the status of women in the Mughal court, especially of the royal house, writers have appreciated the overbearing hold and influence of the women and the richness of the personalities it displayed. "The emperors led the way, but others jostle behind them and the interest extends behind the purdah curtain itself, in the age of secluded women, to the great Mughal ladies. Nur Jahan, Jahanara and Zeb-un-Nisa hold their own with Akbar and Shah Jahan"[9]. Though confined to the royal household, this is a clear shift from the social practices that India had both in the ancient period and in the early medieval period. But such a social situation with high status to women was generally limited to the four walls of their palace or living apartments. Women commonly did not enjoy any type of freedom since they are controlled by religious tenets. *Fatwas* (religions ordinances) are often imposed by the Ulemas over women who are marginalised and socially and economically below. In fact women in India enjoyed at least in theory an honourable status in society. The advent of Turks and Mughals brought about a change in the attitude of women in general and Muslim women in particular. The customs and traditions of the country in addition to the religious dictates, pushed the women behind the curtain stamping a stigma of mental deficiency and this created in them a profound sense of inferiority and inactivity. Though women were still treated with respect, the birth of a female child was looked upon with displeasure and discredit to the whole family. Even Amir Khusrao (1253-1325), a poet with the highest poetic calibre, laments by hearing the birth of his daughter, "I wish you were not born and if you were, it would have been better if you had been a boy. No one can alter the decree of fate."[10].

Purdah as a social custom was accepted and observed by Muslim women in India as some Hindu women who belonged to the upper and well-to-do classes. Poor women belonging to any religious group did not observe prudah because it inhibits the free movement of such women who seek employment or to earn a livelihood. If it is a religious imposition, these women, universally might have observed it without objections. Purdah and seclusion certainly restrict all types of freedom especially the freedom of movement. Women of poor economic standing, especially in rural areas, who had to work outdoors for their maintenance, could not have afforded to observe the rules of purdah or to remain in seclusion. Purdah as observed by Muslim women is with greater rigidity. Both indigenous literature and accounts of travellers vouch for the existence of a rigid system of purdah in India. Manucci refers to that the Muslim women do not allow their faces to be seen by any one. Women of higher social rank travelled only in covered palanquins (Palkis) strictly observing seclusion. There are different varieties in the texture of the purdah throughout the world, of which an Indian variety is the 'Ghoonghat'. In this case the face veil is comparatively thin and transparent. Hindu women of higher social rank also wore the same, especially in the occasion of the marriage. Purdah is also associated with the practice of 'harem' life among Muslims where women are segregated from public life. There hundreds of women are allowed to live in a separate apartment attached to the royal houses exclusively to the pleasures of men. The 'harem' life really reveals the laxity in the morals of the emperors, nobles and the rich people who led a life of ease and pleasure. Inside the harem, women, whether concubines or slaves, enjoyed 'freedom' which they could not expose outside. They also played the role of guards of their apartments, kings and nobles, along with the eunuchs. These women-guards often acted as detectives to find out the possible plots which may often arise from the royal household. But these women did not veil themselves to anybody[11]. On the whole, the practice of purdah, in whatever form they might be, hampered the progress of women denying them all sorts of freedom and proper education and to the complete subordination of them to the whims and fancies of men.

Early and child marriages were common in the Islamic society of India as Brahmins and other higher social classes among the Hindus of that period. This practice also lowered down the status of women in society leading to a corresponding increase in the number of widows and licentious women. Emperor Akbar is believed to have been the first among the Mughals who tried to abolish the child marriage among the Muslims and the Hindus. He not only strongly opposed to the marriages between men and women before the age of puberty[12], but even forbade the marriages of girls before fourteen and boys before sixteen years of age[13]. The system of dowry found in various forms badly affected the condition of women in the Mughal period. Nizamudin Ahmed refers to this practice among the Muslims of high rank during Akbar's period, eventhough the emperor did not agree with the payment of heavy dowries[14]. Both Jahangir and Aurengazeb also found it as a great evil. Polygamy also was prevalent among the rich and the poor alike. Though a privilege to the rich and the rulers, this practice also was condemned and discouraged by emperors like Akbar. These practices in toto, acted as impediments to the freedom and status of women in the medieval society of India.

Women in the Colonial System

The condition of Muslim women did not improve considerably in the early colonial period. Instead, the situation further worsened due to their enmity towards the British. The British, being considered as those who snatched the power enjoyed for centuries by Muslims, were treated with animosity and whatever they introduced here were opposed. Thus were denied the opportunities of modern education to the Muslims in general and their women in particular. The Muslims, at the beginning, stood alone to resist and to defend the life and culture that they evolved for centuries. The entry of the Europeans created in Malabar some hard core divisions among them which finally culminated in the revolts of 1921. In the late nineteenth century two streams of thought among Muslims could be seen, one represented by the loyalists like Sir Syed Ahmed Khan and his Aligarh movement, and the other the Deoband School initiated by Rashid Ahmed and Qasin Nanawtawi in 1867. Sir Syed's motive was to make the upper class Muslims aware of the fruits of the British administration, especially English Education. Thus was formed the Anglo-Mohammedan Oriental College, later transformed into the popular Aligarh Muslim University. This led to a sense of separatism which developed "not for reasons of backwardness," as Sumit Sarkar pointed out, but because traditional elite felt that they are threatened by the growing Hindu economically powerful class of traders, money lenders and professionals[15]. Deoband, comparatively a centre of poor students who could not afford western education, while opposing Aligarh loyalists, supported the Congress nationalists. This created a double-edged ideology of Pan Islamism on one side and an anti-British nationalist move on the other, but with a consistent attack on modernism.

It is also interesting to note that even for an ardent reformer like Sir Syed, issues of Muslim women were only secondary. Whenever he stressed on the importance of education, he meant it only for men and that too unsuited to the domestic and social requirements of the Muslim community. Minhaj al Ta'leem, a publication of the literary society of Bareilly, in 1870 has this to say: "Once women would learn to read and write, they no longer would be under the control of men; would become very clever and would entertain immodest expectations will communicate with letters and thus honour and family name would be at stake and subsequently much chaos would be spread out"[16]. He was against the system of education sponsored by the government and advocated a traditional system of education for Muslim girls or else they would become immoral[17]. Such an attitude of Sir Syed is often justified by some that he did not want the Muslim community to be more estranged from his own movement by giving some more chances to the orthodox for criticism. But this seems to be more strange because Sir Syed, as a reformer was journeying all along through his conservative community with hardships and opposition. While Sir Syed and other reformers were reluctant to impart modern education to their women with the availability of their own separate institutions, the reform leaders among Hindus like Ram Mohan Roy instituted several free schools of primary and secondary education to the Hindu girls as his own initiative advocating their "right to education and enlightenment" [18]. India had a brilliant tradition of female education to all the communities in the past. The Auxiliary committee of the Indian Statutory Commission in 1929 reports that there is nothing inherent either in the Hindu or in the Muslim religion which militates against the education of women. But this was only an intellectual exercise, particularly in classical and sacred literature, in the upper class circles of both the communities. What we could see in the nineteenth century is the revival of Hindu community including women, by several of the socio-religious movements and the establishments of educational institutions.

The reverse looking attitude, especially in the case of Muslim women, was partly due to the fear of the infiltration of modernism and the 19th century liberalism, about which they have an anathema. Moreover, the colonial education system in India was mainly managed and operated by the Christian missionaries who have an additional agenda of proselytisation and the negation of national and religious identities other than that of theirs. The disgusted, Muslim community who already had animosity towards the British with the feelings of the loss of their empire, on the whole, turned their back towards all sorts of progressivism, sacrificing everything including their own development, to the cause of religion and identity. The control of ulemas and other religous functionaries over the community as a whole, particularly on females dictated dogmas imposing the veil, highly detrimental to free education and freedom of movement. Realising the importance of female education., the Hunter Commission on Education appointed by Lord Ripon in 1882 recommended that "female education should receive special encouragement and be treated with special liberality. Yet, as it was rightly pointed out in the Education Resolutions issued by Curzon's administration, much remained to be done in the case of female education." Moreover, while others were utilising the governmental machinery and fund for equipping women with higher education, the Muslim leadership, still in the stronghold of their traditional believes, never realised this colossal failure on their part, pushing them further to the labyrinth of ignorance and inactivity.

The twin evils of purdah, illiteracy and ignorance among the Muslim women of India, found their fiercest test in the second half of the nineteenth century, especially during the days of the Great Famine of 1896. A major section of Muslim women in North-West Provinces and Oudh could not come out in public and receive food grains and financial aid given by the government and other voluntary organisations due to the observance of purdah. Shortage of crop even led to grain riots in places like Agra. A major section of 'purdah-nashin' women belonged to the highly respectable families and the relatives of the later generations of Mughal nobles and generals were greatly affected by the new situation. Their lineage with the old royal families and aristocracies never allowed them to come in public and receive charitable aid. Those who belonged to the lower rank especially in the villages did not observe purdah, and hence they enjoyed the benefits available to them. Women of highly respectable origin were compelled to live in unhealthy conditions of the towns with hunger and deceases. The seclusion of such women also made it difficult to ascertain the number of persons who required relief. Moreover, they want the relief measures, if any, essentially off the record because they never wanted to publicise their names and addresses. Several such insistances were reported from Agra, Lucknow and Fatehpur Sikri that the 'pardah-nashin' women refused to accept doles when they heard that their names were recorded as recipients of charity[19]. But this made the government machinery in a dilemma because all their activities must be accountable and transparent. The post Mughal period in India was so pathetic that these women of the 'once rulers' became the weakest women in the society, being languished at home and eventually perished. This is a miserable saga of the 'pardah-nashin' women extensively found in colonial India. Again, unlike their Hindu sisters, these women, shut up in their apartments, seldom go for work outside cherishing the memory of their proud past. The ignorant, poor, but distinctively nostalgic Muslim women of post Revolt (1857) India led a life of helpnessess and uneasiness as described by Dalrymple[20]. When the Muslims as a community lost their privileges under the Mughals, the situation more adversely affected their women folk who could not even go for a menial job for survival.

The life of Muslim women in the colonial period has no basic change compared to the one that they led in the medieval period. All the more, their condition has been worsoned due to the colonial economic and cultural situations when they lost security and peace especially when they could not compete with their Hindu sisters with total ignorance and the inborn interior cultural baggage. The rise of 'Mehfils' (Music-cum-Dance halls), Qawwali-Ghazal Khanas and such other private apartments owned by courtesans, from where recrection and entertainments for men generated, reflected the socio-economic decadence of the Indo-Muslim Society of the period. Muslim literature, particularly 'the holy' urdu, took a new dimension by retreating from its classical nature, revealed the 'licenciousness"of a patriarchal but sensuous society. Even a separate branch in urdu literature called 'Rekhti' became popular in places like Lucknow, Oudh, Agra and Delhi in the North and Bijapur and Hyderabad in the South[21]. These erotic poems represent love between women and reveal the life of women in the elite Indo-Muslim households. Male poets wrote *Ghazals* on women and their beauty with a motive to rejuvenate erotic thoughts among men and women through a woman to woman dialogue. Exposition of sexual desire in both males and females among themselves is the major aim of such works since heterosex or *zina* (prostitution) is prohibited in Islam. Hence some of the poets have taken lesbianism or varieties of female homosexualities as theme for their poetry. While describing the Zenanas (lady's apartments) and the milieu that created by it, the poet considers lesbian desire as accepted and an inevitable product of life[22]. They too have an excuse that the love between a man and a woman (other than the married), as found in love poems, is unislarmic and hence prohibited.

The concern here is only to juxtapose what Muslim women had been in the early colonial period and how far her position differed from the pre-Revolt age or the later Mughal period. Both the literature and the contemporary chronicles reveal that it was almost the same. The Muslim woman was only a victim of the milieu and what amazing us is that, with all the oppressive ideologies of the period, they find a path which spells dignity and power through their involvement in public spaces like the Zenanas and Mehfils as victors. This dichotomy of womanhood with a dogmatic submission on the one side, and the feminal extravaganza on the other, explicitly highlights the colonial socio-cultural situations. But such upperclass aberrations could not be taken as a standard for a common estimation or understanding of a community. The issue here is how to overcome the barriers that obstruct women coming from the less privileged classes. Gender desparity often works as an additional contributor to social inequality. It does not act independent of classes. Both class deprivation and gender discrimination can destroy the lives of poorer women very severely. The interactive presence of these two features of deprivation—being the unprivileged and being the female—can massively impoverish women from the neglected lower classes[23]. It is from this hangover of the old empire [of the Mughals] and the lethargy that followed as a result of European colonialism, that Muslim women are stepping into the socio-economic realities of Modern India. In the colonial period, with the formation of an Islamic law, the *Shariah* (which need not be to the true spirits of the Quranic tenets and the traditions/*hadith* of the Prophet), a politically motivated Islamic code of conduct, new norms and dictums have been imposed on the Islamic society with the gavel of religion. This hammer of religion is often put on women all the time, being the weaker and more sensitive section of society, who are almost mute and unopposed. In the colonial period, being the times of conflict, what we could experience is that women become both the symbol of honour and the target to be dishonoured.

Society in Transition

The reason for the drastic changes in the status of Muslim women in the colonial period is mainly due to the European occupation of the land once owned by them. The British colonisation virtually affected the social fabric of India, internally and externally. The loss of confidence resulted in the loss of tolerance. Muslim men reacted to this loss by doing what they thought was necessary for the protection and integrity of their families. They secluded their women from the eyes of foreign troops and imposed pardah over them. Women were restricted in the home. When Muslim society is confident and in a state of balance, it treats women with fairness and respect. When Muslim Society is threatened and feels vulnerable, it treats women with indifference and harshness[24]. It is true that the impact of colonialism is responsible for this state of affairs in a country like that of ours and it was the Muslim society that affected gravely as our experience shows in the last centuries. Colonialism imposed foreign values, which the Muslim society, being conservative, could not accommodate easily. Muslim society is found totally dejected and collapsed and unsure of its destiny as explained in one of the letters of Mirza Ghalib, the noted poet, written in the aftermath of the Revolt of 1857. He notes the pity and the miserable tale of the descendants of the Mughals and their nobles, most of them, particularly the women folk, waiting for some men for sharing what they have, only to earn a square meal for a simple existence[25]. While men retreated into the shell of rigid customs and sterile ritual, they forced their women to hide behind the burkhahs, or shuttlecock veils. "It was a bad time for Islam, a time of retreat. When the European masters began to leave from the middle of the twentieth century Muslim women were to be glimpsed still in various degrees of deprivation and subjugation. They still have to recover"[26].

The condition of Muslim women in the post independent India, especially immediately after Independence, is not at all encouraging. The Government of India have appointed several commissions including Sachar in recent years, as a fitting testimony to vouch for this. The issue of the status of Muslim women and defining it cross-culturally is rather complicated. The traditional definition of the status of both men and women has been reckoned in terms of the degree to which a person possesses the qualities or attributes which are considered valuable in a particular society. The basic factors that determine the status of a person are mainly education and the occupation one possesses. Rigid religious practices and lack of education increased the degeneration and degradation of the status of women. Moreover, men encroached their spaces qualifying them with high reverence and applying the 'weaker sex' theory and finally pushing them to the showcases with the freedom totally curtailed. Since Muslim society being patriarchal, men seems to have dominated every aspects of their life. Muslim women are among the most backward sections of Indian society. They have not received adequate attention either of the Government or of any NGOs. Lack of education, poverty, economic dependency and above all, ignorance of their rights have made them more vulnerable to exploitation.

In India, women in general and Muslim women in particular are more down-trodden than any other community. Demographical and statistical studies have brought to light appalling facts that Muslim women are much more backward than women of other communities. Socially, they are the most depressed class of Indian society for various reasons other than their own. Their problems are complex and for that matter, more difficult to comprehend. The backwardness of Muslims as a community and its women folk in particular has to be viewed both in historical perspective and in the light of the social and political forces that determine the general retardation of the community in the present day situations. Several studies on women's education brought forth a fact that the condition of Muslim women is more deplorable than the position of the scheduled castes and scheduled tribes. The recently published Sachar Commission report also reveals this fact and suggests several remedial measures to uplift the women of the Muslim community. It is the religion as interpreted by the ulemas pulls the Muslim women back all the time and hence they could not think liberally or otherwise. With all the efforts of the governmental machineries, what the Muslim girls get is the primary or the basic education to a minimum of five or six years, and while they come up to think, it is stopped once for all. As per the surveys conducted in different parts of the country, Muslim girls are not getting free and liberal education in the higher level including secondary. This lacunae of not getting opportunities for higher and secular education for the girl students virtually destroy the future of women and the growth of their faculties in different levels of life. The world in front of them totally becomes dark and blind. While others make strides, they can't even walk. Such ignorance generating some kind of innocence, not only mislead them, but even take them to the corridors of superstition and blind believes. They could never experience or enjoy the fast growing world, but become an easy prey to the mockery of those who made the best use of it. Liberal or secular education has been considered as an important tool for bringing social and human development. Though basic education is the foundation, higher education is its superstructure and an essential constituent of every human being. A girl or a woman, after getting educated, becomes self contented and acts liberally. Higher education is an important agent of social mobility and instrument of social change. It is also a great source of empowerment. Such educated women can very easily share the decision making with regard to family planning, education of the children, financial management and to know the modern world better. In the graph of education and employment, Muslim women are found at the lowest, below 5 per cent.

Partition of India in 1947 awarded unending miseries and a life of uncertainty to the women of the border states as discussed in detail by writers like Mushirul Hasan, Farzana Sheikh and Ritu Menon in several of their studies.

Farzana endorses the Muslim separatist tendencies as expressed in the opposition of western representation in line with the political norms of Islam[27]. Partition affected so worsely on women that thousands of them either killed or abducted in the horrible holocaust that followed[28]. Hence women, especially Muslim women in India, after partition, could not rise up to the occasion from its long standing sluggishness and shock. Women with a feeling of doubt and uncertainty never thought of a better life when they themselves were struggling to live. They could not come out of their shells, particularly when they were 'protected' and 'owned' by their men, often as a property with the fear of losing them. Education also was one among many things that denied to them. The centrality of the problem debated on Muslim women always is the negation of education to them. In the post-colonial period, other issues like the partition trauma added to the intensity of the problem. Moreover, Islamic society in India often attaches its identity with global Islam and Indian Muslims only as a microcosm of its homogeny. This is purely on account of the wrong reading and understanding of Islamic history considering it as a monolithic culture universally. Though Islam as a religion found new frontiers, the culture and tradition of the region made its identities diverse in different diasporas.

Muslims, not Islam, in the periphery [beyond the heartland] are found varied and dissimilar in life and culture. It stretches from West Africa to South East Asia comprising USSR, China, North Africa, Indian Sub continent, Malay Penisula, Philippines and Indonesia. As far as Indian Muslims are concerned, the attempts of unity and uniformity began with the revivalism, initiated by Jamaludin Afghani and Mohammed Abduh in West Asia, and imported to Penisular India by various revivalist agencies. This was really an 'attack' on individual/singular cultural identities retained in the periphery of Islam. Revivalism, instead of strengthening regional specialities, virtually revitalised new artificial homogeneity which is alien and unaccommodative to many within the orbit of the Islamic society and outside. This created, or still are creating a social and cultural distance which often kills the pluralistic way of life. In fact, Muslim society of the periphery are the part and parcel of the region or state where they exist. They always remained out of the main stream of the Islamic world for centuries without knowing or experiencing the halo and glamour of the 'glorious empires' developed in the name of Islam. Even to the Muslims of the South of India, the Mughal Empire of the North is alien. Before the advent of revivalism, for long, this fictitious and fabricated web of unity could not find a space in the Islamic societies of various regions living with the deep rooted cultural distinctiveness of their own. Most importantly, Islam in these areas, instead of innovation, learnt to adapt and grow as a frontier community. Later local adaptations even over powered the main stream ideals as could be seen in the lives of Indonesian Muslims mainly and the Mappilas of Malabar partly, till recently.

After Independence

In Independent India Muslim women still suffer from the so called *Shariah* or "religious laws" which are applied unilaterally over them by the ulemas and those who have power in society. This is an important factor that obstacles Muslim women to come out from their age-old shackles. The over emphasis that the society gives to the Muslim personal law affects mainly its womenfolk pushing them back to lead a life of seclusion and neglect. In India the *Shariah* is framed in the colonial period as a reference alone to the British Courts of law, but nothing to do with the "Spirit" of the Quranic tenets as expected in its enactment. This partisan man-made law has been considered 'divine' by a section of Muslims as reflected in several cases of Polygamy and unilateral divorce. Moreover, the fundamentalists take up the issue as a minority right as manifested in cases like that of Shah Bano (1984) and the Muslim Women (Protection of Rights on Divorce) Act, 1986. While the Shah Bano ruling by the Supreme Court awarded some security for the maintenance of a Muslim divorcee, the Act of 1986 was only to appease the community who by this time have started agitation against it all over the country.

All these Acts and initiatives on the part of the government are centred around the issues of the Muslim Personal Law which is often politicised to the tune of a few and with a gender bias against women. Moreover, most of the explanations given in the *Shariah* law are highly opposed to the fundamental rights of women to have legal equality irrespective of gender and religion. Writers on Muslim women unanimously agree upon the fact that the Muslim Personal Law contained the corpus of the *Shariah* makes a dangerous harm to Muslim women as a subordinate class to their men folk. While Quran intends to save the women, the *Shariah* subordinates and oppress them. The mysogynist tendency of Shariah could be seen in its approach to the social status of women related to segregation, unilateral divorce of men, and the veil. To examine the issues of Muslim women within the purview of the available Shariah, we must view Muslim women in a general socio-economic context of the country stressing on some focal points to empower them with education and job opportunities. Government, as a people's organ and the protector of the civil rights and democracy, should take brave steps to redraft the Shariah on the basis of Quran and not on the opinions of the ulemas. *Shariah* is mainly based on the oral dictations, *fatwas,* interpretations or resolutions by some ulemas or religious bodies framed to the requirement of the time. *Shariah* is not dogma. It is not the word of God, but the interpretation of the word of God by mortal human beings. Muslims, ignorant of Quran are misled by the self styled Muslim divines (Mullas) by claiming that *'Shariah* is the word of God' and therefore cannot be changed[29]. It is neither written nor codified and not applicable to all in time and space. Most of them are personal in nature and are subjective as found recently on the issue of *Vandemataram*.

The greatest lacuna in the study of Muslim women is that they are often treated by researchers not as a heterogenous entity with multiple socio-cultural traits; instead, envelop them with a monolithic whole to suit to the requirement of Islamic religion only. Muslim women are the poorest and the most disadvantaged group in the country. They are far behind the scheduled castes of India educationally and professionally. While analysing the differences in education status in women, we could realise that Muslim women are more illiterate than Hindu women. A survey even reveal that 59 per cent of them never attended school and those who completed it is only 10 per cent. Very few Muslim girls study beyond the primary stage and even fewer beyond the age of fifteen years[30]. The question of education for Muslim Women is always a burning problem in the Islamic society of India. In all the surveys made nationally and regionally, what we could notice is that a major section of them including mullahs and religious functionaries highlight compulsory religious education simultaneous to the secular education. This perhaps is due to the over emphasis that they give for religion with a fear that women would go astray if they are not properly trained in Islamic religious streams. They have an additional fear of loosing their own age-long grip on the control of society. Even though all agree to educate women, most of them are not ready to send their daughters beyond high school or higher secondary level. As a result, the percentage of Muslim girls attending colleges and universities is not significantly increasing. Some field studies have brought to light majority of the parents of girl students look only for institutions specially, meant for women[31]. The survey reveals about 60 per cent of the parents favours higher education to their daughters of which 10 per cent favoured it only if 'separate' institutions are provided for girl students. This is an alarming situation because, separate institutions for women are only a part of government policy, considering it as economically feasible, taking into the possible number of students enrolled there. Moreover, majority of the respondents belong to the middle and higher classes of society among Muslims to whom higher education is only an ornament, rather than an instrument for employment. If we classify the datas, we could realise that majority of the respondents are illiterate and for that matter they are not favourable to higher or professional education to their daughters. A negligible amount of parents (about 2.5-3%) recommended higher education (preferably professional) to their daughters on economic grounds with a feeling that they would be attracted in the marriage market, even if the parents are poor. As early marriage is the customary practice, the women fail to get professional education which demands continuing study for long duration.

Education in Religious Institutions

The general reluctancy for sending their daughters to co-educational institutions and the pressure of fundamentalists to take them to Madrassas are some of the other reasons for the low percentage of women students in the institutions for higher education. (A new trend could be seen recently for joining faculties like medicine, teacher education and computer learning even in the backward areas). Moreover a good number of parents, especially the poor, fear the ulemas and Mullahs who insist only religious education to girls and also who never agree the girls' move out of their houses after puberty. The poor and illiterate parents, who otherwise won't have any social standing, will be fearful of the possible social taboo or ostracism which may use against them by the rich. The teachings in Madrassas and periodical discourses of the religious functionaries characterise modern education as irreligious and doing great harm not only to the education of girls, but to the growth of the nation as a whole. Such a feeling on education has resulted into a negative growth in the other way (for religious education) particularly among the poor in society. Those who are poor and unable to acquire education in public institutions, since they are costly, and the number of government sponsored institutions are limited or disproportionate to the number of students, a major share of students seek learning in religious institutions where learning, food, clothing and stay are sometimes free. Such institutions thus become a relief for the parents who never realise that their children are going to be trained as fundamentalists and terrorists as experienced in Pakistan and Afghanistan. The former Prime Minister of Pakistan, the late Benazir Bhutto (she herself has been martyred on account of her stand against fundamentalism), vehemently criticised the military regime of Pakistan which nurses the Taliban mode of priesthood which interpret the religion with its various compulsions through the newly emerging Shariah courts, and even warns that, if such extremists are not controlled, instead of a military coup, they (the Islamists) would take up the charge[32]. Soon they become the role models of the extremists all over the world.

In a country like that of India, madrassas and other religious seminaries mostly step into the vacuum of public schools where secular and liberal education is imparted to students of all communities without any discrimination. But now financial constraints often force the government to set up very limited number of public schools and the rural poor thus have no outlet or option to modern education. Such a vacuum compels them to go to madrassas and such other religious institutions, where education (without any approved curriculum), food and clothing are free. "They naturally act as magnets to draw students"[33]. Though girls are not enrolled in madrassas after puberty or marriage, they too have opportunities to attend religious classes or

Quran classes attached to mosques where religious instructions are given periodically by women or male teachers. Apart from religious instructions to those participants who attend such discourses, such centres also encourage mothers to train their children to lead a pure and strict religious life. Children thus trained will not get opportunities to acquire liberal and secular education, so long as they are in the clutches of religious instructors. This is a major danger and a trap from which innocent women and children could not become free and to go for liberal secular learning.

After Independence, there had been great improvement in providing facilities for the education of women. The government of India introduced a new education policy with special concern for women and their socio-economic improvement, equality, gender justice and human rights. It is also envisaged that the national policy on education could be an important strategy for achieving a basic change in the status of women.

Being essential for the growth of human resource, intellectual, social and emotional development, education plays an important role in building up a strong nation. Women, constituting nearly 50 per cent of the nation, have a greater role, being the home-maker and thereby creating a healthy and vibrant society. If we compare Muslim women with the women of other communities, they are found far lagging behind in all spheres of life, in education, employment, public life and politics. Women in Islamic society of India are to be categorised as a separate group of marginalised and free from the socio-economic linkages of the nation. This handicap to Muslim women of the country is not caused by the nations' fault, but by their own community, who have not yet been able to take full advantage of the modernisation that takes place in India. Ofcourse these are due to certain social and cultural factors like pre-puberty and early marriages, negligence of secular education, reluctance to go to public and co-educational institutions, licencious marriages like polygamy, segregation in social life and purdah system. There is pressing necessity of change in social and educational attitudes of Muslim women. Their problems should be viewed in proper perspective both by the government and by their own community. Knowing all these limitations of the community for its backwardness, no systematic efforts have been made by any agencies, including from their own, to get rid of these draw backs and bring them to the level of women of other communities. The low economic status of the community, indifference to education, lack of any organised effort on the part of the community, and above all, the socio-religious pressures are some of the main reasons for this miserable condition of Muslim women in India.

Cultural Diversity

Further more, we know, from the very beginning of Islam, it never imposed a static legal system to be followed by all in all time and spaces. Both the Prophet and the Khulafa-ul-Rashidin (the four orthodox Caliphs immediately followed the Prophet) both *Ijma* (consensus of the people) and *Ijthihad* (reasonable interpretation of scholars) to be accepted where Quran and Hadith are found silent. This shows the flexibility of religion and its laws wherever Islam had its hand. Even the four canonical streams of Islam—the Shafi, Hanafi, Hambali and Maliki—never agree on many of the Islamic dictations supposed to be supported by the verses of the Quran and traditions of the Prophet. Later Imams like Ibn Taimiyya and Al Ghazzali differ on may issues exposing that Islamic ideology also is not a monolith. Hence Islam as a religion is always found to be receptive of all changes required by social forces in the religious practices whereever it has infiltrated. Best examples of its assimilation could be seen in Byzantium, Egypt, West Africa, Turkey and South East Asia in the primacy of its suzerainty. Hence the early Islam offers the quality of cultural diversity and synthesis parallelly keeping the religious identity. The role of Muslim woman in Kerala as head of the family, as the Nair women in Matrilineal system, is a fitting testimony to the local adaptation of systems followed by the Mappila Muslims as a cultural heritage, ofcourse, against the dictums of the religion. The Sakka Muslims of Uttar Pradesh still observe the Hindu practice of carrying fire as a part of their wedding ceremony along with the Muslim *Nikah*[34]. Such instances of accepting local practices like *Tali Kettu* of Hindus are very common among the Muslims of Kerala, particularly in the southern parts. But the Mappila Muslims of North Malabar who have more an Arab influence, particularly of the Shafiite lineages, do not follow such rituals. The absence of a uniformity in the case of the application of *Shariah* in different parts of India virtually exposes the possible laxity and freedom that various Muslim societies could enjoy regionally. Reformist Leaders like Sir Syed Ahmed Khan even declared that the British have not yet realised that the new age demanded totally a new legal system to deal with social, political and administrative affairs. He even called upon Muslims to formulate a new legal code suited to their present requirements. There were several Muslim leaders to follow Sir Syed like Justice Karamat Husain from U.P., Abbas Taiyyabji from Bombay, Sayed Amir Ali from Calcutta, Sir Mohammed Shafi from Lahore, and a host of others.

If *Shariah*, as often claimed, is based on Quran and Sunnah, and is divine and unchangeable, how can this has been modified in India in 1937, 1939 and in several other situations without notice? The Shariah Act of 1937 demanded that the share of the daughter in the father's property has to be restored. The Muslim Marriage Act (Dissolution) of 1939, meant a great relief to Muslim women who were threatened by unilateral divorce. By this act, women obtained the right for dissolution of her marriage. The conditions of dissolution are: (1) If whereabouts of husband unknown for four years. (2) failure of husband to provide maintenance for two years. (3) Imprisonment of husband about seven years. (4) Impotency of husband (5) If the husband suffer from insanity, leprosy, or venereal disease. (6) Girls' early marriage and her repudiation before 18 years of age. (7) Husband's cruelty towards wife, etc. Again, eventhough Quran unequivocally declared the maintenance as an obligation of the husbands to the divorced wife through the verse 241 of the Chapter *Al-Baqra* (The Cow),[35] Muslim men generally waived it for their convenience. But it was made effective in India by Section 125 of the Code of Criminal Procedure in 1973 inviting much criticism from the Muslim masses with their routine complaint of 'encroaching' the 'divine' *Shariah*. This is another example of Islamic andro-centrism exploiting religion and thereby women.

Since Muslims in India (especially Sunnis) follow varied streams of laws as per the conventional Imamates (Shafi, Hanafi, Hambali and Maliki), and a uniform law in full consensus with all the sects could not be codified for practical purposes. A code accepted by one need not be agreed by the other. The same is the case with the Shiites, who also forms a major section of Muslims in India with diverse religious laws keeping their identity as the *Ithna Ash'ari* (Twelvers) and Ismailis with micro sects like the Fatimites and the Bohras of Mumbai. It is wondering to state that those who insist on Islamic law never knew that in India all the Muslims are not governed by the Muslim Personal law. For example, there are so many states like Goa, Kashmir, Tamil Nadu and Kerala which follow their own individualistic practices with regional affiliation and identities.

The conditions of the Muslims of Goa, Pondicherry and Jammu and Kashmir clearly reveal the urge for keeping their identities irrespective of the Islamic law that imposed over the Muslims as a whole[36]. The Kerala Muslims have retained their Marumakkathayam system based on the Nair Hindu custom of the region which is characterised 'unIslamic' by others, particularly the Islamists.

Quranic Verse Distorted

As polygamy is allowed under some specific conditions, divorce also is allowed out of sheer contingency. Prophet Mohammed condemned it as the most disgraceful or objectionable of things permitted. There is a procedural pattern for divorce which should be followed very strictly stage after stage. It is never a right for the husband to be done freely at any moment out of excitement or furore. It provides enough space for waiting and arbitration. The Quranic Verse in *Al Baqra*' virtually confirms this point when it says "Divorced women must wait for three monthly periods before remarrying,... their husbands would do better to take them back during this period, provided they wish to put things right..."[37]. But here men often misinterpret and misuse it for their own gains. At the sametime Quranic law makes women's rights of dissolving a marriage comparatively simple and shows more sympathy towards women. The Muslim Shariah Act of 1937 and the Dissolution of Muslim Marriage Act of 1939 are still followed without much changes in the courts of our country, both often becoming negative to the rights of women. Moreover, the man (husband) has an opportunity to go to a court for divorce and that can never be questioned. If the Government, through some law, insist the husband to present the matter before a court or judicial council, the hazards may sometimes reverse him for proceeding further, and thereby could save atleast some women from the horrors of divorce. The Muslim Ulema is also found alert must be alert on such issues concerning women and acts in favour of the innocent women who often become victims to such inhuman practices. Man's freedom of oral 'Talaq' (Tripple Talaq) must be banned immediately without further thinking. Again if any such incident is noticed, the judiciary of the country should be given all rights to interfere in such cases.

In India when other women enjoy all kinds of freedom and opportunity to protest, Muslim women suffer from disabilities like the lack of freedom of expression, education, inequality in civil rights and social justice, and as a result of all, they easily become prey to negligence and atrocities from their society itself. Majority of crimes against Muslim women are associated with Personal Law (for many, the *Shariah*), child marriage, *mehr*, divorce, custody of children, widow maintenance, dowry deaths etc. In 1980s, a lot of controvercy has developed in India related to the maintenance of divorced Muslim women, particularly after the Shah Bano case. They are being deprived of the right of maintenance all on a sudden by passing Protection of Muslim Divorced Women Bill Act of 1986. Compared to other women, they lost the privilege of maintenance due to this Act. The Act even takes away the Quranic allowance of maintenance in the *Idda* period (nearly for three months). Moreover, these poor, illiterate women are not at all aware of the various criminal laws to protect them from such atrocities and to get natural justice. Even if anybody attempts to object this, she will be singled out and further oppressed and treated as an outcaste. The pity is that it was the leaders in the community and the Qazis and Mullahs often take the lead and harass them. To avoid after-divorce problems, some men deliberately do not divorce their wives, instead, they will be harassed and neglected without even providing the bearest minimum for livelihood. The number of such women are increasig alarmingly in the Muslim community as "victims" of the reformed laws of the government.

In India, both poverty and dowry system compells parents to give their daughters in marriage to comparatively elderly men. The ignorant and poor parents, without the awareness of family planning and having more children, often resort to such marriages to "solve" the "burden" of the family. This creates a large contingent of "young widows" at an early age whose later life is in complete darkness. While analysing reasons to the increase in the number of Muslim women prostitutes in Ganga-Jamuna area of Nagpur, Seema Sakhare of the Legal Literacy Movement in Maharashtra, finds that girls who were deceived in the name of love and deserted as a result of early marriages constitute most of them[38]. Lack of legal literacy is a major cause for such incidents.

As suggested earlier, lack of education is the most important handicap which obstructs Muslim women to their employment and development. While examining such a crucial problem, we have to take into account several factors that accentuated to reach into such a miserable situation like socio-economic, cultural and historical. Muslim women, unlike others, have some additional problems, as imposed by their religious institutions and traditional underpinnings. The continuous Madrassah education for years which is compulsorily imposed over all children in early childhood itself bags a lot of time and human resource, the impact of which will be affecting heavily to those who search for modern education. Most of the Muslim girls are not yet free from the clutches of Arabic-Urdu languages, in addition to their general aversion to English language which is essential for modern secular studies. The Muslim animosity towards western education is historical, because both in the colonial and post colonial period, they believe, that the British colonizers are responsible for the whole sorry scheme of things of the Muslims of India for centuries. Moreover, seclusion and purdah system as a mark of their identity also became an impediment in Muslim women's educational attainments. Such a situation of separatism and communal exclusiveness also alienated them from the common people (here the major community, the Hindu women) resulting into the formation of a minority psyche, undesirable to the common good. Some grievances and complaints have been reported on discrimination in the case of admissions in educational institutions and in the area of employment. Therefore, a study on Muslim women naturally leads the investigator to examine various socio- cultural factors to assess the status of their education based on economic levels and to identify factors that hinges education and employment.

The observance of purdah and early marriage directly affect a major section of Muslim girls going for higher or professional education. The so-called Islamic dress code highly limits Muslim women's freedom of movement and free will. Recently in India a new tendency of imposing the veil on women has come in the banner of an 'Islamic dress code'. As we have discussed in the earlier chapter, no such code on dress is stipulated either by the Quran or by the Sunnah of the Prophet. A single piece dress like the 'shuttle cock' purdah covering from top to toe is neither universal nor compulsory. It is purely a regional variation with tradition and not religious, as commonly found in countries like Saudi Arabia, Iran and the Gulf region. In countries like Indonesia, Pakistan, India, Bangladesh and Central Asia such a *hijab* or veil is not in common use of Muslim women. In India, even in Kashmir where Muslims are in a majority, such a veil is not in prevalence. But the neo-revivalists, recently in India, with the idea of keeping up the 'Islamic identity', insists this on women including the Tennis Player, Sania Mirza, supported by the religious *fatwas* issued by the ulemas. But they do not realise the foolish and impractical attitude when they take on a sports woman in the name of religion. Such a veil is meant only for a woman who just does move and not for those attending a work place where they require physical exertions. Can we think of the hazard to a completely veiled woman in a cultivating field where she is compelled to work in mud and waters? How a female gymnastic or a circus woman or a film star could work with the veil? Have the *fatwa* holders ever thought of it? The answers always will be negative.

This precarious situation of Muslim women the world over, analysing the issue to veil or not to veil, has been taken up by the noted Lebanese feminist Nazira Zein-ed-Din in her writings on Hijab. She was motivated by the contrast between the recent incidents in Syria, where women were prevented from leaving their homes without veil, and Turkey, where secular reformers encouraged women to remove the veil. Nazira argued that veiling was anachronistic and that Islam, properly understood, treats women as the equals of men. Veiling (Niqab), according to her, is an "Insult to Men and Women".

> It greatly harms the two sexes that every man continues to insult his mother, daughter, wife and sister, suspiciously accusing them of bad morals and keeping them confined to a cage....[39.]

To substantiate her argument, Nazira quotes from Quasim Amin, the noted women's reformer of Egypt (1865-1908), who said:

> [Men Insult] with their wings cut off, heads bent down, and eyes closed. For him (man) is freedom and for them (women) enslavement. For his is education and for them ignorance. For him is sound reasoning and for them inferior reasoning. For him is Light and open space and for them darkness and imprisonment. For him are orders and for them obedience and patience. For him is everything in the universe, and for them part of the whole he has captured[40].

This holds good still in the case of Muslim women in India. Does the veil constitute the woman's decorum, chastity and modesty? Practically not, because the world confers on both the genders equal duties and responsibilities from which nobody could escape. Hence either a conceptual or a hermeneutical approach on Muslim women in Indian situations is not well enough to explain their role in the socio-economic ethos that prevails here. It is true that when analysing the status of women in the primitive society, Engels has brought forth the theory of enslavement associated with property. Women's transition from freedom to slavery originated with the rise of the family as an institution and the private property that the male has acquired by force. By force, again, they monopolised women as any other property, classifying as their own. The perceived need of raising the family within the confines of the household accelerated the process of domestication of women. While the male made a quarter of their own in the basic production activity in various fields, the women folk also joined with them strengthening the financial set up, but ofcourse, without giving any strength for the individual female. Whether urban or rural, the great challenge to Muslim women is her transformation from dependency to freedom in all spheres of life.

By seeing the miserable and extremely backward situation of the Muslim minority community, the Government of India has taken the initiative to uplift them by appointing a committee, the Sachar Committee on 9 March 2005, to present a report to the same. Though the Government of India on the recommendation of the Sachar Commission Report (17th November, 2006) has introduced several measures to this effect, it is not properly materialised till date. It recommended special schools exclusively for Muslim girls and literacy training centres in selected places where there is density of Muslim population. Among the 20,000 students of the minority community to whom have been given merit-cum-means scholarships, Muslim girls are eligible to enjoy 30 per cent of it. There is also a decision to constitute finance institutions to encourage micro finance among the women of the minority community[41]. But most of the measures of the government are still in papers alone. The problem here is that women of the community, particularly of the rural areas, are not at all aware of such measures introduced by the Government to uplift them. At the sametime, Muslim leaders in some particular pockets have tried to utilise the fund to improve Madrassah education to their requirements and ignored the other aspects which are more cardinal to the growth of the minority community.

The issue of the overplay of religion in a civic secular society as that of India is a very serious thing to be discussed. In one way, the complaints are often lodged with the constitutional protection of a community (minority) with an intention to be 'served' and to be 'saved' to which they themselves have no initiative. The Mullahs represent only the upper strata of Muslim society and their demand is always reserved for such a class ignoring the mass. The advocates of the Muslim Personal Law believe that the case of the Shah Bano has damaged considerably the "spirit" of it and the Supreme Court has no jurisdiction to adjudicate Muslim procedural law. It also failed to take into cognizance the spirit of the Islamic law in its totality[42]. Here lies the ambiguity of the "spirit of the Islamic law", about which nobody knows empirically. But the pity is that these claims are all made in the name of Islam and the Sunnah. Islam as an ideology offers sufficient scope for adjustments and adaptations as per the complex situations, which may arise from regional specialities, without prohibiting them either from modernisation or adoption to the needs of society. Hence modernisation may draw their women to the job market, although their economic roles conflict with their roles as house keepers and baby sitters which their male folk had imposed on them. It is true that the cultural ethos of the oriental society is totally different from the West. Naturally women too have become an early prey to it without an easy escape. To Edward Said, Orient itself was an exclusive male province to which he sought the support of fantasy writers like Flaubert who made amazing stories of Egyptian women[43]. Here also woman has been taken as a barometer to mark the quality of society. But they ignore the fact that irrespective of region or religion, decadence takes place first in the corridors of women where they are misused by the supremacy of the males blessed with 'authority' and orthodoxy.

The cultural constructs, instead of unifying also divides people as "ours" and "theirs" with western prerogatives[44]. Ofcourse, Huntington puts India in the category of 'Hindu Civilization'. How can this be applied to a country with multifaceted cultures as that of India? Huntington's dichotomy of cultures and clashes is also questioned on various grounds in Indian situations. A secular democracy as that of India which gives equal space to every citizen irrespective of his religion and tradition cannot be fairly defined in terms of the majority religion of the country. A majority Hindu population in a secular state is never equivalent to a theocratic Hindu state [45]. Hence religious divide can not be equated with a cultural separatism as experienced in many parts of our country. Indian Muslims are mostly converts from Hinduism from the beginning of its history, living with a continuity of the nation's regional cultural ethos. The Indian population as a whole is not exposed to any intensive developmental process and the Muslims are no exception. At the same time, a great change could be seen in the case of some Muslims living with an exposure of urbanisation and the consequent modernisation in tune with the situation required. There the pressures of modern life naturally evaporates the religious rigidity especially when it confronts with hard realities of life. Both the *Shariah* based Imams and the Muslim Personal Law Board have their hold in rural areas and the urban centres have practically become free from such obscurantist clutch.

Moreover, non-interference of the government and its assurance not to interfere in issues connected with the Muslim Personal Law greatly damaged the peaceful co-existence of Muslims in different parts of India including Industrial cities like Ahemedbad, Jamshedpur and Bhiwandi and many other industrial spots inviting communal tension and riots. Such policies of the government are looked upon by the Hindus as 'appeasment' of Muslims[46]. The Shah Bano case emerged during this time and the decision of the court to give maintenance to Shah Bano, an elderly Muslim lady, was opposed by the Muslim leaders complaining that the court is interfering in the Muslim Personal Law. Finally the government yielded to the demands of the leaders with vested interests and enacted Muslim Women (Protection of Rights on Divorce) Law which exempted them from all such laws to make their men 'free' from such 'entanglements'. In fact such a law further deepened the poverty and misery of the divorced women in the Islamic Community. It was an unwelcome step by a welfare democratic state. However this move on the part of the government was looked upon by the Hindus as 'uncivic' and 'un-Indian', and the hostile attitude propagated by the Sangh Parivar logically found new outlets in communal tensions and riots including the Mandir-Masjid issues. In such situations, how could one expect reforms concerning women be realised without protest and blood shed? In this dilemma the community itself should realise the seriousness of the problem and an initiative from within could be done providing awareness and education, even by restructuring the so called 'Holy' Shariah or Personal Law, dangerously harming women of the Muslim community.

Specific Problems

Muslim women in India are facing two important pressures that make their life hard and strenuous. If one is the unavoidable socio-economic inequalities which pervade the whole community on a national level, the other is the inequality and injustice sponsored by the Muslim Personal Law on a community level. The Muslims in principle believe and fear that a unified civil code is detrimental to their identity. The disparities in belief methodology and the observational diversities that found among the various sections of the Sunniites clearly reveal that they are not led either by the holy scripture Quran or the Sunnah of the Prophet. Therefore, as suggested earlier, the Shariah is not acceptable to all uniformly, since differences are couspicuoulsy earmarked as 'unIslamic' to the other. There are fundamental differences between Shiites and Sunniites as revealed by the scriptures and by the experiences of followers of both sects. The Shariah Act of 1937 in India, though claims to be applicable to all Muslims of India, practically could not be applied to all sections of Muslims including Sunnis and Shiahs and their sub sections in different parts of the country. For example, the Hanafis of the Sunni sect have different laws with regard to marriage, divorce and dowry laws from those of the Shafiites. Various sects of the Shiahs like the Ismailites, Ithna Ash'aris (Twelvers), etc. also have some differences. But when compared to the four main sects of the Sunnis (Shafi, Hanafi, Hambali and Maliki), it is minimal. Again, unlike the

Shafiites, divorce among the Hanafiites are very simple and could be done very easily even without the presence of witnesses or the Qazi. Hence the Hanafiite women are always at the mercy of their men living with fear and anxiety. All Musim women, except the Hanafiites, have the right of 'Kula' (divorce by wife) which is also sanctioned by Quran. Thus women enjoyed the right of divorce, eventhough husbands did not often agree to it. But in this case she has to forego her 'Mahar' and sometimes they were even compelled to pay a price for her freedom[47]. This clearly indicates that in Islam, separation by 'Kula' is permissible and it attaches great importance to the happiness of the spouses in married life and does not force them to live a miserable life simply in order to maintain the union so mechanically.

With the enactment of the Dissolution of Marriage Act of 1939, Muslim woman has to present reasons if she desires to have a divorce. She loses both the 'Mahar' and the court expenses. Moreover, she has to pay a huge amount as 'Marriage expenditure' to the man as he demands. To avoid such commitments, usually the woman goes to her parents without seeking a divorce. Though this may minimise the number of divorces, it enhances family issues creating further socio-legal problems, if not settled in a given time. All sections of Shiahs and the Shafiites of the Sunniite sect believe that the women have their right to choose their partners. They have even the right to nullify such contracts if they have been brought into wedlock by the pressures of parents or members of the family.

Moreover, several works on Muslim law in India have distorted the permissiveness of extra judicial divorce in Islam. The distinction between the male and the female in the matter of divorce and the other legal requirements are often ignored. It is a well known fact that the males are favoured in all such cases. The pity after independence in India is, in the absence of any serious work on Islamic law, even the judiciary follow such works of much less inferior status to do away with several complicated cases. The man need not go to a court to get a divorce and the divorcee can not be challenged for a unilateral divorce with the belief that it is accepted both by the religious laws and hence the Indian judiciary. Several cases from different parts of India have been reported in like manner.

Similarly women often becomes victims of oppression due to illiteracy and economic backwardness. If women are not educated and employed, they are far away from economic independence and free will. Prevalence of purdah practically curtails the freedom of movement creating less opportunities for quality education and public life including politics. Hence so many factors are intertwined in the practice of such laws contributing only to the rescue of the other. Benazir Bhutto, the former Prime Minister of Pakistan and a victim of political Islam, argues that Islamic law does not treat women as inferior to men or incapable of leadership[48]. Ofcourse, the fear and the belief that the continuation of a woman's rule in the Islamic Pakistan might have been responsible for her assassination at the hands of the obscurantists. Several Muslim women leaders had come up in India in the colonial period in the decades before independence, like Begum Hazrat Mohani (Delhi), Sa'dat Bano Kitchlu (Aligarh) and Bibi Shafa'atunnisa (Ludhiana). The mother of Ali Brothers, Bi'Ma, Amina Taybji, Sakina Lukmani, Amina Qureshi and Fatima Ismail of Bombay were the noted Muslim women leaders who actively co-operated with the Congress and became the part of social activism in anti-colonial struggles. But these rare 'specimens' hailed mostly from aristocratic and feudal classes, which would not in any way help to create a generalisation where we could claim that the Muslim women are all safe and advanced in their society without any social and religious encumbrances. Moreover, the situation in the post-independent period became more deplorable due to several socio-economic factors as revealed through the Commissions like the Sachar in recent times[49].

While Making studies on socio-economic conditions of Muslim women in independant India, the results found are not at all encouraging or welcomable to a social scientist. It is true that, as seen in the cases of all atrocities and excesses, it was the women who suffered most in such disturbed situations as experienced from the agonies of the partition that the country went through, not only in 1940s, but till today. Most of the commissions appointed earlier have brought out a fact that the present day misery, sluggishness and backwardness are not confined to religious reasons alone, but they are also basically interlinked with the liabilities of the colonial rule, the horrors of the partition, and primarily and more importantly, the pressures of tradition and socio-economic baggages. Thousands of women, both Hindus and Muslims, met with rape, death and other atrocities in the borders as victims of mob violence[50]. "All of them treat women's bodies as territory to be conquered"[51]. 'Dishonouring' women of the "other" community is the 'moral practice' in a situation of violence and crime and that pattern continued during and after the partition affecting women of all communities. We have stories of women molested, sexually assaulted, and even stripped "just as bananas peeled"[52]. As Begum Anis Kidwai writes,

> There are many young, half mad women Who keep laughing- perhaps at all of us, at the country, at religion and the propagators of these religions, at governments and their laws. May be they laugh at freedom- Who knows what they are laughing at?[53]

This reveals the misery and agony of women who have become both psychotic and lunatic due to the horrible experiences they had from their own people, later compelled to lead a life of neglect and disregard without any concern for religion, government or laws, or even to the freedom for which they are sacrificed. It is a question to the community and to the nation at large in which they live in and a question never to be answered. It is also a subtle cry of the marginalised with much grief, frustration and dejection.

After Indian Independence, for those who have opted this nation as their own country, still have grievances and a feeling that they are only second class citizens or people of inferior status. This feeling of alienation has both a psychological and institutional imperative to which the government has to involve and take necessary steps to redress their grievances at the earliest. Because, such imperatives include the feelings of a minority psyche, possibly developing into fundamentalism and as recently taken, towards terrorism. This also has an opposite dimension which works often as a counter with the nomenclature of 'majority communalism' symbolized in working groups like the 'Sangh Parivar'. The backwardness of the Muslims particularly of the women folk consciously or unconsciously deposits on the majority community who is believed to have snatched of their rights (mainly of education and employment). This retardation of Muslim women is a result of so many socio-religious and economic factors from which they could not become free. The gender bias of the Muslim Personal Law is still a contentious issue which also is strengthening the already institutionalized societies in various levels of Muslim life in the Indian context. Both the governmental machinery (including courts) and the religion-oriented community, who are entitled to save this precarious situation, often look upon this issue with minimal seriousness, as it is not their concern. Even the Sachar Commission appointed by the government of India is of recent origin and the results of which are yet to be seen. Always the commission reports are found better ways to sleep on a burning issue like this.

In the analyses of the issues of Muslim women in India (and elsewhere in the world over), some stereo types are projected through the Personal Law enveloped by the so called Shariah, with its protruding nails like the purdah, polygamy and Muttalaq. Most of the social scientists revolve around these factors without an empirical Perspective. A more serious study on Muslim women recently brought out the fact that they constitute the poorest and the most disadvantaged, destined to be suffered from patriarchy, gender inequality and discrimination in various socio-economic levels including education and employment[54]. The educational status of Muslim women all over the country is so minimal and deplorable that they are found comparatively more illiterate than the backward classes among the Hidnus. Muslim women respond very miserably compared to the average Hindu women in all strata of education and for that matter, the lliving standard of them is generally poor and much below than that of the other backward communities[55]. It is a fact that Muslim girls, particularly in backward areas where low economic classes live, are compelled to be married in their early teens. In most cases such girls even become mothers with two or three children before the age of 20. We have several such instances in the backward districts like that of Malappuram in Kerala, Murshidabad and 24 parganas in Bengal, Hyderabad in Andhra Pradesh and in many Muslim ghettos or Mohallas found in Bihar and Uttar Pradesh. Parental poverty, increase in the number of children, especially females, illiteracy, poor health, lack of employment opportunities are all inter-linked to create a vicious circle from which nothing could be possible towards the formation of a dynamic society, especially when they themselves were struggling to survive. While evaluating female literacy and education among Muslims in the rural areas of our country, analysists have found the town girls' participation beyond the school level was very dismal. The majority of Muslims did not consider modern education as an important asset for their women. This leads us to a conclsion that poor economic condition of parents, socio-cultural aspects, negative attitude of parents towards female education, lack of education among the family members and non-availability of girls schools are some oft-repeated reasons for the low enrolment of Muslim girls in our country, particularly in the rural situations[56].

Moreover, in our country, the condition of women in general is very poor and the majority of them are still illiterate, "negative, passive and powerless". The Indian women (including their men) generally have a feeling that practices like dowry and purdah, instead of creating "cultural restraints", keep their identity as "agents of culture"[57]. In rural areas the situation is much worse when compared to the urban centres. Literacy rate in urban areas is better than the rural areas since the urban centres have more educational opportunities for those who are economically sound. Cities and towns are also the centres of modern way of life with more employment opportunities. These facilities are utilised only by middle clas and above middle class people. The community in urban areas comparatively become more open with a compulsion of mixing with multiculturalism. Although there have been a large number of universities and colleges in these areas, the percentage of girls enrolment is not more than 50 per cent of total population except in states like Kerala. But the growth of Muslim communities in such urban centres and industrial cities have even led to communal polarisation. The newly emerging classes with more economic power thus become targets of the opposing classes leading to tension and conflicts often characterising as 'communal' to exploit the religious sentiments of both the communities. If we make an analysis of most of the communal conflicts in India after independence, this economic and social aspects are to be seen working dominantly in depth, though not found in the surface of the issues. Such economic divides often lead to violence. Development causes for significant shifts in the socio-economic structure which benefit some group naturally harming the other[58]. Such situations create an atmosphere of insecurity, fear complex and an overall discomfort to the mobility of the community, especially of the womenfolk. Here the question of religious identity also loom large with significant shift from the hitherto circumstances finally retrieving from the currence of socio-economic life.

The Psyche of the Community

This complex situation of fear and suspicioun with an urge for identity generated a new psyche in the Muslim masses which is often expressed in a feeling of alienation. As in all other communities, it was the females of the community who becomes the victims of such situations. Though not widely accepted, the veil was insisted, curtailing freedom and movement to a large extent. Meanwhile Mullahs and other religious functionaries were trying to revive the religious institutions like Madrassas and seminaries to educate and equip their followers to the benefits of the other world which is "permanent" and "immortal". Even the available educational facilities were practically denied atleast to the women folk of the Muslim community of the urban population. The rural women also suffered from the same problem. Moreover, being poor, they do not have access to resources dominated by the high investments done by the rich and the privileged who do not have any sympathy or concern towards the poor and the marginalised.

In India, even after the reformation movement initiated by Raja Ram Mohan Roy, the condition of women in all classes did not improve drastically or in the same degree as found in Europe. But among the Hindu women, after acquiring modern education, a lot of improvement could be seen. Among Muslims modern English education has become a taboo due to several socio-economic and historical factors as suggested earlier. As in other societies in India, Muslim women too became the part of the patriarchal joint family system. Though the law provides gender equality, a wide gap still remains between reality and the ideal, mostly because of historical and social reasons. For a traditional and religious society as that of Muslims, there is least chance for their women becoming empowered or even to think independently.

To Gerda Lerner, patriarchal system always dominates a subordinate group considering it far inferior, but mitigated by mutual obligations and reciprocal rights. Moreover, the dominated exchange submission for protection and unpaid labour for maintenance. In the patriarchal family, responsibilities and obligations are not equally distributed among those to be protected. The basis of paternalism is an unwritten contract for exchange; economic support and protection given by the male for subordination in all matters including sexual service, and unpaid domestic service given by the female[59]. This is exactly what experiences Indian women, and more deplorably Muslim women. Even the governmental initiative does not work well for women's empowerment. It was one of the principal objectives of the 9th Five Year Plan (1997-2002). It aims to create a psycho-emotional environment to empower women as agents of social change. Women's empowerment could be achieved only when they gain greater share of control over resources - such as material, human, intellectual and financial resources like money and access to money-and control over decision making in the home and community at large[60]. It is true that a section of reactionary and backward looking Mullahs consider education, employment and empowerment of women only to give them power to dominate men. As Farida Akhtar observes, "we would not like women's empowerment to result in women's taking over men's powers within the same exploitative and corrupt society"[61]. Empowerment to women is not for its abuse or for exploitation. It is to empower herself and to overpower men[62]. The propaganda by some hard-core Islamists often go to the dimension of curtailing even the basics of human rights to their women folk without any sympathy in their persons whatsoever. The question here is of the "liberation" of Muslim women from the age-old believes and oppressive practices at the 'excuse' of religion. These 'rules' of the religions as dictated by the ulemas and other religious functionaries are all confined to a class of Muslims who can afford life without the involvement or participation of women. But those who live in poor conditions have to search their livelihood without caring the social stigma like purdah or seclusion imposed over them. Majority Muslim women desire to have good employment in one way, for economic reasons to share the family burden of their husbands, and in another, to have a better social status. Those who are employed will be looked upon with respect both in the family and in the society. But, more often, both society and their own family do not agree or permit to seek such jobs of independent nature designating them 'unIslamic' and their women throwing themselves to the hell of agony and sufference. This results in the stunning of her family including children without any hope of development. Such women are tied up in their home engaged in domestic labour, child care, cooking etc.

In the rural sector, for Muslim women, employment opportunities are comparatively very limited. Most of them being illiterate get jobs in agricultural fields, construction areas, and in fisheries. Their wages are also very low, compared to men, and are compelled to work in unhealthy situations. Illiteracy and ignorance of labour laws make their life more deplorable, always looking at the mercy of their masters. Such flock of women never experience what freedom is, and their life rolls on unendingly till they become finally free from their life. Amartya Sen, the noted economist, sees development as freedom which in turn empowers all. He observes, "Indeed, the empowerment of women is one of the central issues in the process of development for many countries in the world today"[63].

Lack of awareness of law, human rights and illiteracy lead Muslim women also as the victims of domestic violence in different parts of India. It is true that violence against women is also an expression of patriarchal dominance which is perpetuated through social conditioning and the enforcement of custom that control women's behaviour. Moreover, it is a manifestation of the traditional power relationship between men and women. Illiterate women become vulnerable to acts of violence in the family or in the community comparatively easier. As Shireen Jejeebhoy observed:

> In most of India, both north and south, and among both Hindus and Muslims, the family is mainly patriarchal, patrilocal, and patrilineal and the reason is well known for the kinds of inegalitarian gender relations that are related to gender violence. Women are defined as inferior, husbands are assumed to 'own' women, and have the right to dominate them, 'including through the use of force[64].

Surveys and studies also suggest that there is no significant decline in the incidence of domestic violence against women of all communities, classes and status of society. Many conservative Muslims argue that women's subordination is divinely ordained, since it is codified in Shariah. But as referred to earlier, Shariah is a product of human interpretation of Islamic laws in different parts of Islamic world. As Fatou Sow observes, there is no such thing as 'the Muslim Woman'.

> There is not one type of Muslim woman; they differ according to their countries, culture, language and other influences. The Shariah law are interpreted differently within these influences and resolve issues in different ways. The Muslim world is not one world, but exists in different places[65].

Such generalization on Muslim women globally is highly essential for a study and evaluation of their counter parts in India. The status of women in Muslim society reflects the destiny of a practicing Islam. When Islam is secure so are its women, and when Islam is under pressure and threat, they too are so[66].

Today, in India, political leaders and power masters won't take drastic steps to the reform of Muslim laws, since they are fearful of their vote bank. They could not stand for a change. Therefore the initiative for a change should come from the community first, and more specifically, from the women folk itself. Other women's organisations also must take up the challenge to educate, organize and to provide legal assistance to all their sisters living in the shackles of the religion and tradition. For Muslim women, like women of all other societies, the essential factor to improve their condition is make them aware of their rights and to create a consciousness that they are equal to men of their community. To achieve their goal they should be ready to take new challenges. Of course, some analysts finally and conclusively find fault with European colonialism when they analyze the condition of Muslim women in India. According to them, even after independance, Muslims as a community continued the same ethos of life without much change. The Muslim leadership (both spiritual and political) do not care whatever happened to the women of their own community. The belief that a girl child is a burden and often unwanted, still hold good in almost all communities in India, including Muslims. Though the major share of the Muslim community all over India is still not free from the overall control of their religion and its ideologies, it is not totally stagnant or turn face against the new trends going on throughout the world. Changes could be seen in urban centres, particularly where socio-economic developments have penetrated in the living conditions of the people. Such few segments found in the economically potent sectors have no reluctancy to imbibe modern and progressive elements emanated by the new social order now linked with globalisation. The government also is taking effective steps to an immediate transformation of the community and it is now upto the community to decide whether they should co-operate with the new situations or to stay with the old concepts. No doubt, it is the option of the society to go for a radical structural change as a primordial for creating an open society accepting the realities of the modern world.

Notes and References

1. Fathima Mernissi, "A Feminist Interpretation of Women's Rights in Islam" in Charles Kurzman (ed.) *Liberal Islam,* Oxford University Press, 1998, pp. 114-16.
2. Beniprasad, *History of Jahangir,* Allahabad, 1940, pp. 157-58. See also Khafi Khan. I, pp. 270-71.
3. Muhammed Saqi, Mustaid Khan, *Ma'assir-i-Alamgiri,* Eng. Trans. J.N. Sarkar, p. 322.
4. Albert Hourani, *A History of the Arab Peoples,* Faber and Faber, London, 2002, pp. 119-20.
5. Ibn al-Hajj, *al Madkhal,* Cairo, 1929, Vol. I, pp. 245-46.
6. *Quran*, Chapter 16, Verse 97 reads: "To whoever, male or female, does good deeds and has faith, we shall give a good life and reward them according to the best of their actions." Chapter 40 Verse 40 also reads: "Whoever does evil will be repaid with its like; whoever does good and believes, be it a man or woman, will enter paradise and be provided for without measure".
7. Abul Fazl, *Ain-i-Akbari,* p. 342.
8. Beniprasad, *op. cit.,* p. 158.
9. Percival Spear, *A History of India,* Vol. II, Penguin, 1970, p. 26.
10. Shibli-'*Shair-ul-Ajam;* II, p. 123.
11. Abul Fazl, *op. cit.,* p. 47.
12. *Ibid.*, p. 287.
13. Abdul Khader Badaoni, *Muntakhab-ut-Tawarikh* Trans., p. 315.

14. Nizamudin Ahmed, *Tabaqat-i-Akbari,* Vol. II, Trans., p. 599.
15. Sumit Sarkar, *Modern India: 1885-1947,* Macmillan, 1983, p. 77.
16. Quoted in Tahera Aftab, "Negotiating with Patriarchy: South Asian Muslim Women and the Appeal to Syed Ahmed Khan" *Women's History Review,* Vol. 14, No. 1, 2005.
17. Sheikh Mohammed Abdullah (founder of Women's College, Aligarh), *Mushahadat Va Ta'asurat,* Aligarh, 1969, p. 205.
18. Shivanath Shastri, *History of the Brahma Samaj,* Vol. I, p. 47.
19. *Report of the Indian Famine Charitable Relief Fund,* Calcutta, 1897, p. 67.
20. William Dalrymple, *The Last Mughal—The fall of a Dynasty,* Bloomsburg, London, 2007, pp. 372-87.
21. *Rekhti* is a form of erotic Urdu poetry originated in late 18th century. It portrays the love and relationship among females. Saadat Khan Rangeen (1755-01835), Insha Allah Khan (1756-1817) Shaikh Qalandar (1748-1810) were its early exponents.
22. Vanita Ruth, *Love's Rite: Same-Sex Marriage in India and the West,* 2005, pp. 248-52. See also Manjari Srivastava, "Lesbianism in Nineteenth Century Erotic Urdu poetry Rekhti" in *Proceedings of IHC; 2008,* p. 986.
23. Amartya Sen, *The Argumentative Indian,* Penguin, London, 2006, p. 207.
24. Akbar, S. Ahmed, *Islam Under Seige,* Cambridge, 2005, p. 116.
25. Akbar, S. Ahmed, *Discovering Islam, Making Sense of Muslim History and Society,* Routledge, London, 2002, p. 122.
26. *Ibid.*, p. 185.
27. Farzana Shaikh, "Muslims and Political Representation in India. The Making of Pakistan" in Mushirul Hasan (ed.), *India's Partition,* Oxford University Press, Delhi, 1993.
28. Anis Kidwai, *Azad ki Chaon Mein,* [In the shadow of Freedom] National Book Trust, Delhi, 1990, p. 306. For a detailed study, See Ritu Menon and Kamla Bhasin, *Borders and Boundaries, Women in India's Partition,* Kali for Women, New Delhi, 2000.
29. Zarina Bhatty, "Socio-Economic Status of Muslim Women", in Zakia, A. Siddiqui and Anwar Jahan Zuberi (ed.), *Muslim Women, Problems and Prospects,* MD Publications, New Delhi, 1993, p. 13.
30. Zoya Hasan and Ritu Menon, *Unequal Citizens—A Study of Muslim Women in India,* Oxford University Press, New Delhi, 2006, p. 233.
31. The present writer has made a sample survey with regard to higher education prospects among girl students in Calicut city, being a major Muslim populated centre of Kerala. The responses found are not very encouraging. *See* Chapter Three.
32. Benazir Bhutto, "Letter from Pakistan, *Mathrubhoomi* (Mal.), 30 May, 2007. She complains about the Islamist squads (including girl students) who lead processions threatening the barbers and beauticians in Pakistan where beauty aids are sold. She further quotes the divisive activities of the chief priests of Lal Mosque and Jamia Hafsah Mosque in Pakistan. Later, out of sheer protests the Musharraf regime cleared off the terrorists from the Mosque and Seminaries with much casualities including the death of the Chief Qazi of Lal Mosque.

33. S.K. Datta and Rajeev Sharma, *Pakistan from Jinnah to Jehad,* New Delhi, 2002, p. 216.
34. Zarina Bhatty, *op. cit.*, p. 13.
35. The Verse reads: Divorced Women shall also have such maintenance as is considered fair: this is a duty for those who are mindful of God" (*Surah* II, Verse 241)
36. Tahir Mahmood, *Personal Law in Crisis,* Delhi, 1986, pp. 23-46.
37. *Quran,* Chapter, *Al Baqra*, Verse 228.
38. Seema Sakhare, "Atrocities Against Muslim Women" in *Muslim Women, Problems and Prospects, op. cit.,* pp. 63-64.
39. Nazira Zein-ed-Din, "Unveiling and Veiling" in Charles Kurzman *op. cit.,* 1998, p. 103.
40. Qasim Amin, in Charles Kurzman *op. cit.,* p. 103.
41. Decisions of the Ministry for Minority Affairs, Government of India, published in *Mathrubhoomi Daily,* 2 December 2007.
42. Anis Ahmed, *Women and Social Justice in Islam*, Naushaba, New Delhi, 1994, p. 51.
43. Edward W. Said, *Orientalism,* Penguin, 2003 (edn) p. 207. Whenever he explains the Orient, Said attaches it with terms like degenerate, backward, uncivilized, retarded, inequality etc.
44. Edward, W. Said, *Culture and Imperialism,* Vintage, London, 1994, p. 368, Lately Samuel P. Huntington revived it in his controversial work, *Clash of Civilizations and the Remaking World Order,* Simon & Schuster, New York, 1996.
45. Amartya Sen, *The Argumentative Indian,* Penguin, London, 2006, p. 54.
46. Asghar Ali Engineer, *Lifting the Veil*, Sangam Books, Hyderabad, p. 35.
47. Ramola, M. Buxamusa, in *Muslim Women, op. cit.,* p. 35. Ramola reiterates her argument in a paper titled "Muslim Personal Law in India—A Historical Perspective" presented in the National Women's Conference, Trivandrum (April 1984), sponsored by Indian Association for Women Studies.
48. Benazir Bhutto, "The Fight for the Liberation of Women", *Women's Studies Quarterly,* Vol. 24, 1996, pp. 91-97. See also "Her Final Words on Islam, Democracy and the West" in her monumental work *Reconciliation*, Simon and Schuster, London, 2008, particularly the Chapter, "The Battle within Islam: Democracy Versus Dictatorship, Moderation Versus Extremism."
49. The Report of the Commission submitted in 17 November 2006, analizes various issues concerning Muslim girls and women and suggested intensive action plans for their upliftment on a war footing.
50. See Mushirul Hasan (ed.) *India's Partition: Process, Strategy and Mobilization* Oxford University Press, Delhi, 1993. Again, Hasan, *Legacy of a Divided Nation: India's Muslims Since Independance,* Oxford University Press, Delhi, 1997.
51. Ritu Menon and Kamla Bhasin, *op. cit.,* p. 43.
52. Shorish Kashmiri, "Humiliated and Harassed they Left", in Mushirul Hasan, *op. cit.,* p. 156.
53. Anis Kidwai, quoted in Ritu Menon and Kamla Bhasin, *op. cit.*, p. 66.
54. For a detailed study, *see* Zoya Hasan and Ritu Menon, *Unequal Citizens: A Study of Muslim Women in India,* Oxford University Press, 2006.

55. *Ibid.*, p. 232.
56. Archana Chaturvedi, *Muslim Women and Development* (ed.), Commonwealth, New Delhi, 2004, p. 43.
57. Julia Leslie, "Introduction", *Roles and Rituals of Hindu Women* (ed.), Motilal Banarasi Das, Delhi, 1992, p. 3.
58. Asghar Ali Engineer, *op. cit,*. p. 17.
59. Gerda Lerner, *Creation of Patriarchy,* pp. 217-18.
60. Amartya Sen, *Development As Freedom*, Oxford University Press, New Delhi, 1999, p. 202.
61. Farida Akhtar, *Personal Communication*, Batliwala (ed.),1994, p.30.
62. Anand A.S., *Dynamics of Gender Justice: Crimes Against Women*, Bodhraj Memorial Oration, New Delhi, 2000, p.10.
63. Amartya Sen, *op. cit.*, p. 203
64. Shireen Jejeebhoy, *Population and Development Review*, December, 2000.
65. Fatou Sow, in *Dawn* Special Supplement, World Social Forum, Mumbai, Jan., 2004.
66. Akbar S. Ahmed, *Discovering Islam*, Routledge, London, 2003, p. 84.

3

Muslim Women in Kerala

Life Culture and Value

Muslim Women in Kerala, after conversion, did not have much sociological segregation, and continued to live for centuries with their traditional and cultural baggage in the same society. Many, being local converts, could enjoy their age old practices as others in the parallel societies. Even purdah in the strictest form was not insisted. Matriliny as a socio-hierarchical institution, which is basically opposed to the tenets of Islam, was continued in the Islamic society of Kerala, but without the conspicuous hegemony of the women as embedded in that system as followed by their Hindu counterparts. Women in the early Islamic society of Kerala also observed the erstwhile traditional believes and practices including the dress habits of their counterparts. Without the face-veil or purdah, they stick to the 'hijab' or modest clothing. The common folk among Muslim women were also not prevented from leaving their homes without the veil. But a marked change in this attitude could be seen concerning purdah, mobility and freedom, only in recent times, with the imposition of revivalist and puritanic ideologies.

Tradition and Challenge

Among the social problems and challenges that the Mappila Muslim women of Kerala face today is centred around the negation of freedom insisted by an Ulema-oriented society which greatly affected their freedom of movement, education and free will. They still suffer from several phychological and attitudinal problems thrust upon them mostly as a residue of the dogmatic past. Such issues concerning teenagers arise out of early marriage and dropping out of educational institutions are causing to the curtailment of juvenile freedom, further pushing them to phychological pressures and disappointments. The dowry deaths and violence are so rampant among them and excessive dowry demands make the parents impoverished. To overcome this burden many families go for sex-selective abortions, ofcourse, not seeking the consent of Shariah. At the same time the outdated theological stipulations of the Shariah are easily targeted against women than men since they are easily vulnerable. This ofcourse retarded their growth which could never be visualised in a developing society. Therefore, a structural analysis of the society of Muslim women in Kerala and its varying degrees of conflicts are to be debated for having a scientific hypothesis.

Both sociologists and reformists have identified the fact that the lack of education is the prime reason for the backwardness of Muslim women in Kerala. Education has been considered as an important tool for bringing socio-economic development. A major section of Muslim girls in Kerala did not have even the basic or primary education, probably due to the negligence of their parents who themselves are the victims of the situations prevalent in that society for centuries. When we come to their status in higher education, the situation is more pitiable. Higher education is the basic requisition of any society in modern life as an important agent of social mobility and instrument of change. It is significant to note that higher and professional education are highly essential for the overall development of women, not only as a source of livelihood but as a bulwark of empowerment. Educated women are better off in decision making, finance management and family planning, compared to the less educated who often become a 'burden' for others. No doubt education equips the women to know the world around them rationally and to play their role more effectively and independently.

In Kerala, especially in northern districts, majority of Muslim girls are kept out of secular learning due to several factors including social, economic, religious and even cultural. Generally in Indian situations, education for girls is often viewed as a wasteful expenditure. It is true that several studies have come after independence on all India level like that of Qurratulain Hyder (1975) Indu Menon (1981) and Sushila Jain (1986). Recently the Government of India has appointed Justice Sachar to examine the case seeking a report.[1] All their conclusions are disheartening that the number of Muslim girls seeking higher education is below 5 per cent.

This study on the situations of the Muslim girls in Kerala is mainly concentrated in the backward districts like Malappuram, Calicut, Wayanad Kannur and Kasaragod, all formerly of the British Malabar. It aims mainly,

(a) to study the attitude of Muslims as a class towards the education of women.
(b) to evaluate the approach of parents or guardians towards the higher education of girls.
(c) to examine the role of ulemas and other religious functionaries towards the education of girls.

(d) to findout the reasons for not sending girls to schools or colleges, and

(e) to analyse the social situation in toto with an insight a peep into remedial measures.

While analysing the condition of the Mappilas of Malabar (in 1887), William Logan, the Collector of Malabar, has this to say:

> They are moreover, as a class nearly almost, if not altogether, illiterate. The early education received is a parrot-like recitation of portions of the Koran, which, being in Arabic, none of them understand. The scruples of the parents prevent them from permitting their children to attend the vernacular schools of the Hindus. A fairly successful attempt has however been made to reach them by giving grants to their own teachers on condition that they must show results. The teachers being as illiterate as their pupils except in knowledge of Koran recitations, usually employ Hindu youths to teach the pupils and so earn the results grants. And some of the pupils, are now being taught teaching as a profession in special normal schools. The number of Mappilas who have advanced so far as to learn to read and write English in the schools could very probably be counted on the fingers of two hands[2].

This clearly reveals the miserable condition of the Mappila Muslim learning in Malabar in the colonial period. The same situation continued in the twentieth century and even after independence. If this was the picture of the Mappila Muslims in general, the condition of their women folk was so deplorable than we could imagine. As an administrator, Logan highlights the prevalence of perennial poverty and sense of insecurity among the Mappilas who live in a feudal setup controlled by the Hindu lords and crowned by the British Raj. Thus education becomes the least and the last thing that the Mappilas could accomplish in such a situation of crisis and anxiety. Though Logan was instrumental for the establishment of primary schools exclusively for the Mappilas in Malabar, he realised the futility of starting schools for starving people in the context of riots and disturbances through out Malabar[3]. No doubt that the Mappilas looked upon the colonial rule with suspicion and revenge, not only with socio-political reasons, but with cultural and religious animosity. Their education, being propagated by the missionaries, was opposed greatly on religious grounds characterising it un-Islamic. The conflict with modernity and liberalism found new dimensions with more transparency when the issue of girls' education loomed large. Hence the reverse looking attitude of the Mappila Muslims in Kerala has to be analysed in a wider historical perspective. New issues like the Khilafat developed in the national level also found new roots in places like Malabar generating a new psyche among Muslims alienating all progressive elements with an opposing ideology of 'resist' and 'revolt'. The post - Rebellion situation in Kerala exhibit a retarded, frustrated and religiously emotional group rather than an enlightened and liberal class of people. "A dearth of rational and pragmatic elements among the Muslim leadership"[4] was highly wanting in such a situation. Moreover, poverty, illiteracy and the all pervading religiosity made the situation further worse. When religion and its tradition have been taken as an instrument of solace to save the critical situation, it was the women folk of the community that suffered most as in all other societies. They have neither voice to react nor resources to supplant.

Thus was emerged numerous Madrassahs, Darses (Mosque seminaries) and Orphanages in different parts of Malabar as an after effect of the rebellion to "protect" the lowly and the lost, in the early phase of the 20th century. They were controlled by the religious functionaries like the Mullas, Musaliars and Thangals who have no other perception than religion and its paraphernalia. The lop-sided educational system prevailed in the community for such a long time without any structural reform was the potent cause for the degeneration of the community. Due to general socio-economic reasons, there developed a negative attitude on the part of the Mappila Muslims of Kerala in the acceptability of English education and the parents were prevented from sending their children to schools established by the government and Christian missionaries. They were looked upon with disfavour and those who sent their children, especially girls, were ostracised.

Islam as a religion attaches great value to education and prescribes it as the duty of both men and women alike to accomplish it. This has been specified through several verses of the Quran and by the sayings of the Prophet. The first revealed word to the Prophet is 'Iqra' which means 'read'; Prophet also said, "Seek knowledge even if you are compelled to go to China". According to him, Knowledge lights the way to heaven, it is our friend in the desert, our society in solitude and guides us to happiness. Again "Knowledge is the lost wealth of a believer; Fetch it whereever it is found". He sees no gender difference in acquiring knowledge. But such injuctions are often ignored when the question of education of women comes in all Islamic societies.

Negligence of Female Education

Though reformers like Sanaullah Makthi Thangal, Chalilakath Kunhammed Haji and Vakkom Abdul Khader Maulavi have attempted in this direction positively, their impact was alarmingly minimal, particularly in the case of girls' education. The reformist ideologies from outside especially of Jamaluddin Afghani, Mohammed Abduh, Abul A'la Maududi and others also infiltrated simultaneously in Muslim society to push them further back to the rigidity of puritanic Islam. Those who preached this new ideology of "Islamic modernism" (considering Islam as the most modern and based on reason and science) did greater harm to the Muslim community never allowing them to turn to secular and liberal education. The so called 'refined' but revivalist Muslims of Kerala also have taken initiative to form their own cages of learning to train the pupils in their direction on the excuse of "saving" the religion from the "attack" of the West and to create an ideal Muslim society as "envisioned" in the Quran. Education and the new trends created by the impact of the West broughtout a marked change in the socio-political structure of Muslim community in Kerala in the 20th century. But it remained peripheral so that it could not penetrate deep into the society since both the women and the commons were kept out of its orbit. Moreover, the beneficiaries of western education were the upper class Muslim elites who were never interested in the upliftment of their poor brothers of the lower strata of society.

The negligence of female education is often linked with several socio-cultural traditions continued for centuries with the backing of reactionary ideologies centered around purdah, ignorance and freedom. The question of social change among Muslims, particularly among their women in Kerala, is not merely associated with religion or education alone but also to its attitudinal velocity in the changing situation of modernity. Even reservation, for the community is not a solution. Lack of awareness and educational laxity make educational employment opportunities beyond the reach of the claimants.

As the Narendran Commission in Kerala, observes,

> Even with the reservation, most of the communities are not getting adequate representation in all the categories of posts. We conclude the report by pointing out that reservation for backward classes is only a means to an end and not an end in itself. It can not be a permanent feature[5].

It is true that the condition of Muslims after Indian Independence was not at all hopeful even with the Commissions and their recommendations appointed to bring the community to the forefront along with others. As referred to earlier, Muslims approached education (here western/secular) with a taboo on account of various socio-cultural factors. The first experience of a Muslim, whether boy or girl, in Kerala, is to learn the rudiments of Arabic, not as a language, but as a gateway to the study of Quran and thereby the religion. The teacher here will be a country Mulla or Musaliar who knew nothing but some recitations of Quran and the elementary aspects of *deeniyat* (concerning religious believes) and *Amaliyat* (concerning religious practices and rituals). His mode of teaching was very crude and unimpressive to the taste of pupils. In olden times most of them stopped with this type of learning with which they could claim to be a practicing Muslim. But those who want to study more in religion with the aim of a practicing Mulla, would attend the next stage of religious learning called *Dars* learning. *Dars* meaning 'class' is attached to a mosque, usually in the upper storey of the building. This was a residential type of learning where students stayed and studied as if in a modern hostel. The students will sit in a semi-circle in front of a lamp, usually a traditional lamp called *Nilavilakku,* in the centre, facing the *ustad* (guru). Ponnani, the great centre of Islamic learning and the seat of Makhdoom family, and many other traditional centres in Kerala, still follow this type of learning even today. The syllabus contained are moral science (*Akhalaq*), mysticism (*Tasawwuf*), and grammar. Moreover, these students who depend on the local houses for their food and money, most of them develop some kind of servitude to the feudal class and Muslim landlords as depicted in the novel of Moidu Padiyath, *Yateem* (The Orphan).

Since Dars system follows a residential pattern, such a type of religious learning is denied to females. They found solace in the much known and popular *Othupalli* (A school only meant for reading of Vedas like Quran). This single teacher institution also was attached to a mosque. Later, writing also has been introduced by using Malayalam in Arabic script, known as Arabi - Malayalam. Most of such othupallis were later converted into primary schools in Malabar by the British introducing subjects like Mathematics, Malayalam, elementary science and civics in addition to religious education. Such schools were great boon for Muslim girls who have no opportunity of acquiring learning from elsewhere. Most of the girls who underwent studies in these schools were also compelled to stop education particularly when their parents were aware of their age and to "dispose them off" with marriage. Those parents who sent their wards to higher schools also earned criticism, rarely even ostracism, from their own community controlled by the Mullahs. Such instances made the female education rather impossible for a long time in Kerala Muslim society. Reformers like Makthi Thangal, Chalilakath Kunhammad Haji, Vakkom Maulavi earlier,[6] and the veteran playwright K.T. Mohammed later, protested and criticised such system of education through their writings[7]. Recently a very impressive film has come in Kerala, though criticised by the orthodoxies and traditionalists, namely "Lesson one—A. Lamentation", highlighting the perennial grief and gloom a Muslim girl suffers early in her age due to the lack of education with the pressures of country priests and illiterate parents.

This is the social milieu that faces the females of the Islamic community of Kerala even today. The impact of the West influenced the Muslim leaders and the religious functionaries to reform their erstwhile methods of education and to improve for the present day Madrassah type of learning. This move greatly challenged the old *Dars* and *Othupally* systems, articulating a system framing new syllabi and curriculum and also with text book teaching. Though such madrassahs have their origin in North Malabar in places like Cannanore, Badagara and Calicut, South Malabar (the present Malappuram district) became their chief centres of efflorescence[8]. Simultaneous to the growth of Madrassahs, Arabic colleges, being higher education centres, also sprang up in different parts of Kerala, most of them again in South Malabar. All the sectarian groups in Kerala like the Mujahids, Jama'atis and Sunnis have their own madrassahs and Arabic colleges. Some of them have even Women's Colleges. It is true that since most of these institutions are centred around religion and Arabic language, they are neither liberal nor secular. The overwhelming growth of Madrassahs and Arabic Colleges greatly affected the wide acceptance of state owned and aided colleges in these areas and the Muslim enrollment, particularly that of girls, was so poor, leading to their continuous backwardness. The lull that followed the Rebellion of 1921, the fear complex and the animosity towards the British, the deep rooted religious and political prejudices were all responsible to create such a state of affairs in the Mappila Muslim psyche towards modern education.

This is the social scenario in Kerala when the Muslim females are totally kept out of education with which they have great utility in their future life. Muslims constitute about one fourth of the population of Kerala in which the female is round about 50 per cent. All the census report since independence reveal a fact that Muslims are far behind in literacy compared to all other communities including scheduled castes. The highest number of unemployed women are found among Muslims, that too in the four districts of Malabar, namely Malappuram, Calicut, Kannur and Kasaragod. Here the females constitute more than 90 per cent as unemployed. This situation is due to the lack of modern education. The Mappila Muslims of northern side of Kerala face the problem of employment, which often does not realise both by the community and by the governance. Since the Muslims of the Southern part of Kerala are comparatively educated and aware of employment opportunities, they are getting privilege of securing maximum reservation available for Muslims in general. This regional disparity continues even now in Kerala Muslims. This reservation originally initiated for the Mappilas of the British Malabar in the early period, thus jeopardises the very spirit and purpose of it further pushing the Mappilas of Malabar back to the old standard. This is a major lacuna that developed after independence as a result of the new nomenclature of reservation communities making very backward Mappilas in the common category of "Muslims". Even community leaders and Muslim League who have more hold and vote bank in the northern region and who always lament and plead for the upliftment of the community, never realised this aspect of the "robbering" of the opportunities by a microscopic minority of the South and from the shares of the real minority group of the Mappilas of

Malabar who really deserves the reservation both in professional education and the quotas in government employment. This intra-regional difference in the policy of reservation of a particular community adversely affects the Muslim women also in Malabar.

Many adverse conditions are also facing the community limiting their presence in all walks of life. The Ulemas and traditionalists take such situations in favour of their spaces recruiting them to the Madrassahs where the "safety" of the soul is reserved for the other world which is permanent. Such an attitude of "retreat" also developed among the Muslims of the region particularly in colonial context. The same situation continued after independence without much basic change. Moreover, in Kerala Muslim Society, an additional weightage always has been given to religious education for girls, especially when they are taught that the very life of them is built in developing a family life of husband and children. A dichotomous division of two strong stands, one to educate on modern lines, and the other on traditional pattern, always worked diametrically opposed to each other without offering any practical solution for any live issues of society. It is also true that the attempts of Britishers to propagate English education did not find any fruit in the case of Malabar Muslims on account of several socio-historical reasons. They opposed both the 1823 and 1854 schemes because they failed to provide any facility for religious learning. Realising this handicap, the British in 1870 introduced a new scheme incorporating Muslim religious teaching including languages like Arabic and Persian. Moreover, provision was made for grant-in-aid for starting "Mohammedan Schools". But such efforts on the part of the Government also was in vain. The percentage of the Muslim students' presence in the schools clearly reveal this aspect that in most of the institutions the attendance is below 5 per cent. The recommendation of the Hunter Commission (1882) observes that Muslim parents give least attention to modern education and give more priority to religious education, and complains that the religious education takes a lot of time and there by it kills the faculty of the student who goes for modern education. Moreover, he leaves the institute pretty earlier making his modern education incomplete. Therefore its recommendation include provision for special time-table for Muslim education since all of them attend Madrassahs either in the morning or in the evening. It also suggested some provision for giving scholarships and to institute special officers to inspect and monitor such schools in backward areas[9].

Some statistics of the Muslim education in the 2nd half of the 19th century, reveal the pitiable condition of Muslim girls whose presence is nil in almost all the schools in Malabar region.

The following tables are good examples to illustrate this.

Table 3.1: Muslim Education in the 2nd half of the 19th Century

Year	*Hindus*		*Christians*		*Mappilas*		*Total*	
	Boys	*Girls*	*Boys*	*Girls*	*Boys*	*Girls*	*Boys*	*Girls*
1868-69	9649	360	1589	417	309	NIL	11547	777
1869-70	11412	583	1870	469	348	NIL	13630	1052
1870-71	11439	603	1898	389	369	NIL	13706	992

Source: Report of the Inspector of Schools in Malabar (Madras Presidency) for the years 1868-1871.

As suggested earlier, this poor condition of Muslim education in general and girls in particular in the 19th century, are not due to socio-economic reasons alone, but historical and attitudinal. Whatever introduced by the British, like education, employment, modernity and even language, were opposed bluntly by the Muslims. The ulemas among them also have additional responsibility in alienating them from the British because they feared the loss of their hold on society. Further, the English education was looked upon as a method of Christianising people, and to introduce into a new culture never to compromise with the socio-cultural ethos of the Mappilas. The situation continued without much change in the post-revolt period also. In 1930s and 40s slight improvement could be seen in the education of girls when some special schemes on the part of the government like the grant-in-aid and special schools system in backward areas were introduced. This slight rise in the graph of Muslim education (both of boys and girls) is also due to the encouragement given by religious reformers and community leaders like Makthi Thangal, Chalilakath Kunhammad Haji and Vakkom Maulavi. These leaders fought against superstitions which made the community backward and retarded. Organisations like Muslim Aikya Sangham and Muslim Majlis took the lead for the propagation of education among Muslim girls. Thus a resurgence of Muslims to acquire education, though slightly, could be seen in places like Calicut, Tirur, Malappuram, Tellicherry, Cannanore and Kasargod in Malabar, and Alwaye, Ernakulam, Quilon and Trivandrum in Central and South Kerala.

The basic reasons to the reluctance of the parents to send their children to schools are to be understood seriously. Most of the parents were very poor to meet even the meagre expenses of their wards like the cost of books, dress and other items, connected with school going. The number of the children in a family also was a factor for the parents who cared them. They were also not aware of the value of education and the time that spends in school for modern education is found unproductive for a poor parent who often depends on their children as a work - force. Further, the education of a girl-child is not at all lucrative, since she is going to be an asset in another house after marriage, particularly in a society where the marriageable age of a girl is in the early teens. The government have taken several administrative measures to combat such socio-economic issues by appointing commissions including official and non-official members. Hence the Grieve Commission of 1931 made some proposals which for the first time recoganized religious education for Muslim students, and that too incorporating within the time span of the general curriculum of such schools where they are in majority. Moreover, the religious teachers of such schools called Mullas or Musaliars were given training so that they could feel that they are also protected and treated as other teachers[10]. This experiment was found very effective in all Malabar region and both governmental and non-governmental agencies have started schools in such models. However with all such encouragements, the condition of girls' enrolment in schools did not improve substantially. Even if they are enrolled in standard I, a good number of them became dropouts before reaching IVth or Vth standards, due to several economic reasons and social pressures.

Though several Muslim organisations like the Muslim Aikya Sangham[11] did yeomen service to the propagation of education among Muslims, it also did not find fruit as expected, especially in the case of girls. As a sectarian revivalist group, the Mujahids were the first to give importance for education among Muslims as a part of their campaign against superstitions among the Muslims of Kerala. But their attempts were mainly concentrated to eradicate blind beliefs and superstitions and to combat Sunnism practically, rather than the spread of modern education among Muslims. Jama'at e' Islami also followed the same path in Kerala, virtually becoming the enemies of Sunnis. Moreover, the Sunnis, who form the major share of the Muslims of Kerala, looked upon both of these revivalist sects with suspicion and opposed all their educational activities as an attempt against puritanic Islam. Hence in one sense, both the Mujahids and the Jama'atis did a disservice to modern secular education in Kerala by giving too much stress to revivalism, ignoring the general Muslim mass and their psyche. Resurgence and revival, for them, meant not that of the Muslims, but that of Islam and its ideology. Such a move adversely affected the general Muslim attitude who sought modern and secular education. Moreover the conservative ulemas and religious functionaries highlighted this "dangerous" aspect of revivalist modernity without religion, and with a fear of losing all their followers leading them towards "heresy" by the Mujahids and Jama'atis. Thus the Sunniites in the early stage also developed an aversion to modern education criticising the neo revivalists and those who go for modern English education. Such a development among them is often linked with the Muslim hostility of British colonialism which was responsible for the end of the Mughals in India and the disappearance of the Caliphate from the Islamic World.

Again, the statistics on Muslim literacy often centred around the males of their community and as per one survey of 1931, the female literacy among

Muslims was only eleven per one thousand taking the whole population together. It becomes further less, taking into account the literates in English and above the primary level education[12]. Moreover, the survey reveals that literacy meant the ability of a person to read and write alone. When the question of higher education comes the graph suddenly goes down even in the case of secondary education. The following table will give a communitywise growth of literacy in the Post Rebellion period in Kerala and the low level of literacy among Muslim girls (Table 3.2).

The same was the situation in the Central and Southern part of Kerala. The percentage of Muslim girls there also was very low when compared to the other communities in those regions. While the percentage of school-going children are taken, the Muslim girls form so low a position (23.3) when compared to Hindus (53.3) and Christians (74.2)[13]. Various Census Reports of the period reveal the fact that Mappilas showed little interest in acquiring English

Table 3.2: Communitywise Growth of Literacy in the Post Rebellion period in Kerala

	Name of the Community	*No. of Literates*		*Literates/1000*		*Literate in English*	
		Male	*Female*	*Male*	*Female*	*Male*	*Female*
1921	Hindus	244081	66529	247	63	21344	2286
	Muslims	58820	3565	119	7	1198	29
	Christians	12944	8567	451	293	4128	2813
1931	Hindus	296341	7956	266	82	34751	5874
	Muslims	80876	6818	142	11	3204	96
	Christians	15873	10847	499	329	4751	3032

Source: Malabar District Gazette Vol. II, Madras.

or secular education in these days of uncertainty and social crisis created by Malabar Rebellion. In the period under report the Mappila literacy altogether was so insignificant that their literacy has been calculated in 1:6 ratio[14] against 1:2 ratio of Muslim-Hindu population. This state of affairs was due to certain ideological and sociological factors from which they could not make free by themselves. Unlike in the other places, the socialisation of the Mappilas began within the religious frame work alone, and continued within the parameters of its ideology[15].

The census of the later periods also reveal the appalling fact that the Muslim girls are still very low in acquiring modern education. The study, particularly for girls, is not at all having any utility to seek employment because employment for them was denied either as a social taboo or an "undesirable" asset for a girl, By this time she will be dragged towards a marriage tie. Moreover, the Mappilas, in that particular socio-cultural structure, were compelled to rely on the guidance and leadership of Muslim traditional intellectuals, since there is no other alternative as others have.

The decades following the Revolt of 1921 was one of crisis to the Mappilas of Malabar on account of several socio-economic aspects. The indolence created by the revolt made them more lethargic and inactive even in their approaches to life. The disbelief in governance led them more to a state of frustration and backward looking.

Radical Changes

After independence, Kerala showed a great leap in socio-economic development, particularly after the formation of the state on linguistic basis in 1956 and the coming up of the first elected government under E.M.S. Namboodiripad in 1957. The government introduced several measures for the upliftment of the backward classes in acquiring education and employment. The major scheme included reservation as per the population ratio to the deserving communities, both in educational institutions and in employment. Moreover the government gave thrust in allocating higher educational institutions including professional colleges more in backward areas, both in private and public sectors, and where such centres were not there before independence. But the benefit of such a policy of the government has been fully utilised by the communities like Ezhavas and Christians. Muslims still were not aware of the new developments and were not free from their attitudes of the previous decades. This made their educational status more appalling than the scheduled castes and tribes. A survey made on the numerical strength of the Muslim students (both boys and girls) reveal that those who are enrolled in the 1st standard could not complete even the Vth standard. When it comes to the high school level the percentage of the pupils is less than ten percent of the original who sought admission in the Ist standard. If we analyse the drop out of girls, it is further deplorable, particularly when it reaches to the Xth standard. For example a study on school-going children in 1964-65 shows that if their enrolment in Ist standard is 1,34,202, in V standard it is 46,775 and in VIII standard 18,085, in the X standard it is 8,562 only. It is far below and disproportionate to population, compared to the Christians and the Hindus.

Though the exact numbers of girls are not available in the case of Muslim students, the drop-outs of girls will be several times greater than other communities. The important factor to be noted here is the equilibrium that kept by the Christian community in almost all classes, eventhough they form a religious minority with a lesser percentage of population compared to Muslims.

A study of 1990 reveals that there were 6.51 lakhs Muslim girl students in Kerala Schools representing about 25 per cent of the corresponding population of school going girls. As mentioned earlier, dropouts could be seen when they go to higher classes. When it was 27.60 per cent at the Lower Primary level, it falls to 17.79 per cent when it comes to the High School level[26]. This is a major draw back in the status of Muslim girls education in the state of Kerala, all along in their journey for education.

The feed back received to the Questionnaire distributed clearly reveal some important factors with regard to the reasons for the educational backwardness of Mappilas of the northern region of Kerala. The response generally from the women of the middle class (uneducated) is comparatively poor. But some selective women with moderate education responded with great enthusiasm. They mainly belong to Calicut and Cannanore districts who have the facility and encouragement from families to acquire modern learning and employments. Though their percentage is low (37%), they form a potential group mainly of teachers, doctors and other professionals. What we could read from their attitude is that they are dominant not only in their families, but even in society in which they live, and enjoying a say in all their dealings whether social, economic or cultural. This educational empowerment made them strong and most of them being employed, also are economically sound to lead the family. The educational empowerment of women benefited the society in two dimensions—one the development of womenhood themselves, and the other, upbringing their children with education and modern outlook. This is a great change earmarked in Muslim societies where women are properly educated, even if all of them are not employed.

Several causes have been highlighted by the respondents to the backwardness of Muslim women in the Malabar region. Nearly 15 per cent, from whom opinions sought, were reluctant to respond. At the same time a major share found orthodoxy and illiteracy as the basic factor for this state of affairs (40%). While a good number of them found poverty as the major reason (15%), some stressed on child marriage (10%) as a factor allied with poverty, particularly in backward rural areas. The indifference of parents (8%) and non availability and inaccessibility of educational institutions (12%) also form sufficient reason for the pathetic situation among the Mappilas to reach out modern education (Table 3.3).

Table 3.3: Reasons for Backwardness

1.	Orthodoxy and illiteracy	40 p.c
2.	Poverty	15 p.c
3.	Child marriage	10 p.c
4.	Indifference of parents	8 p.c
5.	Non-availability and Inaccessibility of Educational Institutions	12 p.c
	Non-Response	15 p.c
	Total	100

Reasons for backwardness as responded provided in the survey in Calicut, Cannanore, Kasargod, Malappuram and Wynad districts.

Though this is the general scenario found in all these districts, a slight variation could be seen from district to district like Wynad and Kasaragod. This fluctuation in the percentage is partially in accordance with the reasons already provided and the nature of settlements as in urban and in rural areas. Surveys are also made in cities and rural areas and the table of which will be given separately

Studies and surveys on Mappila Muslim women have also brought out several interesting aspects with regard to their life style and home management, apart from all such handicaps arose as a result of the lack of proper education. This situation of women involvement in home affairs has come out of sheer contingency when their men folk was out of station due to employment, particularly after 1970 with the Gulf boom. The inflow of money also compelled them to go for banking, shopping, etc., where financial management is required. The frequent house visits of relatives and social get together also gave them some kind of an exposure which could not have been possible in earlier days, especially for those old generation who followed strict 'ghosha' system also became aware of the child care reposed on them with full responsibility including education. But this does not mean that they are all free from social stigmas and the rigidity of traditional practices. Recently a much publicised news have come on literacy of Muslim women in Malappuram and Kasaragod districts where they suffered the worst in education and socialisation. But this is only one aspect of the economic growth which is mechanically shooted up as a result of the extensive use of computers and cell phones. evidently not in touch with the information technology to which it is meant. Those who have computers and laptops are now further pushed back to their secret cells, ofcourse with convenience of chatting with their spouses or relatives. This indicate a negative growth and development without any chance of intermingling with others. Such a mechanised life never brought them to the wide world of liberal education highly essential for the development of any society.

Moreover, in such societies, economic growth made them more lethargic and inattentive to education creating a useless class of unemployed youth who could be useful only for anti-social and terrorist activities. The excess money they gain from various sources is often spent for disruptive and undesirable channels creating an unhealthy social ethos, which Kerala had never experienced before. Such a generation, lacking proper guardianship and leadership, soon become the most undesirable and unfit class of miscreants who could never be controlled by their uneducated women living in home. The survey analysis in districts of Kasaragod, Kannur and Malappuram reveal that almost all homesteads have all modern accessories and living conditions with vehicles (cars and two wheelers), computers, most advanced individual cell phones, apart from other routine household articles required for modern living. Some houses have two-three motor cars or two wheelers individually. The so-called label of 'backwardness', at least in the sense of economy, could not be taken in the case of about 60 per cent of families in such regions[16].

The condition of Malappuram is partly different. There, the women being mostly from the lower middleclass and who have the opportunity atleast to acquire primary and secondary education generally have attempted for preparing a new generation equipped with modern professional education. The gulf boom did not affect this zone as in Kasaragod, and as a result, more attention to female education is imparted. Though there also the computer literacy is a much acclaimed weapon, the magnitude of its growth is comparatively minimal. Except some towns likes Manjeri, Mannarghat Tanur, Tirur and Parappanangadi and Perinthalmanna, the majority (about 60%) life is still in poor conditions and in perennial poverty is in the rural areas. They suffer the maximum social exploitation from the rich, including the reservation claims. An important crisis that faces the poor Mappilas of Kerala is that they are not getting their due share or percentage of seats in higher education institutions and colleges owned and acquired in the name of their own communities. All such institutions have to allot 20 per cent of the seats in the category of 'community quotas' to which the institution is allotted. This is apart from the 20 per cent management quota again meant for the same community. Practically 40 percentage of seats could be claimed by the community apart from the general merit. Usually what we experience is the management quota totally will be sold out for money often by the authorities and those poor who could not afford such liabilities again will be outside the campus and their agony is never attended by these community leaders who often lament in the name of community reservation in other public sectors. This contradiction is experienced throughout Kerala in the allotment of higher educational institutions and with allocation of seats on community basis. Such anomalies have been noticed in the case of professional colleges, including medical and engineering, in the recent past. Thus the poor, though qualified, are always kept out of the orbit of higher education including professional education. Studies made in Malappuram, Kasaragod, Kannur and Kozhikode districts bring out appalling instances of such injustice done towards the poor in the community[17]. Malappuram in Kerala comes 2nd in Muslim population districtwise which amounts to 25 lakhs, second to Murshidabad in West Bengal (37.4%). In the percentage of Muslim population, this district comes 11th with a percentage of 68.5, leaving some of the districts of Jammu Kashmir and Lakshadweep (95.5%). Next comes Kozhikode (37.5%), Kasaragod (34.3%) and Mahe (31%) lying in between Kozhikode and Kannur districts, a Malayalam speaking region under the union territory of Pondicherry[18].

The imbalance in the presence of educational institutions proportionate to population also has been highlighted by many eventhough the Muslims, especially the females, are reluctant to utilise the available opportunities in such areas. As the report reveals,

> The all India picture shows significant gap between Muslims, SCs/STs and all others in the 1960s. Literacy levels among SCs/STs have increased at a faster rate than for other SRCs. This enabled them to overtake Muslims at the all India level by mid 1990s, while reducing the gap with 'All Others' also. Thus communities with a relatively high literacy level have continued to improve over the years. The SCs/STs have also benefited from measures like reservation. Muslims, on the otherland, have failed to improve their educational status. Consequently, their gap vis-a-vis the group labelled 'All Others' (with initially high literacy levels) has increased further, particularly since the 1980s[19].

The educational problems of Muslims in Kerala is not equivalent to the situations in the other parts of the country. There the Muslims live by developing an identity of their own in their outfits and in selecting habitats. They prefer to live in exclusive Mohallahs or Ghettos, often highlighting the sense of security from the police or district officials. The inferiority complex thus developed further shrinks them from the common spaces leading to more disadvantages like neglect by local authorities in providing civic amenities, sanitation, schools, dispensaries etc. Such a situation naturally takes their children to the local Madrassas where they are taught in a primitive way and their opportunity for secular education ends forever.

The Muslim diaspora in Kerala, except in some rural areas of Malappuram (there too it is fast disappearing or changing), is as any other community both in villages and urban centres. There they mingle with other communities without any feeling of differences and they enjoy all fruits of governance as others. If any violation or variation in this state of affairs are there, it is of their own attitude or ignorance that is to be responsible. Moreover, as in other parts of the country, female education has become the hallmark to identify the standard of the community. Here also, as discussed earlier, for a long time they were shut up in the four walls of the houses without any freedom to move either for education or for employment. In Muslim society women are not counted for employment and they were kept out of the work force. When such was the situation elsewhere, here Muslim women, observing limited seclusion, were engaged in traditional home-centred jobs like sewing, sigar rolling and knotting fish net etc., all in a contractual basis mainly concentrating the coastal areas. But in the interior, the poor naturally joined their sisters of other communities in agricultural labour, particularly in region like Malappuram.

But with the change of technology and mechanisation, such low-skilled jobs have disappeared, further pushing them to greater poverty.

New Aspirations for Change

It is often said that the Muslim community is always backward looking and is very slow in progress particularly in womens' education, employment and their rehabilitation. But the situation after independence in Kerala is highly encouraging to their upliftment, eventhough they could not utilise it fully in accordance with dreams of the administrators and social activists. A drastic change took place in the activities of women in Kerala after the three-tier panchayath system with a stress on the compulsory reservation of women in representing elected bodies of Panchayat—the local, block and district. When a stipulated number of women representing the wards, a good number of Muslim women are also represented to the Panchayaths where Muslims are in majority and to the seats reserved for women. Several women from different Panchayath wards have thus become members and where the chairmanship reserved for woman is occupied by Muslim women. This is a great change which could be realised by the representation of women in local administration which also transformed the whole system of village administration which was considered as a mirage decades ago. The new political participation of women, especially of Muslim women, thus became a reality in this segmentary state where the weaker sex for the first time got an opportunity to mingle with others. The new class of women thus occupied in local administration have got a rapport with others who have been elected democratically. The new class while occupying important position also became aware of our democratic values and socialist ideologies other than the traditions taught by religion for centuries. A new world of dialogues and consensus has been opened before them for their own good and development.

Recently Muslim women in Kerala have got an opportunity to indulge in socio-political activities as a result of the reservation in the Three-tier Panchayath system and the much acclaimed 'Kudumbasree'. An important instrument of the District Panchayat Council which augmented the women participation in general, and Muslim women's involvement in particular, could be easily studied by examining various 'kudumbasree' projects exclusively managed by women, sharing the issues of common women and in participating the social service activities. In several Panchayaths we could realise the miraculous success of programmes by the untiring activities of women with high sounding social interactions without any taboo of socio-religious nature or prohibitions. Such projects have brought them to the forefront of socio-cultural activities without any communal or class barriers. A community marriage recently organized at Nadapuram (Calicut) with the initiative of several NGOs including 'Kudumbasree' is a fitting testimony to such a social service. Ten orphan girls have the fortune of getting married with gifts of gold ornaments, bridal dress and a sumptuous meal for thousands of participants. This was a philanthropic work of a single gulf-based business man of the locality. A point to be noted here is that all the brides wore saris only as the bridal dress in Kerala style without any lineage to purdah[20]. This marriage *mela* takes place yearly in the region for the last few years with thousands of womens' participation of all communities.

No doubt that a lot of social change has come in several backward areas where Muslim women formerly have no opportunity to educate themselves. Both upper primary and secondary schools have been started in almost all the Panchayats after independence. But a great drive in education could be seen in Kerala with the formation of the left-front government under EMS Namboodiripad in 1957. All the governments after him, gave great thrust for education in backward areas like Malappuram, Kasaragod, Kozhikode and Kannur. It is true that Malappuram being he Muslim dominant district of the state with 67 per cent of their population, got particular attention during the period of the coalition ministry of EMS Namboodiripad[21]. Now the Muslim mass, particularly the females have been conscious of education considering it as an important instrument for bringing social change and human resource development.

Higher education, including professional education like medicine, engineering and information technology, has been regarded as a primary source of standard of life and earning livelihood. It also became an important aspect for social mobility and change. For the overall growth of women, higher education is so cardinal that it is the source of empowerment in a highly competitive society as that of Kerala. One important factor noted in the survey is that girls who seek higher education are belonging to the higher classes which means educationally sound and urbanised. Several data have been given earlier regarding their lowest percentage when compared to other communities. A case-study has been done in Calicut city as a model, since it is a core centre of Muslim education including professional, for most of the surrounding backward districts and rural areas. In this study, stress has been given to:

1) The attitude of the community towards higher education for women.
2) The attitude of parents towards their daughter's education.
3) An examination of the attitude of the religious functionaries like Mullahs in the education of Muslim girls.

By applying a quota sampling method, information has been collected from 150 men and 100 women through a questionnaire. These include different classes of women like housewives, (both literate and illiterate), coolies and part-time petty labourers, (literate and illiterate), home nurses, employed women from the lowest fourth class to doctors, engineers and college professors and students acquiring higher education.

Thrust has been given in opinion seeking since they are decision makers with regard to their person and profession, and their overall development including the education faculty. The men selected are from various streams of social life like professionals, labourers, traders, religious functionaries. They are also categorised as rural and urban, illiterate. All respondents consider education unavoidable to women, but some of them including religious leaders, prefer to have a simultaneous religious education to all of them. A good number of them wanted to teach their girls in separate institutions exclusively meant for them (nearly 20%). Female respondents are greater than the males with regard to higher education (about 70%). A noted higher education centre in Calicut is Farook College, a 1st grade college under Calicut University with a national accreditation of 'A' Grade and having almost all courses, in undergraduate and post graduate level. It has a Muslim student strength of more than 70 per cent of which the girls form more than 50 per cent of it. This is the same case with the colleges of the Muslim Educational Society[22] and a number of other colleges under Muslim managements. In all districts of Kerala Muslim educational institutions are available and with appreciable Muslim students' strength. Moreover, in Calicut city, there are Higher Secondary Schools, exclusively meant for Muslim girls like Calicut Girls School, Kundungal, (Calicut Beach) where 96 per cent of them are Muslim girls. Anoted Higher Secondary School under the Muslim management is the Himayatul Islam School in the heart of Calicut city where the Muslim population is in majority. Here also the Muslim girls form the major student strength. The Mappila School at Kuttichira, is also in the ghetto of the Muslims of the region, almost exclusively filled up by Muslim girls for their higher secondary studies[23].

Moreover, in the field of Higher Education also the Muslims of Calicut city has improved a lot due to the establishment of women's colleges by educational organisations like the Muslim Educational Society (MES) and the Muslim Service Society (MSS). The Women's College of the MES in the city, though unaided, is a leading educational institution for accommodating Muslim girls. The Marzook College for women started by the MSS also is doing yeoman service to the higher education for Muslim girls in the city of Calicut. In both these Women's Colleges, the strength of Muslim girls exceeds 60 percentage of the total seats allotted for various courses[24].

A striking fact in the growth of Muslim women's education could be seen after independence, ofcourse, by the cumulative effort of the government, local NGOs and social organisations. A significant change could be seen in the attitude of the community. After the formation of the Farook College (1948) a large student migration from different parts of Kerala, especially from the northern districts, is experienced in acquiring modern education. Of the students they enrolled, form a major share of girls. This is on account of their feeling that the college is their own and will be secure since it is working within the orbit of Muslim culture. The same is the case with the various MES Colleges and Colleges managed by various Muslim Associations mainly functioning in Calicut, Malappuram and Cannanore districts.

The following table will reveal substantial increase in the educational status of Muslim girls in the institutions of the two major agencies and other Institutions in Calicut.

Table 3.4: Educational Status of Muslim Girls in the Institutions

Name of Institutions	*No. of Boys*	*No. of Girls*
Farook College Institutions	2275	2568
MES Institutions	1849	1647
Colleges other than Muslims in the city of Calicut		
Malabar Christian College		
Govt. Arts College		
Providence College (Women)		
Guruvayurappan College	471	360
Five Secondary Schools (Other than Muslim Schools)		
Total	1435	1928

Source: Records and Registers kept in the various Educational Institutions (2008-2009).

The study in Cannanore and Kasaragod reveal a fact that they are comparatively backward in women education both in secondary and collegiate levels. This is mainly on account of the non-availability of enough schools and colleges proportionate to their population. A major educational institution in the Cannanore city is the Higher Secondary School run by the Deenul Islam Sabha, now having Plus-Two and English medium, situated near the Arakkal palace in the old Cannanore city. Here the Muslim girls' student strength is more than 70 per cent. A major change in higher education took place in Kerala as a result of the education policy adopted by the Communist Party (Marxist) after 1957. Several schools and colleges in Cannanore district were started under the Muslim managements. A major initiative in Muslim womens' education came after the establishment of the Sir Syed College in Taliparamba, a very backward area in Cannanore district[25]. A major leap could be seen on account of this institution in the growth of higher education among Muslim women not only in the Kannur area, but even in the neighbouring districts like Kasaragod, Wayanad, Calicut and Malappuram.

While examining the reason for dropping outs and a retreat in the educational advancement of girls, several factors are to be evaluated as reflected in the responses of various classes in the Muslim community of Kerala. Eventhough all the respondents considered women's education essential, most of them are not in a position to send their daughters beyond higher secondary or Plus-two, to which they project reasons of their choice like the absence of separate institution for girls, lack of Islamic studies in secular institutions, social problem of an educated girl in getting suitable partners after marriageable age, challenge to wear purdah etc. It is also interesting to note that, from the datas collected, distinct variables are seen in the responses of males and females, married and unmarried. While 60 per cent of the respondents among females are in favour of educating their daughters, only 40 per cent of males are in favour. This has a logic that men are more concerned about the future of their daughters not allowing them to derail from religious practices and finally to give them in marriage traditionally. They are suppose to answer the issues brought forth by the community and by the religious leaders and the wrath of both. Nearly 12 per cent of the respondents stressed the lack of separate institutions for females a cardinal reason for their reluctancy. They feared that their daughters would become wicked in the situations of co-educational institutions with a possibility of trespassing Islam and dismissing symbols like the veil. Moreover, the parents, particularly males in Kerala, fear that their educated daughters may become a burden without getting educated boys as life partners. The surveys in the northern districts of Kerala like Kasaragod, Kannur and Malappuram districts reveal the same. The boys in such districts usually are far behind higher education and most of them without having professional education are put up in unskilled occupations, but with an attraction of the volume of money they acquire. This imbalance in education negatively affect the future of educated girls and much to the argument of their parents. Moreover, a small section of the respondents (nearly 8 p.c) highlighted economic backwardness or poverty of the family as an additional reason for not sending their daughters for higher education.

In a general analysis, what we could find in the attitude of Muslim men towards women are more conservative. In such a context, when we asked about their attitude, the respondents (both male and female) revealed that men are opposed to the higher education of girls. In the Kasaragod and Cannanore districts, where we used quota sampling method, the response was appalling. It includes housewives (literate and illiterate) of both urban and rural streams, employed and college going girls. More than 30 per cent of the female respondents stated that men oppose to the higher education of women mainly on account of their lack of education, economic backwardness and partly due to rigid religious attitudes. The following table will disclose a sample data taken from the districts (Cannanore and Kasaragod) illustrating the variables in urban and rural areas.

Table 3.5: Variables in Urban and Rural Areas

Opposition (Reasons)	*Urban*	*Rural*
Lack of education	45%	55%
Economic reasons	40%	60%
Religious Reasons	30%	70%
Indifferent/Unknown reasons	20%	80%

Source: Responses to the Questionnaire supplied.

Thus it is fascinating to note that Muslim men are also equally responsible for the low percentage of girls education particularly in the higher and professional levels. In the rural areas 70 per cent of the respondents object to the women education due to religious reasons. Thus it is necessary to effect radical classes in the religious attitudes also.

Whose Responsibility?

The backwardness of Muslim girls in continuing education is also considerably associated with the negative attitude that Muslim ulemas and religious functionaries show towards them since they have a major role in the day-today life of the Muslim communities. This situation has been aggrevated after the issues like that of the Shah Bano and the uproar for a uniform civil code in the Indian context. Our observations and respondents' perceptions in various districts of north Kerala, particularly in the Malappuram district clearly reveal the new shift from the already existing ethosthat the community had with some trends of modernisation. These ulemas through their routine religious discourses highlight all such incidents as outside inroads towards religion and the "hazards" being irreligious or heretic. The Mosques and the Ulemas have their special mechanism of night speeches on religious issues and epic stories, for Muslim community. These speeches help extending the orthodoxy in the community. More lectures influence the males who put pressures on females especially when they come through religious draconism. The religious functionaries always stress on the importance of religious education on girls and negating the liberal and secular education. This attitude basically pushes the girls in the four walls of their apartments, particularly when they attain puberty. Moreover, as a safety valve, they with the help of the parents, detain such young girls in the entanglements of the wedlock from which they could never be free. This is one of the cardinal reasons for the backwardness of Muslim girls who seek higher or professional education.

Though the Muslims generally oppose them, these ulemas still have their influences in the economically and socially undeveloped homesteads and regions. Majority of the respondents are of the view that these religious functionaries discourage Muslim girls from acquiring higher learning apart from the persuation they often give to parents with a belief pattern that it is a rightful "religious duty".

Table 3.6: Reflections on the Attitude of Religious functionaries towards female education

Districts		*Favourable*	*Unfavourable*	*Indifferent*
Calicut	Male	15%	40%	45%
	Female	16%	45%	39%
Cannanore	Male	17%	42%	41%
	Female	20%	40%	40%
Malappuram	Male	18%	60%	22%
	Female	15%	55%	30%

Source: Data generated through field work.

A very interesting aspect to be seen in the Calicut city is the wide gulf in the attitude of Muslims (both male + female) that the old city of Calicut including places like Kuttichira, Itiyangara, Mukhadar, Pallikkandy, Kundungal etc. to acquire higher education is comparably very low eventhough they have half a day schools including secondary where Muslim girls are in majority. Our study of the region led to a terrifying truth that mostly the girls in these schools are either not allowed to go for higher studies or they themselves are not mentally prepared for choosing their future by higher education or for employment. From our interviews with some girls who have completed their Higher Secondary, what we could understand is that for most of them, education partly is a pastime till they attain the marriageable age. More than 95 per cent of the families of these girls belong to the commercial class and for that matter, the grooms of these girls come from that stream. The non-availability of qualified grooms for better qualified girls may also be a reason for such a situation that developed into traditional commercial communities spread over the whole of western side of Calicut city starting from Beypore in the South to Vellayil in the North.

The condition of a small ghetto within this geosphere in the city is also noticeable on account of its total negligence in health, hygene and education, where the Muslims form 80 per cent of the population. This notorious part of the city, nicknamed as "Bengladesh Colony" is still beyond the reach of development and civic amenities. The place is also noted for the grooming ground of outlaws where major cases of immoral and drug trafficking and opiation in the region are reported. Most of the houses seemed to be the centres of miscreants where outsiders were not even allowed to enter and each such house is within the control of an elderly woman, though restrained, often a Muslim. An interview with such a woman revealed the hard realities of juvenile girls in the colony, who never had even the opportunity of getting primary education, either religious or secular. Such girls and their male counterparts easily become the prey of miscreants and anti-social elements working as carriers of drugs and victims of immoral trafficking[27].

While analysed the educational and economic status of Muslim women in Vatakara Municipality (northern side of Calicut District) the experience is not much different from the seashore of Calicut Corporation. A small fishermen colony in the beach towards north, locally known as 'Sainande Valappu' (The compound of Saina) is a very backward area where Muslim and Hindu fishermen live in clusters, and in unhealthy situation. This area also has been in the same condition as the ghetto in Calicut. The Muslims of this part, particularly ladies, are also innocent of education and the situation continued for years. The symptoms of immoral and drug trafficking, in addition to robbery and theft with casualities of criminal nature, nurtured from this area for years. Our observation of the attendance of Muslim girls in the neighbourhood lower primary school is not at all hopeful because they form less than 5 per cent of the school's girls students' strength. Here also poverty and parents's ignorance are the major factors for such a situation. Recently there are rare cases of migration to gulf countries from this region which finally may result with some economic betterment and overall development of the region[28].

Moreover, while analysing the educational status of Muslim girls in the Calicut city particularly in the coastal areas, Zoya Hasan and Ritu Menon also give due weightage to poverty apart from early marriage and lack of awareness among parents. From their study in different areas of Calicut and Malappuram, they could find out early marriage as the main obstruction to the continuation of education by Muslim girls[29].

The survey in the Malappuram district particularly in the coastal area, where Muslim population is comparatively high, is most fascinating. In the sample survey done in the Municipal coastal towns like Tirur and Ponnani, the educational status and employment potential of Muslim women are very poor. Again, as seen in Calicut, the coastal belt dominated by the fishermen community, still shows the deplorable condition of Muslim women especially of younger generation without having proper education, but wedlocked at an early age of fourteen or fifteen to our amazement. But these towns taken together generally, are coming up with strong economic background as a result of the gulf boom. Ponnani, with a background of the Makhdoomean orthodoxy, is found fast growing into modernity with education and reform and also by the wide acceptance of leftist ideologies. This is a significant change which could be noted and analysed amongst a variety of contributory factors. Except in coastal areas, the percentage of school-going Muslim girls has been raised to 80-85 in urban centres and 60-65 in rural areas. This is a marked change from the earlier conditions when modern education was treated as a taboo. This change also could be seen in the percentage of dropouts especially from the middle to the higher secondary. This is a general trend that Kerala poses with regard to the Muslim female education in toto. Mushirul Hasan, while comparing the dropout of girls from higher classes in Karnataka, Tamil Nadu, Andhra Pradesh and West Bengal, draws of the graph of Kerala with a lesser gender disparity[30]. Here the percentage of girls' enrolment in schools is increasing and there is a subsequent decrease both in drop outs in higher classes and the under age marriages. This adds more confidence for Muslim girls and their families to a better life and to restructure the future.

From the ongoing analysis what we can hypothesise is that the low level of education among Muslim girls is due to several factors existing in their society. Firstly, the economic backwardness of the community never allows them to accept modern education which is very costly and unapproachable to them. Secondly, ulemas and other religious functionaries dictate the community, especially the girls, not to go for higher education which, they fear, may damage the religious ethos and moral life of the women folk. This virtually isolate the community from others and from the trend of modern life. Thirdly, the early marriages of girls obstruct them from the chances of going for higher education and closes all opportunities of seeing an open world. This causes more sufferance to the girls and young women pushing them to have more children and more misery in the family life. This creates a vicious circle denying their children a better life later who live in poor conditions, without getting modern education and a healthy and comfortable life. Fourthly, illiteracy prevalent among parents widely affect the education of their girl children because they are totally ignorant of the importance of education and its value in society. Finally, as the Muslims themselves claim, lack of separate institutions for girls is a handicap for those who seek modern education. This, further, is a part of the value system that prevails in that society who still cling to purdah and seclusion.

Moreover, the reverse looking Muslim community never consider modern and higher education as a means of livelihood for the future generation. This is linked with several factors that haunts the society, of which the role of purdah or early marriage and religious compulsions are not of lesser importance. It is a fact that the issues of Muslim women, whether in India or elsewhere, are more complex and divergent to comprehend. Several commissions, lately that of Sachar,. repeatedly highlighted this aspect of the Muslim community, particularly of their women, in highsounding words with remedial measures. But as a closed society governed by religious dogmas and traditional beliefs, it could not be touched easily with the beams of enlightenment. As referred to earlier, their women folk suffer the most and they are the most depressed class of Indian society. This has to be viewed both in historical perspective and in the light of socio-economic backwardness. The fundamentalists make the people believe that modern education is undesirable for girls. Virtually education equips an individual to have a better life with self reliance. It is a fact that Islam considers learning compulsory both for male and female as revealed through several verses of the Quran and the traditions of the prophet (vide Chapter-I). This wailful situation is to be valued not on the account of religion but of the value system that the Islamic society followed for centuries in different continents with the pressures of fastidious historicity. In their long journey of strife and struggles, women as a weaker sex have been marginalised everywhere branding them inferior to men. Hence they were denied all opportunities of education and thereby to achieve professional and personal excellence.

Absence in the Mainstream

The absence of Muslim women in the mainstream, especially in a region like Kerala, is also extensively affected by the feeling that they belong to a minority community, and hence are expected to be treated or 'protected' specially, providing the opportunities usually not available to them. But this marginalization is not of the government policy alone, but of the attitude of their own community which itself imposes several restrictions on their womenfolk misguiding them to be within the framework of religion and 'moral' values. But one could not be blind to the fact that with the expansion of Islam the world over, it also underwent several changes within the regions that penetrated as found in India and South East Asia. Even the ideology of Islam and its observance, apart from its basics, have been transformed by the interaction with other societies and cultures. This we could experience in the nature of the spread of Islam other than the Arab World, especially in Africa, Central Asia and South East Asia, where they have their political dominance too. Even in the Arab World and in its periphery, this metamorphosis could be seen in different times under various Caliphates and Imamates. While accepting various tribals and cultural groups into the fold of Islam, the Prophet himself has given due weightage to this regional milieu that crept into the fold from regions like Egypt or Asia minor or Africa or less cultural groups like the Berbers and Slavs.

The advent of Islam in Kerala created a new cultural group among Muslims called Mappilas. Their identity in Kerala has been ascertained by a sociological integration of two elements, the regional ethos and the Islamic faith. This is a case not only of Kerala alone, but the whole of Asia, particularly of Indonesia where the regional elements dominated over everything including religion. This also is an aberration to the belief that the semitic religions like Islam will not have any compromise with the regionalism or the cultural traits other than theirs. Likewise, we have living examples in countries like Indonesia where Hindu names are extensively used like Sukarnaputri and Meghavati. for Muslims. They still cherish the stories of Ramayana as a part of cultural ethos developed with the "Greater Indian" culture spread over there particularly in the time of Chola expansion. In Kerala also Mappila Muslims had names like Pathummakutty (instead of Fathima) and Kuttiacha (instead of Aisha). For males they used Kunhi Ahammed and Ahammed Kutty adding Kutty as prefix and suffix. Even Mappila Muslim literature in Arabi Malayalam has the influence of Hindu culture The "Mappila Ramayanam" has become very popular in Malabar constituting an important part of the corpus of "Mappilappattu". As noted earlier, in the prime days of Islam, places like Turkey and Syria evolved new religious experiments with a conglomeration of their own local elements. But as in any community the chores are found among the women folk alone since they are found everywhere within the confines of the household. They enjoyed limited freedom in such situations while the opposite sex have the privilege of dictating things.

Muslim women in Kerala basically suffer from stubborn patriarchy often justified on the line of religious tenets. But this state of affairs is not attained as a result of religious dictates alone, but evolved due to several socio-economic factors too. Islam as an ideology does not interfere in the socio-economic activities of women on the excuse of gender speciality alone and their status hike is, in all respects equal to men. It also teaches to acquire maximum adjustment and accommodation when confronts with opposing situations including modernisation. The changes found in the behavioural pattern of Muslim women are the result of their responses "to contextual requirements rather than moulded by an ideology and tradition"[31]. Hence this attitude could better be reflected in issues like education, marriageable age, employment and family planning. in the socio-economic situations that developed around them rather than the much publicised religious stigma alone. The study shows that in majority cases the ulemas and other religious functionaries exploit such a situation to their requirements. Therefore, in places like Malabar (northern part of Kerala), inspite of the education some of them acquired, the general life style of Muslim women is still in a religious-based pattern from which they could not be free easily. Even for those who are educated, the level of freedom they enjoy is very limited as a result of the patriarchal control over them.

Impact of Social Moorings

Practices like matri-local system, further, curtails the independent life of women and their mobility in social life. Here, though they get more economic and familial security, they could not lead an independent life, highly essential for its growth as a microcosmic unit. Moreover, major share of the Muslim women in the backward districts under study are not at all aware of family planning or the ways and means to population control. This is not because that they are reluctant to accept such methods, but either the ignorance of the contraceptives or their non-availability or inaccessibility may be the reason. Again, these women rarely attend health education classes or visit hospitals. The girls who are destined to be married in their early teens and conceived often in a childish embarrassment certainly will have no seriousness either of the gynaec problems or childcare, the negligence of which may even threaten their own life. The study in the backward areas of Malappuram and the interiors of Calicut, Cannanore and Kasargod districts reveals the disdainful and jeering situations that the women community among Muslims face with sheer disgust and loath. Nobody comes either from their own community or from outside to rescue such innocent and helpless women from this miserable state of affairs that haunt them for years. But the problem of such incidents of early marriages and an early divorce is often legitimised by the sanction of religion as interpreted by fake ulemas or religious functionaries with the support of community leaders who accommodate such "divinities" for gaining their own end. The Thangals and other priests even enjoy greater control over the community.

When we analyse the pattern of dress that Mulim women in Kerala accepted, we have to realise the fact that they have absorbed more from locally than from outside. Their common dress include a white *mundu* (lower garment) often with a coloured border popularly known as *kaachi* in Calicut area. The upper garment include a jacket with long sleeves stretching to the palm with decorative embroidary work round over to the neck and the collar. The head cover is simply a *thattam* or a white scarf with borders of different colours rarely golden. The beauty and texture of the dress varies on account of the age and occasions. Hence a bridal dress is more colourful with the costliest of the silks and embroidaries. It includes a special dress like the *mathappu* (very colourful ornated texture, usually blue, red or green) and *ponchappam* (usually in gold and purple). It is also a fact that with all such Mappila Muslim specialities, Muslim women still prefer to have sarees as a common dress of their own for the marriage and for the day to day usage. Even those who wear purdah, use either sarees or churidars as inner garments. These are all very common in the dress style of the Muslim women in Calicut, Tellicherry and Cannanore.

A distinction could also be noticed in the life style of Muslim women both in the coastal areas and its interiors. Trend towards modernism in dress and outlook could best be noticed among the Muslim family of these areas, particularly among the women of the Koyas of Calicut, the Keyis of Tellicherry and the sophisticated women in Cannanore and Mahe areas. In their fondness in wearing gold ornaments too, there is no distinction in the varieties of the ornaments of their sisters in other communities. This could also better be noticed in the bridal collections that Muslim ladies prefer to have in their purchases. The ornaments that the Muslim women wore in olden times like *alikathu* (small rings with glittering gold pieces wore on the upper part of the ear, usually 5-7 in each ear) and some peculiar ornaments in the ear lap are all now disappeared and all have now common ornaments as others have in the society.

Our field study on the peculiarities of life of Muslim women in the coastal areas of Calicut, particularly in *Thekkepuram* (Kuttichira, Kundungal, Mukhadar, Idiyangara, Pallikkandi etc.) also brought to light some strange practices that they observed till recently, but not totally disappeared. It is associated with the marriage ceremonies and some women-centred professions, particularly among the Koyas of Calicut. These women in the service sector are called *vilikkarathi* (paid women deputed to invite for marriages at a time when marriage invitations were not popular), *thunakkarathi* (women helpers in the marriage pandal, particularly being the associate of the bride, often acting also as a beautician), *kalikkarathi* (the professional player in the *oppana* group song standing along the bride). *Eettukarathi* is another type of women, lesser in social status, who mostly act as nurses to attend the delivered women for forty days. Some of these women also act as cooks in the kitchen of the Muslim houses on special occasions. All of them are almost in extinct as a result of modern life and with the rise of micro families.

Like their sisters in other parts of the country, Muslim women in Kerala face a host of problems against the general perception that they face only issues centred around Shariah including divorce and inheritance. As noted earlier, here, their issues are more deeper, even reaching to the point of human rights. Most of their problems are associated with socio-economic factors that generally push them to extreme poverty and backwardness. The much discussed issues like *Muthalaq* (Tripple Divorce)' and Muslim Personal Law in the general Indian context, are not coming to the limelight heavily, partly as a result of religious revivalist ideologies, and to some extent, by the interference of progressive ideologies and the secular governance. Denial of education and employment, early marriage, imposition of purdah, male-female relationship and freedom of movement are to be considered as major issues related to the total upliftment of Muslim women in Kerala. All these factors have to be addressed very seriously in the light of human rights. Commissions, including Sachaar, have categorised these poor mass of women worse than that of scheduled tribes, and it is more so in the case of Kerala. The conservative attitude of the family including patriarchal dictates and the societal antagonism are the greatest hurdles found in the way of girls' educational and professional attainments.

The issue related to inheritance and property rights are also the factors that affected the familial constructs of Muslim women in Kerala. Many a family suffer from this old system of the division of property as per the law of inheritance practiced in Islam at a time when there was no property right for women in the tribal society in Arabia. In the present global circumstances, where the whole concept of family, capital accumulation, life style, employment, industrial capitalism and all the more, the restructured human relations, such as law of inheritance is found impractical, and illogical, and for that matter, unlawful and a moral wrong. It should be remembered that Quranic articulations are often specific to the time and circumstances of its revelation. This aspect has been ascertained by the Prophet saying that, after all types of interpretations on the principles of Quran and traditions, great weightage should be given to *Ijthihad* (scholarly/reasonable interpretation) and *Ijma* (consensus of the people). Writers like Amina Wadud argues that there must be continuous re-evaluation of even fundamental principles, from the time of their specific embodiment throughout the challenges, changes and limitations of history[32]. As legal codes are major concerns to human polity and social order, no single set of legal codes could ever be expected to support the universal law in the complex situations of changes in human life. Moreover, understanding and implementing the fundamental values should be in accordance with the circumstances and dictates of human life. Such an approach of the universal application of the so called 'universal phenomenon' of religious halo greatly affected the poor masses of Muslims in Kerala also in their socio-economic life. Women, particularly of the lower section of society, not having proper economic background, carried on their livelihood with frustration, while their male partners, may be their brothers or their own husbands, enjoyed the fruits of such allowances with a negative attitude. Such mere imitations of the past virtually minimises even the human rights of women and their status and bargaining power in society. These aspects have been discussed in detail by writers like Mir Hosseini who argues that gender rights are neither fixed, nor absolute. They are, on the contrary, cultural and legal constructs which are asserted, negotiated and subject to change. She also examines and exposes the validity of such rules and bias of Islamic *fiqh* and their inner contradictions[33].

Muslim women in Kerala are far inferior to their menfolk (including husbands) due to several socio-economic compulsions and restrictions. Being unemployed and illiterate, they are supposed to depend on their men for everything in the household. They have no access to resources and men dictate things in the family and women's position here is bordering on to servitude. With a weaker bargaining power, they could not in any way dominate in the family. The situation, thus created by socio-economic factors, become more intensified when religious tenets are unequivocally imposed over them. Such 'impositions' have their own logic of 'protection' in a state of 'insecurity', possibly compelled to live facing an 'alien' or opposing culture. This could be found in the Taliban -led Afghanistan which exposed the gender regime in its fiercest form, instructing women to cover completely and remain inside the houses. This is merely a gender aggression in a political deal. But the pity is that such actions are often legitimised by men in the excuse of religion, to which, originally it has no role.

But in urban situations things are different on several factors including socio-economic. The situation is further better and favourable to women, particularly if she is propertied and has the control of resources. The matrilocal system, in one sense, also strengthens the cause of women when their spouses are only 'visitors' with lesser claim on resources and bargaining power. The issues like polygamy and unilateral divorce are also almost nil in such circumstances. Statistics taken from Kasaragod to the border of Malappuram districts, especially in the coastal area where matrilineal system prevailed once, the Muslim households are still keeping the same pattern (Matrilocal) without much change. The situation of women further improved in these regions due to development of education and by the wide acceptance of micro family system. But women with an urge to preserve class and social purity with economic power are found facing more restrictions on their mobility than the lower sections. Seclusion and purdah are more found on them, probably as a mark of their superior status, and to safeguard the morals and purity of such groups. But this superior status, instead of making them free, pushes them more to observe seclusion and live passive. This also reminds us, with a new insight that mere economic progress or educational upliftment do not necessarily reduce gender inequalities. This partly corroborates the theory of Maria Mies who in her study on Indian women argues that the most cruel form of violence are to be found in areas where great "development" and new form of wealth are appeared with cinemas, alcohol, television and such other consumer goods introduced as indicators of modernisation[34]. That means, to some extent, in an urban society, irrespective of class, consumerism, that developed as a result of modernisation, creates a lot of socio-economic disparities and some kind of gender tension on issues like free marriage, divorce and inheritance right.

No doubt majority of the issues and the claims for such gender rights naturally arise out of sheer economic and social pressures. The male's enquiry to acquire whatever resources possible in a given living situation in a competitive society of wants is a common phenomenon, particularly in urban centres. But Kerala, being a region without much difference of urban and rural, represents such an elitist culture basically in the life style of people without much class or religions differences.

Interestingly, in all our study area, the response among women regarding the inheritance and property rights is very poor. Most of them do not know what this right itself is and are ignorant of the ratio of their share even. It is true that Islam prescribes shares in the property to all varieties of females specifically denoting wife, mother, sister and daughter. However, this rule is often found violated making it the victim of unreasonable practices. This, ofcourse, is based on a belief that sons, rather than daughters support and look after parents in their old age. But this is not a general rule to be applied with in the case of Malabar Muslims who still follows the matrilocal system in which wives are retained in their own houses. Hence what we have experienced in our study is that there are instances of parcelling out the whole property of the parents, particularly the living compound and house to those who occupy the house traditionally. It is a common sight in Malabar where the compound family system is still prevalent as a heritage of the matrilineal system of the past. The Mappila households of the Koyas of Calicut and the Keyis of Tellicherry are living examples of such a mode of life. In such households the parents with their daughters and their husbands and children live together very harmoniously. Such a system becomes more effective particularly when their brothers seek their asylum in their wives' houses as a corresponding and parallel practice giving great relief for all. Heavy expenses in the Muslim marriages and several unnecessary practices often go against the cause of women. Most of them also believe that whatever the property rights they had is only as a result of the clemency the parents showed towards them. Only 2.5 per cent women have shown the audacity to claim their property and that too with the pressures of either husbands or matured children.

The response with regard to Muslim Personal Law, virtually a male-dominated, the much acclaimed 'Shariah-based product of the North Indian Muslims, is also highly fascinating to our observations. In the area under study, nearly 95 per cent of Muslim women, both urban and rural, rich and poor, did not know what the Shariah is or to what purpose it is framed. Since these areas are dominated by the Sunniites, majority of them never heard of it. But in the revivalist Mujahid and Jama'at circles, small section of educated women only know its presence in areas, particularly in the north, where it acts as a fighting force against liberal Islam and often as an exploiter of women's rights[35]. Those who are aware of it, even have the feeling that it (Shariah/Muslim Personal Law) is the most holiest than the Quran and the traditions, and could not be violated at any cost. They also consider it as a symbol of Muslim identity. They never knew that on this issue a great divide has taken place among communities in India leading to a polarisation, from which the country even now could not be relieved. Our enquiry, whether the law is gender-friendly or not, is quite appalling because most of them believe that, since Muslim Personal Law imbibes the spirit of Shariah, it is gender-just and universally applicable without any compromise. This is a great challenge to the claim of a uniform civil code and the secularisation of law. What they stress is a community intervention rather than that of a democratic government to which the Muslim Personal Law could never be tolerated in an open civil society. Though the Muslim Personal Law seems to be gender-just providing some rights to women, in reality, it often works against them. Since women are unaware of their rights, they never go against it. Moreover, the patriarchal nature of society and the limited rights of mobility rather limit them not to go outside their homes for education and employment. Many consider going outside the house itself is a violation of Islamic law on the basis of a verse found in the Quran revealed specially to warn the wives of the Prophet which reads: "Stay at home, and do not flaunt your finery as they used to in the pagan past"[37].

In the final analysis, what we can observe is that the issues concerning Muslim women are not to be taken in isolation because they are closely associated with the questions of womens' rights in general, and for that matter, they should be evaluated in a wider perspective of human relationships irrespective of gender, class, community or religion. Muslim women, particularly those living in backward areas, have to be taught the true spirit of Islamic laws and the misuse of the 'Shariah' by men with a feeling of superiority and domineering nature. Institutions like marriage and family life are not to be treated as a check on life and progress, and a wide world of freedom has to be opened before them. They (women) must also be aware of their ignorance and illiteracy and the socio-economic factors that always push them to timidity and backwardness. The community also has an additional responsibility to prepare these innocent and mute masses towards progress and development. They must also be informed of the sultry and fake ulemas and leaders who claim to be the "protectors" of the women folk who always stick to a literal interpretation of the tenets and traditions, instead of making them more pragmatic and humane. Such a new wave is indispensable in a region like Kerala where religious fundamentalism takes new shape and dimensions, posing overwhelming threats to the lives of all, without band or barriers.

Notes and References

1. The Sachaar Committee Report was issued in November, 2006. It runs to 285 pages and is divided into 12 chapters. It also contain very useful handy tables and graphs. Apart from the Chairman Justice Rajindar Sachar, the other members were Syed Hamid, Dr. T.K. Oommen, M.A. Basith, Dr. R. Besant, Dr. Akhtar Majeed and Dr. Abu Saleh Shariff (Member Secretary).
2. William Logan *Malabar Manual*, Vol. I, Reprint, Delhi, 2009, p. 198.
3. *Ibid.*, p. 594.
4. Asghar Ali Engineer, *Lifting the Veil,* Hyderabad, 1995, p. 43.
5. Report of Justice K.K. Narendran, 11th Feb; 2000.
6. Makthi Thangal (1847-1912) was a great reformer and an ardent critic of Christian missionaries. He wrote more than 24 renowned works and encouraged translation of Quran. His concern for Female education could be detected from the slogan found in his journal *Tuhfat-ul-Aqyar* written in Arabi-Malayalam. It reads:
   Did not leave the kitchen; Did not meet Scholars;
   Did not learn any thing; But no dearth for *fatwas* (religious ordinances)
   Chalilakath Kunhammed Haji (1866-1919), a noted reformer and a multilinguist who also wrote several works on Islamic jurisprudence. He introduced blackboard for teaching The Khibla Controvency (A conflict on the issue of the direction while one prays turning to the side of Ka'aba in Mecca) was an issue of his time. An advocate of modern Madrasah type of education. Vakkom Abdul Khader Maulavi (1873-1932) was a noted reformer from Travancore. A Scholar with the knowledge in Arabic, Sanskrit, English and Urdu. Started *Swadeshabhimani* and patronised Ramakrishna Pillai as the editor of this journal.
7. K.T. Mohammed wrote dramas like *This is Earth* (1953) criticising the feudal characteristics of Muslim Society in Kerala and its illiterate religious functionaries. Through a character in this drama, K.T. declares the liberation of Muslim Women. It reads:
   "The hands holding spoons are rising; The giggling bangles in the hands make noises. The blackish spoons lifting as flags; Ready for a war leaving the black kitchen." K.T.'s work reminds the message of V.T. Bhattathiripad who wrote *From Kitchen to Stage* (Mal.) (1929) to reform the Brahmins of Kerala.
8. C.K. Kareem (ed.), *Kerala Muslim Directory,* Cochin, 1991, p. 311. See also C.N. Ahmed Maulavi, *Great Mappila Literary Tradition* (Mal.) 1978, and Syed Mohideen Shah, *Islam in Kerala.*
9. Proceedings of the Education Department, Government of India 15th July, 1885, p. 33.
10. G.O. No. 1371 (Education), dt. 1st June, 1934.
11. The first Conference of the Sangham was held at Eriyad under the presidency of Vakkom Moulavi. Other leaders of the Movement were P. Kunhammad Haji (Manappat), K.M. Moulavi, E.K. Moulavi, Seethi Muhammed and Sheikh Hamadani etc.
12. Research Project, The Socio-educational progress of the *Backwards of Malabar*, Table 2.2. Calicut University, 2002, p. 46. The initiative to this project was

taken up by K.K.N. Kurup, the Vice Chancellor, with a thrust to the condition of the Muslims of the region after the formation of the University of Calicut.

13. Administration Report of Education Department (1943-44), The Superintendent, Government Press, Ernakulam, 1945, p. 31.
14. *Census Report* of 1921, p. 350.
15. K.N. Panikkar; *Against Lord and State*, Oxford University Press, 1989 pp. 54-55.
16. The towns of Kasaragod, Kanhangad, Mogral, Padanna upto Mangalore are dominant by these newly emerged class who have an economic priority compared to their brotheren of other communities except some Konkani Brahmin businessmen of the coast. The recent communal tensions in Mangalore and its outskirts are the result of the economic or trade rivalry with these groups particularly with the emergence of the BJP government in Karnataka.
17. Speeches of community leaders as representatives of the Managements of affiliated colleges, *The New Indian Express* 10th July, 2008. This aspect has been highlighted by the Minority Commission on several occasions in their reports.
18. *Sachar Committee Report,* Government of India, Nov., 2006, pp. 15-16.
19. *Ibid.,* p. 18.
20. The news of the Community marriage has been publicised with photograph in all the regional newspapers on 10-4-2010, One Soopi Haji, a philanthropist of Vanimel in Calicut District, took the initiative for such a venture.
21. The Muslim League leader C.H. Mohammed Koya, a representative from Malappuram, became the education minister in two consecutive terms, which made him a stalwart of Muslim education not only in Malappuram District, but even in other backward areas of Kerala. The educational consciousness of Muslims was regenerated as a result of the availability of a number of schools, colleges and other higher educational institutions in other parts of Kerala.
22. Muslim Education Society was started in 1964 in Calicut with the initiative of some Muslim philanthropists. Its first President was Dr. P.K. Abdul Ghafoor, a physician by profession. Now they have more than 20 institutions, including a medical college and an engineering college, both in the Malappuram district.
23. Other schools where Muslim girls' strength forms more than 50 per cent is the M.M. High School in the city. Other institutions are also utilised for the education of girls who wanted to have their studies till plus-two level, when most of them are either married or stopped studying.
24. These Women's Colleges in Calicut City are unaided/self financed and affiliated to the University of Calicut.
25. The foundation stone of the College was laid down by E.M.S. Namboodiripad, the Chief Minister, under the Presidency of C.H. Mohammed Koya, the Education Minister, in June, 1967. Now this is the largest educational institution with a multi-centre campus under the Kannur University. A post graduate college, An Institute of Technology, A Teacher Education College, A Higher Secondary School etc. are functioning in this campus sponsored by the Cannanore District Muslim Educational Association, initiated by some Muslim philanthropists and educationists of the district. The first President of the Association was A.K.

Kaderkutty, a noted Industrialist and technocrat followed by V. Khalid, a noted Justice of the Supreme Court of India.

26. C.K. Kareem, *Kerala Muslim History, Statistics and Directory* (Mal.), Vol. III, Cochin, 1991. p. 43.
27. Field study and interview with one Fathima (pseudoname), a resident of colony for the last fifteen years, and who also revealed first hand information about several incidents including the 'Icecream episode' of Ragina, a poor Muslim girl originally belonging to that ghetto, and later "saved and protected" by the forces of money and power. The name of a former minister, was also linked with the 'ice cream parlor' case in Calicut, a celebration of the media in 2005-08. Such thickly populated areas in the coastal towns of Tellicherry and Cannanore are also noted with the same pattern of life. Fishing is the main profession where all communities are residing. These areas are also noted as highly sensitive due to the presence of miscreants. Chalil in Tellicherry and Marakkarkandy and Tayyil in Cannanore are examples.
28. Based on the interview with the residents and ward members of the locality. This situation is not of the Muslim community alone, but the whole of fishermen folk (Hindus and Muslims) who depend on sea for their livelihood. After Calicut City, the major drug-trafficking are reported from here. The 80 years old Krishnan Marakkan and Madhavi Amma (pseudo names) revealed several cases of criminal nature, especially with the members coming from outside, occurred in the region for the last twenty years. Now the situation here is fast improving as a result of the interference of local bodies and developmental measures of the government.
29. Zoya Hasan and Ritu Menon, *Educating Muslim Girls—A Comparison of Five Indian Cities,* Women Unlimited, New Delhi, 2005, pp. 134-143.
30. Mushirul Hasan, "Muslims in Secular India, Problems and Prospects in Education" in *Will Secular India Survive?* (ed.), Imprint One, Delhi, 2004, pp. 291-305.
31. Aijaz Ahmed and Nazim Aijaz, "From Dependency to Subordination-Muslim Women in the Rural Setting" in Zakia A. Siddiqi and Anwar Jahan Zuberi (ed.) *Muslim Women, Problems and Prospects,* New Delhi, 1993, p. 89.
32. Amina Wadud, *Inside the Gender Jihad,* One World, Oxford, 2006, p. 43.
33. Ziba Mir Hussaini, "The Construction of Gender in Islamic Legal Thought and Strategies of Reform". *Hawwa: Journal of Women in the Near East and the Islamic World,* 1-1 (2003).
34. Maria Mies, *Women: The Last Colony,* Kali for Women, New Delhi, 1988, p. 137.
35. A forum known as the Muslim Personal Law Board was organsed by some Muslim leaders and Ulemas under the pretext that they are the true protectors of the Shariah and the community in 1972. It became popular after the Shah Bano Case. Infact the law seeks space in Muslim personal life and popularise the misuse of divorce (Triple Talaq), polygamy and law of inheritance. Triple divorce has never been a part of Islamic teachings. Neither the Quran nor the Prophet never accepted it. Being a pre-Islamic Arab customary law, it is quite unfair to apply it on all Muslims universally.
36. *Quran*, Surah 33 *(Al Ahzab*-The Joint Forces), Verse 33. This is a Medinan

Surah which gets its title from the incident of the Battle of the Trench in 627 AD, when the joint forces of various tribes besieged Medina. Also a critical time for Muslims (especially to women) in motion.

37. In this context, a Two-day National Seminar on the "Emergence of Fundamentalism and Terrorism" was organised at Calicut jointly by Maulana Abul Kalam Azam Institute of Asian Studies, Kolkata and Malabar Institute for Research and Development at Calicut on 18th and 19th June, 2010; with the participation of scholars from various streams. It was attended by Dr. H.S. Vasudevan, the Director of MAKAIAS who delivered the Presidential address, Dr. P.K. Maichael Tharakan, the Vice Chancellor, Kannur University and Dr. K.K.N. Kurup, the former Vice Chancellor of Calicut University. This academic seminar was the first of its kind arranged in the whole state of Kerala.

4

Gender and the Reform

Making of a Social Change

Debates over gender relations, the family and the women's rights, are by no means new to the forums of Muslim societies. In recent years the 'Women's question' attracted more attention in backward spaces as that of the Islamic society of Kerala. Scholars of modernity always projected Muslim women as backward looking in all their deliberations with deep concern for reform. Lack of education, early marriage, increased female domesticity, and above all, the hammer of religiosity (Shariah) entangled Muslim women in a cell of their own. These battered women often became a 'private matter' of the male and the household.

We have already seen how women in the Islamic society of Kerala lived in seclusion compared to their sisters living differently in other communities. The socio-religious ethos that pervaded over, greatly pushed them back to the shackles of inertia and indolence for centuries. It is true that all attempts at reform, ofcourse from within, to bring them to reality, failed on account of several reasons, of which the parental and patriarchal hierarchy takes a big toll. Since resources are not reachable to all, an imbalance in all aspects of life could be seen in all societies, ofcourse with cultural and regional variations. Thus the inequality found in families creates some kind of exploitation and even conflicts. This general dictum could be applied to the Muslim society of Kerala as well, perhaps to a greater degree. Writers like Bina Agarwal, a feminist cum economist, has examined this problem in a wider perspective, particularly when she says that gender relations are not equitable in most of the societies in South Asia, living upon "undisputed traditions"[1]. Customers laws and rules played a seminal role in making them effective.

Like any other social group, the life and liberty of Muslim women in Kerala is also closely associated with their education, economic potential or employment which determine greater gender equality leading to social change. Such a change will naturally provide women more respect, bargaining power and the much required exposure in a competitive society. Moreover, such an openness and liberal attitude in the life of the "reformed" women hopefully allow them to cross the gender boundaries. Gender reform also calls for the freedom from complete hijab (veil) which normally separates women from the world of men. In one sense, as Mernissi observes, it (the veil) can be treated as a symbol for the collective fantasy of the Muslim community "to eliminate them from communal life, to regulate them to an easily controllable terrain, the home, to prevent them from moving about, and to highlight their illegal position on male territory by means of a mask"[2]. The ambivalent attitude towards Muslim women followed by their own menfolk is highly discernible in a practicing society especially when it is confronting with modernism. This is because some section of the reformers among Muslims argue for a 'restricted' *hijab* about which they themselves are enigmatic, and for them the veil is never a symbol of subjugation.

Reform and Politics of Gender

In Kerala opposition against real reform and freedom emanates from the feeling that any such attempts are only towards westernisation of the community. It is true that the colonized have acquired several things from the colonizers as in education, dress and habits. Changes effected as a result of European innovation were mainly in the category of upper and middle class Muslims living in urban situations. If Islam preaches a genderless equity for all, and if it treats justice as a part of religious morality, surely women of the community must get their unequivocal rights in discharging their duties as good citizens of a civilized society. This is the major handicap that the women of the Muslim society of Kerala now suffer. The control on women, their exclusion from socio-economic activities and subjection to a religious code or shariah are all features of a committed Islamic society as found in many Islamized states. A region like Kerala is beyond such politico- religious pressures, though, it still shows the tendencies of Islamism, not by the ruler's hand but by the rigid mechanisms of the revivalist ideologies.

Islamic revivalism found a strong footing in Kerala in the 40s itself in the form of purification and reform. Major movements engineered by the Salafis (Mujahids) and the Jama'atis were attempting to reorient the existing Sunniites living in their own shells. These revivalist ideologies, though first found harmless, now became a burden for many who wanted to have a liberal life. We have our own experience in the post-Revolutionary Iran where revivalism took a new turn by imposing religion in all its rigidities. The incidents in the post revolutionary Iran, particularly in the issues of women, reveal the sum total of a social set up developed there by the reports of Haleh Afghar, who examined the miserable plights of women there. The pronouncements of some religious laws drove women back into the "sphere of domesticity" creating an atmosphere of male aggression toward women[3]. The incidents at Iran created a credo among the already occupied Mujahid-Jama'at revivalists in places like Kerala to work with more vigour. This rejuvenation of the reactionary forces also found their fresh spaces in their educational institutions like the Madrassahs. The early reformers of the Islamic world like Afghani and Abduh opposed all types of liberal Islam and redefined and revitalized the Islam of the prophetic age not allowing to be diluted with innovations even from the cultural zones in which it exists. The final failures of Reza Shah in Iran and Musthafa Kemal in Turkey (in 1925) demonstrate what the Islamists wanted to have by religion in their respective countries. While denouncing the veil, Ata Turk even laments that how women are marginalised and 'domesticated'. He asks, "what are the meaning and sense of this behaviour?... Can the mothers and daughters of a civilized nation adopt this strange manner, this barbarous posture?.... It makes the nation an object of ridicule"[4].

As noted, earlier, in Kerala, the reformist initiative have been taken first by some individual reformers like Syed Sanaullah Makthi Thangal (1847-1921) Chalilakathu Kunhammed Haji (d-1919), Sheikh Mahin Hamadani Thangal (d-1922) Vakkom Abdul Khader Maulavi (1873-1932). Their main target was to resist the colonial and western cultural impact highlighting the religio-cultural supremacy of Islam over all other elements. This attempt of purification and revival virtually led to the creation of a rigid and closed society with embossed identity. Eventhough, some of them have advocated the education of women, the society in toto was not in a position to accept their reforms particularly in the colonial context[5]. But such meagre incidents do not mean that there was phenomenal social transformation in Muslim community in Kerala either in the colonial period or immediately after independence. Islamic social system was still suffering from the worst features of patriliny and religiosity of Islam which has been interpreted in the most negative way possible in the case of women. Both the conventional ulemas and the advocates of revivalism were fearful and to the loss of their identity in the threshold of western colonialism, which they thought, could be saved mainly through the seclusion of their women. The debate over women thus became dominant all over the Islamic society and the veil emerged as a potent signifier, denoting not only the sociology of gender but also matters of cultural import[6].

The move to uplift women initiated by the Salafis and the Jama'atis found no fruit in the Islamic society of Kerala which still was under the grip of the conventional Sunniites. Moreover, to the Orthodox Sunniites, the revivalist ideologues are more dangerous and are to be defeated at any cost, because, being the "virtual enemies" of their religion from within, they could do more harm than others from outside. This sectarian antagonism spread widely in the Islamic society of Kerala to the dismay of all progressives. But such a situation does not last long as a result of the pressures for modernism and its cardinals like democracy, liberalism and secular education emerged with the dawn of independence. The competition by all groups is not to liberate or change the backwardness of their women, but to push them back to the four walls of their habitats with the "divine duty" of a wife or a mother. This traditional resistance to change and sheltered existence of their women led to form a stagnant society and without life and without emancipation. Though some sectarian groups like the Kerala Nadvathul Mujahiddin, Jama'ate' Islami and Samastha Kerala Islam Matha Vidyabyasa Board of the Sunnis have attempted to the upliftment of their girls through education. Whatever progress they have made, showed mainly tendecies of negativism and rigidity opposed to a liberal modern life. Here we get a group educated, but in approach finds rigid and puritan. Can this be encouraged is the question before all in a democratic social environment.

Hence in the Islamic society of Kerala, reform of women with a gender thrust has to be redefined or re-evaluated in a fresh perspective without any preconception or sectarian label. It is also true that all varieties of Islamic institutions, provide facilities for girls'education with more ardour in recent years as a token of their concern of the fair sex. But this education is mostly limited to religious education alone and it never goes beyond the orbit of their beliefs, customs and traditions. It is also a touching sight to see the segregation of sexes in most of the Madrassahs where a curtain divides the innocent children who know not even what gender itself. Such Madrassahs and Arabic Colleges are abundantly found in Muslim majority areas in Malappuram District. Those who get studies and training in such centres will naturally imbibe an asexual attitude leading to a cult of misogyny in future years. Moreover, the syllabi of these institutions, particularly meant for girls, never teach subjects other than religion and traditions branding all others as 'irreligious'and dangerous and unfit to be followed. Both the traditionalists and revivalists exploit the poor financial condition of the major share of the community who out of sheer helplessness allow their children to go for such schools where they get every thing free. The poor parents also find it as a relief to their financial burden. While analysing the mushroom growth of Madrassahs in Pakistan, Benazir Bhutto, highlights this aspect behind the growth of Islamist squads (including girl students) who even led processions threatening barbers and beauticians and stores where beauty aids are sold. Financial constraints often force the government to set up very limited number of public schools and the rural poor have no gateway to modern education. Such vacuum leads them to go to such type of Madrassahs where education, food and clothing are free. They "act as magnets to draw students"[7]. Such issues have to be solved by the government alone with strong constitutional commitment providing all children free and compulsory education without allowing the reactionary forces to invade in others' spaces without call or consent.

Recently, a new trend has developed in Kerala that several private agencies and communal organisations have started schools of their own under the purview of minority reservations as guaranteed in the constitution. The mushroom growth of such schools, unlike in the past, have shown tendencies of separatism, since they are mainly meant for some communities to whom everything is secured, both for teachers and students. There is least chance of intermingling of teachers and students of other communities, since their presence is very limited due to various reasons, including finance. Such schools are also not accessible for all the commons seeking admission from different communities and categories. This is a major lacuna for the healthy growth of secular education for all. Therefore, both the government and the public should take initiative for instituting such schools in public sector for democratising education to the benefit of all sections of people and to avoid sectarianism and segregation among students at least from the field of education which is considered to be the basis of culture and humanism.

It is a pity that girls on account of their gender speciality are collectively recruited in Madrassahs and Arabic Colleges without any scrutiny or scruples. As said earlier, they soon become the victims of the male fancies or patriarchal dictates. In Islamic society, it seems that the females have an additional commitment to follow the dictums of religion and to keep its identity more than their male counterparts. Because from the early student days to adulthood they are destined to suffer more compared to their brothers or mates. The negligence of girls in various stages of their development was a common experience in an average Indian life. But due to various socio-economic reasons, some backward communities like Muslims still stick to such odd practices creating an imbalance in the gender status in the family system as well as in society.

Moreover, while the reformers go for the dichotomy of gender status, more often they are reluctant to offer liberal and secular education for all. Women are instructed with some "dos" and "don'ts" and any minor breach of it are treated 'irreligious' where as men enjoy great immunity from all such taboos. This is evidently reflected in the life style of Muslims found in all spaces with respect to the dress code, mobility, public appearance, marriage and divorce and legal status. This disequilibrium experience in the Muslim gender status has to be examined with its socio-cultural backlash rather than religious moorings. In a society where theocracy dominates, there are issues concerning the equality of women particularly on matters of inheritance, property, divorce, though the Shariah had its own solutions which often do not corroborate with the existing socio-political situations. This situation created a lot of social complexities in a pluralistic society as in Kerala where the Muslim community constitutes a major share. The question here is whether Shariah could be compromised with the reforms among Muslim women who live in a secular legal system which dominates a multifaceted society posing a dual standard. The answer will be possibly negative. Moreover, the social problems and challenges that the Muslim women of Kerala face today is centred around the negation of freedom insisted by the ulema-dominated society which greatly affected their freedom of movement, education and free will. Therefore, women are the worst sufferers from several psychological and attitudinal problems imposed over them mostly as a cultural baggage of the past. The theological impositions are easily targeted against women than men, which ofcourse, adversely affected a developing society.

Any debate on the liberation of Muslim women and their reform in Kerala is associated with the attitude of Muslim society and its intellectuals. A dearth of liberal Muslim intellectuals could evidently be seen in the making of a social change in the post independent era. Instead, such a vacuum has been filled by radical religious reformers like the Salafis and the Jama'atis in addition to the existing tradition-bound ulemas, most of whom belonging to the Sunniite streams. The rigidity of the so-called revivalists often point against the liberality of the traditionalists, who, for others, are subservient to 'shirk' (polytheism). They observed religion as being practiced through what sociology of religions calls its 'priestly function' of celebrating the status quo, whatever it happened be, without regard to its being in the right or in the wrong. The revivalists argue and give more stress to the 'prophetic function' of purification of the existing religious beliefs found among the commons. This often becomes as a vehicle of protest against accepted values of the dominant society. This multitheistic attitude of the traditionalists, they complain, causes more harm to truth and damage humanity than anything else. Thus emerged a new 'idiom or diction in the revivalist corners 'religion Versus religion' as modern Islamic ideologues like Ali Shariati project in all their deliberations. The Islamists and the revivalists highlight the religion as a vehicle of a silent revolution (as found in Iran) against the one which is dead or suppressed. We have already seen how Islamist revivalists like Abduh, Afghani, Rida and Qutub remodelled the religion highlighting the philosophic potential of Islam in an unprecedented way making its reflections throughout the world. Such ideologies have made some inroads in Islamic society of Kerala in its early days itself, though not with much popularity, under the guise of reform and renaissance.

Rediscovery of Islam

This 'rediscovery of Islam' in the Kerala context, instead of making the society reformistic, pulled it back to a medieval theoretical exercise from which it could not yet have been relieved. In a society where women are either totally illiterate or partially educated, these reformers could easily narcotize them by misusing religion. This is merely an exploitation of the ignorance of the people, especially of women in the name of religion and traditional beliefs. After getting training in a rigid religious frame work, the so-called revivalists dominate the poor folk with a conscious reformulation of their thought with new concerns exclusively within the orbit of their committed tradition. All the Islamists in Kerala, as elsewhere, while they go for a reform in women, they never touch the religion they practice, whereas men are at liberty for anything. Often the Ulemas concentrate on women since they are the caretakers of children, particularly keeping in mind the integrity of society and women as its repository. Hence the religion of women got great importance, because they are mutes to the dictates of their religious masters and patriarchy. This particular aspect of religious domestication of women in Muslim societies has been highly used by writers like Robert A. Fernea and Elizabeth Fernea while they examine the "variation in religious observances among Islamic women"[8]. Strict adherence to religious rituals, insistence to observe a rigid dresscode etc. are some of the manifestations of an additional subservience that expect from women by the Islamic society. Compared to men, these impositions are highly disproportionate.

Moreover, ill treatment or denial of equal opportunities to women are a part of concerning human rights. A woman basically has the right to have a life with dignity and honour. She has even the right to live free from violence at the hands of her own husband or parents with self respect. If empowerment of women—educational, economic and occupational—is the motto of any society, they should be treated with equality and enforcement of human rights. It is true that discrimination against women violates the principles of equality of rights and respect for human dignity, and even violates national laws. A major share of Muslim women in the area of our study never knew the freedom and human rights they deserve as per our constitution and international law. This non-awareness is also the result of long standing negligence and ignorance that a male-dominated society often imposed over a section, which believes and rely, above all, on a 'divine providence'. As in the case of other societies, women in the Islamic society also suffer silently all such discriminations and disabilities on account of the reason that they are women alone. In some cases, a gender insensitivity could be seen, especially among the lower/working class people. This unconcern of people around such women develop a gender inactivity leading to a 'culture of silence' as often termed by sociologists. But this is not a part of unwillingness to speakout on the part of women, but the quantum of a benign sufferance that they were continuing all along in a male-dominated society without getting an opportunity either to complain or to protest. When there is understanding, care and respect for women in a society, we could claim that they are treated with dignity and sobriety.

The gender disparity could be seen more explicitly in some poor families where women are always treated as second grade. Our visitations in such families and the interview with some elderly women reveal appalling instances of negligence in health care and nutrition. In most of such families womens' subsistence is mostly on the residual food kept balance after the satisfactory consumption of the males. This certainly causes malnutrition and health hazards for many a women in such families. This ofcourse is not on account of any economic backwardness or inability to feed proper, but a continuatin of a practice for generations as a social system even among higher classes. This may also be partly due to the seclusion followed in such societies. But a gradual change could be seen recently by the attainment of education and awareness. Kerala Muslim society also confront with the new situations developed as a result of social change, particularly with the breaking down of joint family system and to the development of nuclear families. Wide acceptance of family planning leading to the new family system with lesser children, also strengthened the bondage among members with greater integrity and concern. Occupational security and economic growth also resulted in the enhanced standard of living of the people in general.

In places like Kerala, the gulf boom improved the socio-economic status of the women folk, and thereby the whole family system. They acquired some confidence in the management of families, especially of their children. Usually when the men are not available in the houses, it becomes a necessity for the women to manage every thing in the family system including the education of the children. These women are also compelled to go out for banking, health caring, shopping, and for the schooling and educational attainments of their children. This mobility and interaction with others created in them an atmosphere of free mingling and an overall awareness of what is happening in the outside world. Moreover, when such women confront with the hard realities of life, they also imbibe the spirit of self-confidence, independent thinking and a standing on their own potential. They also acquired the bargaining capacity in all the spaces they want to be. This is a major improvement of the faculty of Muslim women, though not much educated, that we could experience in all the areas under study. Today it is a common sight in Kerala, whether it be in banks, hospitals, educational institutions, railway stations, bus stands, airports, shopping malls, restaurants and in streets, Muslim women, though cloaked in purdah, are moving with steps of confidence and freedom. But even when such a situation prevails, the inside story of many a family is with lesser opportunities and economic frailties that demands more concern, by revealing the inherent weaknesses of a tradition-bound society longing for its upliftment.

Data gathered from various areas under study also reveal the fact that for the last thirty/forty years there is considerable development in the position of women in Islamic society of Kerala due to education and the concerted effort on the part of reformers, Muslim intellectuals and, all the more, by the governmental and non-governmental agencies. A World Bank study in 1993 declared that education of girls is one of the most rewarding investments. Moreover, women's educational empowerment helps to reduce infant mortality, better nutrition, health care, equip mother as the trainer of the child and the general improvement in the social status not only as a mother, but even as a protector of human rights in future. This is the "greatest return" that a society can have from the investment in the education of women. While families in India in general are in a transitional condition, Muslim families, particularly in Kerala are not keeping their tempo as others are due to several socio-religious reasons. The religious reformers and the custodians of womens' movements are also fearful to some extent that they may lose their grip of society as a whole, if women are set free liberally. Even early reformers like Sanaullah Makthi Thangal and Vakkom Abdul Khader Maulavi do not agree to have such a state of affairs with regard to the freedom of women. While they advocate for education and reform such reformers thought of keeping the women within the orbit of religion and value-based periphery, if any. The later sectarian reformers like the Salafis and the Jama'atis who emerged more prominently from 1950 onwards, also did the same wrong, always limiting women to their definitions of Islamic law. To Islamist reformers, women never will have equal status with men, to which they brought interpretation of some verses of the Quran and traditions to their requirement. This is a major reason for the marginalization or internalisation of Muslim women in Kerala. Imposing a new frame work of religious values, totally discharging the cultural values which were continuing all along, they present an identity of their own, in the social life of Kerala.

Recently, Islamic Societies, as in Kerala, rely greatly on the revivalist ideologies of sectarian groups in framing the life style of the women than following the dictums of the Quran and the traditions of Prophet. We have already seen what Quranic tenets and the traditions of the prophet have to say with regard to all aspects concerning women. Purdah the cardinal factor linked with the freedom of women, has been regularised as a cultural and regional usage, rather than a religious imposition or instrument of suppression. (A chapter on Purdah is following). Prophet himself was very lenient and considerate towards women and among the two things referred to in his last sermon, one was a warning to protect women by all means. He was very kind and alert to unfortunate women, being exploited in work situations, and commented on the injustices done to women workers as recorded by Muslim, (quoting Aisha in his Sahih) one of the authentic reporters of hadiths.

> Allah will definitely enforce the settlement of the dues of those entitled to receive them on the Day of Judgement, even the wrong done to the hornless goat (the female) by the horned goat (the male) will be redressed.

This tradition analyses the situation of a working class woman who increases the income of her family mingling with male workers. She has the same right as the male worker and should not be taken advantage of, or subjected to any form of harassment. We should remember that if his injunction was enforced by the Prophet they and years before Karl Marx in his manifesto. Prophet also gives great emphasis to the honour of women. The plea for special protection and sympathy and consideration have been misinterpreted by some scholars as if they require protection by segregation. By protection of women, Islam means not a sheltered security, as in a jail but some concern and elemency on the part of the males who are physically more fit.

The local reformers in the name of religion, insisted total veiling of women without proper understanding of the Quranic injunctions and the real merit of it. Any gender reform could be discussed only with a practical definition of Hijab especially when the rigid reformists utilise it as a *coup-de-grace* to achieve their motives. The Quranic verse on Hijab was sent specifically to the Prophet's wives referring to a curtain to have some privacy in their small houses. It was not an item of clothing[9]. The Quranic Verse for others (Surah 24: 30-31) commands that they should draw their veils over their bosoms. Again, there is no specific verse in the Quran requiring Muslim women to veil their faces. A face veil was only a status symbol in Pre-Islamic Arabia preventing the common masses from looking at ladies of high rank.

The issue of veiling is a model in the context of reform among women in the Islamic Society of Kerala. Several such issues are often projected to check further improvement in their social life by the fundamentalists and extreme ideologues. Their discussions on reforms are always centred around the peripheral issues like veil and never get in to the structural aspects of Islamic Society. For example, Abul A'la Maududi, the icon of Jama'at e' Islami, considers Shariah as the Supreme law to be followed by all Muslims. To him, it is the will of God, that frames the source of law in a Muslim Society as a matter of divinity Maududi pronounces,

> If an Islamic Society consciously resolves not to accept the Shariah, and decides to enact its own constitution and laws or borrows them from any other source in disregard of the Shariah, such a society breaks its contract with God and forfeits its right to be called 'Islamic'[10].

Such dictims are the continuation of the concept of a theocratice state and the government. These contentions of Maududi totally negate all laws, constitutions of Parliamentary system, court of law and ultimately democracy in the attempt to the final establishment of Islamic law in the world. Can such an ideology could give any kind of freedom to the women folk of that society without breaking the secular, liberal and democratic systems of a country? As referred to earlier, women naturally will be the first target of attack as we experience in the present day Muslim world. The Mujahids (Salafis) who claim to be the earliest reformers in religion consider Mohammed Abdul Wahab of Saudi Arabia, an advocate of puritanic Islamism, as their spiritual leader. But Islam is opposed to puritanism and extremism. Prophet Mohammed emphatically says,

> Beware of extremism in religion; for it was extremism in religion that destroyed those who went before you.

The reformers always bring Shariah on all issues concerning women, thinking that it is universal and cannot be challenged and changed. Basically, Shariah is the collective opinions of Imams based on Quran and Sunnah framed in the medieval context of Islam. Since it is a practical guide, it contains *Ijthihad* (independent reasoning). *Ijma* (Consensus), *Quiyas* (Analogy), *al-istislah* (public interest) and *al urf* (custom) etc. While the issues on women arise in modern times, the so-called reformers and ideologues totally depend on this Shariah of the bygone age which prescribes archaic crime and punishment laws and antiquated notions of women's rights of a medieval premise. As Ziaudin Sardar observes, "what was originally devised to fight tyranny has become a source of tyranny itself"[11]. Shariah, as many believe, is not meant to be a tool of torture, but it often becomes so in the hands of the puritans when the issues on women 'haunt' the Muslim society. These extremist groups who speak for puritanic Islam energise themselves from the old Kharijites, reignited during the time of Ali, and who believe that all others are apostates. They further legitimise intolerance and violence quoting the Quranic verse which asks the believers "to do good and prevent the evil". Such an ideology of reform abhors history and tradition and drains it off all human content. How can such an ideology rooted in hate and misogyny could protect the women of their society with dignity and honour? The answer certainly will be negative.

Due to several socio-economic factors and by the interference of the governance, the condition of women has been improved easily, particulary in the last three decades. The traditional Shariah notion of a patriarchal system that the husband is the head of the family has gone, and instead the responsibility has come in to the hands of both. Thus women have become partners with men working in all capacities. Recently great shifts have come even in the practice and enactment of Shariah with the timely interference of the civil courts of the country. As per the conventional Shariah, men have a unilateral right to divorce and that has been abandoned. Moreover, women are given the right to divorce, and for men to obtain a divorce, prior authorisation from a court is required. Verbal divorce, rampant among Muslims once, has also been outlawed. Both men and women have got the right to reach with a contract of marriage by themselves without the legal approval of a guardian. An important innovative change could also be seen in the increased financial obligation of the husbands who previously divorced with ease and leisure. Now the husbands are required to meet all the monetary and legal obligations to a divorced wife and children. Polygamy has been restricted, and if any, will be with the consent of the first wife. While allowing the Muslims as a religious minority, the interfence of the court and the government is confirmed in all matters in the application of Shariah with a positive approach concerning women. Many recent court verdicts and legislations are brilliant examples of the obligations and commitment that the government have to protect the women in a developing society where democracy and secularism prevailed.

But such shifts and innovations are not beyond criticism, because, for some, these attempts are encroachments on the 'Divine law' which are not liable to undergo any change or adjustment. Now a new metamorphosis is searched for globally to find a space for accommodating political Islam. As referred to earlier, the pressures more on women for a return to formal or traditional Islam is desired by the reformers with an ambition to achieve a dynamic future and glory for it. In this respect some of the countries in Africa like Sudan and Morocco, and in South and South East Asia like Pakistan and Indonesia have become easily the victims of such an agenda of the neo-reformists. India too is showing tendencies to rally behind these democratically weaker nation states. The fundamentalists usually depend more on slogans than on programme for reform articulating agendas on peripheral issues preaching perpetual conflict in the social system. It is in such a context of a dilemma that confronts Muslim women, a host of Muslim feminist writers emerged with the declared dislike on orthodoxy and puritanic revivalism. Writers like Nawal El Saadawi, Fatima Mernissi, Amina Wadud, Asma Barlas and Ayan Hirsi Ali brought forth a new reform concerning women with a re-reading of Quran. They were seeking fresh spaces for the modern and challenging Muslim women in the era of globalisation. They were also trying to formulate a vibrant Islamic paradigm for the women who want to compete with modernity.

Again, Islamic scholars who argue for the freedom of women do not agree with their employment outside as a bread winner. They consider it as an infringement of the principle of equality because men cannot equally share with them the "responsibility of motherhood". If women are compelled to shoulder economic responsibilities it will lead to "gross and palpable inequality"[12]. This is a curious and grotesque finding of religious scholars who never agree with the mixing of the sexes in work places, which may, according to them, lead to moral deterioration and weakening of family ties. This is merely an androcentric fear developed with misogyny to monopolise the spaces of women and the to achieve universal dominance of the males. Such reactionary arguments have been fought out by several organizations of human rights in countries like Morocco, Nigeria, Turkey, Lebanon and Indonesia. The Nigerian Organisation Baobab is a well known defender of Women's rights under Muslim laws, in particular, the criminal legislation of Shariah passed in Nigeria since 2000. There are several instances of abuse of Shariah by some self-acquired law givers, mostly unemployed young men, policing the dress code of women publicly and harassing and ill treating them for sitting with men in public conveyances. On charges of adultery also, only women were punished by the cruelest way of stonning and flogging publicly without hearing anything from them. The proponents of fundamentalism work at all levels from International forums to the common streets. Moreover, the political manipulation of religion and its laws virtually has put the women's right advocates on the defensive all over the world. The miserable plight of the nineteen year old Yousra Al-Azam who went with her elder sister and the fiance in Gaza city for shopping in April, 2005, is startling eye-opener for all. Yousra, whose hair fully covered by a black scarf, was beaten and shot dead publicly by the so-called 'morality police' without giving any reason[13].

In Kerala also, recently, some issues regarding the divorce and the re-union of couples, raised problems including social ban on some Muslim families. Several Muslim families suffer such hardships for years as a result of the interference of ulemas and Muslim leaders. Actually, the divorce will be valid if it is done by a person consciously (i.e. in a normal state of mind) offering three incidents of divorces within a span of time. It should not be uttered at a stretch successively. Instead, enough time has to be given for rethinking and re-union, to which the law give more importance in such situations. Moreover, if a person, says that it was not done consciously, the Muttalaq is not going to be valid[14]. Again, such unileteral decision of the ulemas is also invalid as per the Quranic injunction, because it wants to appoint two arbiters to reach into a conciliation.

> If you (believers) fear that a couple may break up, appoint one arbiter from his family and one from hers. Then, if the couple want to put things right, God will bring about a reconciliation between them: He is all knowing, all aware[15].

Moreover, in this case, it is not the person alleged to have divorced, but those who have attempted for a permanent dissolution of the marriage are responsible for such crimes. The Prophet says, "Those who interfere for breaking the marriage relations will be out of religion"[16].

Women insult and accusations are common in Kerala, not on religious grounds, but on grudge and selfishness. The weapon, more often, is the allegation of adultery (zina). But the punishment for a false accuser is more heavy than the accused. They are punishable as per the Quranic law which says,

> As for those who accuse chaste women of fornication, and then fail to provide four witnesses, strike them eighty times, and reject their testimony ever afterwards, they are the law breakers[17].

Here, what we could see is, those who talk in the name of religion are either ignorant by themselves or consciously exploit the ignorance and innocence of people. Early women reformers like M. Haleema Beevi, Aysha Mayan, Ansar Beegum and Thankamma Malik did a major role to make Muslim women free from such evil practices through their speeches and writings. They focused against the dominance of priesthood on one side and opposed the prevalence of class distinction on the other. They realised that it is the priests in the Islamic society of Kerala who always supports evil practices like the dowry, polygamy and divorce, all of which are always used against the interests and even to the dignity and honour of women. But no social scientist could claim that all these evils have been eliminated by the work of social reformers as we could realise from the experience and study of similar classes in other societies of the same period. Women as a social class in all segments were suffering from several restrictions and taboos in the colonial situations, and all of which continued unhampered in the post independence India also. Muslim society, comparatively being a closed one with religiosity and traditions, was in its lowest ebb, in places like northern Kerala. The socio-educational institutions like Muslim Educational Society (MES) founded in 1964, gave a new drive for the upliftment of Muslim women, especially through their educational efforts. They started a number of colleges, including for women, which gave a new awareness, among Muslim women of Kerala, not only to educate but to reform themselves.

As mentioned earlier, Muslim male reformers were the advocates of their women's upliftment. The magazine *Muslim* by Vakkom Moulavi was one of the earliest of this kind who strongly pleaded women's reform. All the early reformers have stressed the importance of education among women[18]. In the early decades of the 20th century itself we have ample evidences of Muslim women who protest and resist the indiscreet attempts of men for marriage and dominance over them. Such a story has been revealed in a 'letter song' [19] of

Puthoor Amina written during the time of Malabar Rebellion of 1921. This song is addressed to a depredator who spent several years in a jail at Bellary (Tamilnadu) and wanted to marry her. She denounces the unilateral decision of a man to marry a girl without seeking her consent and criticises the male-centred family life. She also doubts the possibility of divorce after having a number of children as usual. She laments that women are cornered in the kitchen and along with children, they are deserted by men.

All the reformers, irrespective of gender, vehemently opposed some common practices found among Muslim families in Kerala spending a lot of money, but creating much pain and health hazards to girls who underwent 'ear-boring' (making about seven holes each in the upper part of ear). This was observed very ceremoniously by all the families. All early Muslim reformers opposed these practices through their works[20].

Women's reform in Muslim society owes much to the songs, particularly 'Sabeena Songs'written and sung by Muslim women themselves. They give great messages of their urge for freedom and a special space in joint family system, ofcourse, everything within the limits of Islam. It is true that writings of Shujayi Moidu Musliar and Makthi Thangal influenced them for writing such songs by women. An Arabi-Malayalam Magazine exclusively for women *Nisaul Islam* (Muslim Women), popularised such songs in addition to the teaching of religion and morals from Islamic history and traditions [21] P.K. Haleema, Malumma, Jameela Beevi and others were some of the composers and singers of such songs in the early period of 'Sabeenas' and 'Malas'. Some of the songs are devotional in character, for example, *Mohiudin Mala* (Moideen Mala) and *Nafeesathu Mala*. Moideen Mala is based on the great Sufi Mohiudin Abdul Khader Jilani of Baghdad. Nafeesath Mala is centred around the life history of a devout Muslim woman of Egypt, popularly known as Nafeesathul Misri. Since this is a very popular song among women, it is kept very holy and used to sing when Muslim women are toiling with delivery pain, believing that they will get relief from pain.

Role of Orthodoxy

Simultaneously, Islamic society has to fight such orthodoxies also, so embedded with the belief patterns of the Muslim women in Kerala. The reformers found it very difficult to detach such rituals and traditions, since they are all linked, though remote, with some traditional beliefs of Islamic history and culture. Some Islamic myths also have been incorporated in the belief system of the people of Kerala as manifested in the corpus of the ballads like the *Kurathipattu* (a sooth sayer's song) where Fathima, the daughter of the Prophet, is engaged in a dialogue with a soothsayer (here angel Gabrael)[22]. Such songs are surely indicative of the local influences and cultural trends to the religious believes of the people. Though the revivalists and reformers pooh-pooh such regional cultural linkages, they have highly influenced the belief system of local Mappila Muslims of Kerala. It is true that with all such pressures from outside these local cultural traits have survived without much change.

One of the earliest noted reformers among the Muslim women in Kerala was M. Haleema Beevi (1918-2000) of Adoor in Southern Kerala. Her pioneering work is a magazine called *Muslim Woman* started from Tiruvalla in the Alappuzha District. In 1946 she became the editor of a newspaper, *Bharata Chandrika*. In 1972 she began another publication, the *Modern Woman*. But such attempts were stopped on account of economic problems in addition to the harassment to herself and her husband, by the fascist action of Sir C.P. Ramaswamy Iyer in Travancore. In 1938 she organized a Muslim Women's Conference at Tiruvalla, in which several noted women participants like P.G. Kadeejah, Moideen Beevi, Dr. Habshah Marikkar attended. While stressing the importance of education for women, she never satisfies with the formal education with which some qualifications are acquired, but the real education to make them aware of the whole life, and to create woman as an independent individual with all responsibilities in social life equivalent to men. This was the message that she made all along in her speeches wherever she addressed women. In all her speeches she repeatedly advised women to acquire knowledge. For her, *ilm* in Arabic is not religious learning alone, but all types of knowledge that we could achieve in this world. She also vehemently criticised the attitude of men who considered women only as a 'consumer commodity', shut up in houses for their enjoyment and family life. By gender reform they meant growth of education and social change.

Several new generation writers have rallied in the Muslim Women Reform Movements in Kerala providing their own contributions in recent years. But most of them are committed to sectarian groups of the Salafis and the Jama'atis, though a very few are liberal and independent. Both the Salafis and the Jama'atis exploit the situation seeing that the majority of them are ignorant, illiterate and backward. Through their journals and publications, what they intend to have is to impart learning within the frame work of religion and to prepare women to equip to their own sectarian requirements. To achieve this motto, all such groups have instituted Madrassahs and Arabic Colleges throughout the length and breadth of Kerala, some of them exclusively for women alone. Those who are getting training from such institutions are only fit to be their messengers and brand ambassadors of their sects. This virtually lead to a "negative " learning instead of acquiring a liberal education. To combat such lineages of Muslim women with sectarian organisation, some organizations like the *Nisa* have come in cities like Calicut, not only aiming at the reform of women, but fight out and achieve the rights of women particularly in the issues like divorce and the right of maintenance of widows[24]. There are some women's organisations of the Mujahids and Jama'atis started with the intention of uplifting their youth. The Mujahid Girls' Movement and the Girls Islamic Organisation are some of them. They are all strictly functioning under the control of their parent organisations, the Kerala Nadvathul Mujahidin and the Kerala Branch Jama'ate Islam Hind, and for that matter, they could not go with a liberal outlook.

These revivalist and rigid organizations also have favoured for some reform "from within" centred around women's dress code and their madrassah education. While they allow women to go out of their houses, they insisted to wear the so-called 'Islamic dress', to keep the Muslim identity more than anything else. Here a pertinent question arises, what is an 'Islamic dress'? No where in history Islam mentioned the modalities of such a dress. Neither the Quran nor the traditions of the Prophet brought forth a hard and fast rule regarding the dress, except the dictations for keeping 'modesty' in appearance. It varies from region to region, from people to people, and from time to time. In the early days of its expansion, Islam as a religion accommodated all cultural traits and values of the host country which we could experience even today in Africa, West Asia South and South East Asia. Eventhough they have changed their faith, they continued the culture and identity that they have been following for generations. This is the case of Turkey, Lebanon, Egypt, Morocco, India, Indonesia etc. [Details given in the ensuing chapter]. In the case of the Madrassah, unlike the orthodox Sunnittes, what they did is they introduced a reformed syllabus with the translation of the religious texts. Some of them have been transformed into Arabic Colleges and affiliated to the University and other secular institutions. But these institutions, except universities leaving apart their high academic excellence in language and literature and in the study of 'fiqh' are not to be treated as centres of liberal and secular education. Hence, eventhough they seem to be reformed outwardly, the rigidity and puritanic nature of such institutions continued without much changes internally. What we could see in 1960s and 70s is the growth of such institutions in the backward areas where Muslims are in majority. Moreover, such institutions are also getting huge financial assistance from Arab countries due to their commitment to the study of Arabic and Islamics.

It is also a fact that the easy accessibility to Madrassahs and Arabic Colleges adversely affected the secular learning of Muslim students, especially of girls because the routine formalities of admissions are not required to get admission in such institutions. Moreover, since all such institutions are offering free education including boarding facilities, women students extensively utilise such facilities. Those students who acquired training from these institutions are looked upon by society as role models, committed to keep up the Islamic entity in their life, as wife or mother with the strong conviction of upbringing their children into the same fold. This parallel studies in Madrassahs and Arabic Colleges virtually rob the time and effort of the youth in the prime age of the development of their faculties. This is a great lacuna that the Muslim women suffer from, in recent years, in Kerala. This backwardness in education and seclusion in life of women made the European writers to observe the Islamic society much inferior to the European ones. A well known British Orientalist Lane Poole has observed; "The degradation of women in the East is a cranker that begins its destructive work early in childhood, and has eaten into the whole system of Islam" [25]. But this is a partisan attitude of the Westerners when dealing the orient and Islam, always highlighting the west as supreme in all respects. Such an approach is evidently a result of the misunderstanding of Islamic culture as a monolithic one.

Changing Pattern of Life

Apart from the community initiative, other important factors were there for a positive change in the attitude of Muslims towards progress and reform in Kerala. One important factor was the social justice principle that the Communist governments followed in Kerala after 1957. Moreover a 10 per cent reservation for Muslims is also allotted among other backward classes[26]. But the recently developed Gulf factor put virtually the fast development of Muslim education to a reverse gear with a negative impact on women's education, particularly in the poorer sections of society. Fazal Gafoor, the President of MES, has commented, "They make more money by the new venture, but the pity is that they have bypassed education"[27]. But this attitude of Muslims to seek job in the Gulf countries is gradually changing for the last few years on account of job uncertainty and the restrictions of such countries to accommodate unskilled labourers. Hence both men and women now devote themselves for educational qualifications including professional. One important change to be noticed for the last two decades is that girls widely show a tendency to continue their education after marriage. This is in lieu with the demand in gulf countries for professionals and more dearness for couples in the host-country. Moreover, women also have realised the economic value and partnership in profession for a better family life while they are abroad. Unlike the situation in a joint family system, they began to think of building a nuclear family, particularly with the aim of giving better education to their children. This is a marked change in the Muslim family life.

A notable change in the dress habits of girl students also could be seen in the higher secondary schools and colleges. Most of them do not use purdah or even Mufta. Instead, in addition to the churidars, they wear a free flowing shawl or a scarf. Even in Muslim schools (Managed by Muslims), both the teachers and girl students are presently at complete liberty to have their choice in dress. Moreover, students coming from the rich and elite groups never wanted to put a robe like purdah, since such dresses conceal their costly sartorial splendour making them useless and which often limit controlling their life of gay and ease. These new trends found in students and employed women have a great impact on women living in urban centres like Calicut, Tellicherry and Cannanore. But such a new trend found in youngsters and employees have been criticised from "inside" as "westernised" and 'unIslamic' and against their culture and traditions. But those who go after things 'external' like the dress, never search the real problems of their women in the community like education, poverty, harassment of all kinds, domestic violence and denial of human rights, which are so crucial to a free and fair life of women in any society. One must also realise that whatever freedom the Muslim women enjoy at present is, least sanctioned by their own community, but by the governments, activists of human rights, and by the efforts of other organisations of society.

The new situations in Kerala caused to the entry of several Muslim women not only in the field of human right or reform, but even in occupying covetable public positions. Due to the resurgence of education among Muslim women, apart from professionals, a number of women activists and politicians have come out to the lime light in the last 3-4 decades. Moreover, by the enhanced reservation system in all spheres, especially in the representation of the local administration, Muslim women are also getting due share. This is mainly as a result of the political and social pressures generated locally. Recent experiences show that such women working with their colleagues are proving better in discharging their responsibilities with more confidence. Such an awareness of rights concerning themselves and their surroundings is the greatest output that the community has as a result of these reform and change in the Islamic society of Kerala.

In colonial India it is a fact that Muslims in general and women in particular, did not try their fortunes on account of many factors, both historical and cultural. They looked upon both education and employment as fruits of British administration and a legacy of western imperialism. But after independence, situation changed, but still the quantum of Muslim women's participation is very limited compared to other communities. Many are utilising the facilities and opportunities available for them, but many more have yet to come to the stream. In a state like Kerala, and in a society so backward as the Muslims of Kerala, the role of the educated and enlightened becomes so important not only as the model for others but even to be the part and parcel of the total development of society.

In the initial stage, unlike women of other communities, Muslim women require more attention first from their own men and from the entire community. Without the co-operation from men, they cannot achieve success. Dependency on ulemas will certainly divert them, because as mentioned earlier, they have their own agendas, and for that matter, they won't allow others either to interpret Quran or to make decisions independently and liberally. Perhaps a better understanding of the Quranic injunctions and the prescribed laws by both men and women can significantly change the status of women and make them aware of women's rights and their objectives[28]. In Muslim families, in line with the Ulemas, parents usually did not allow girls to go out for education, because they feel that it is a violation of Islamic rules. This objection is based on a Quranic Verse, "O, wives of the Prophet, remain peacefully at home"[29]. This verse is often misused by the ulemas to restrict the women to go out of their house and make public appearance. A strong view among scholars is that this is specially meant for the wives of the Prophet. Thus it is important for the parents and husbands to be aware of the real intention of such tenets to avoid partisan and reactionary intepretations of the religious functionaries to save the women from their sorry state of affairs.

For the last few decades, Muslim women have become the theme of a lively debate in Kerala, ofcourse within an Islamic framework. It is centred on Quran, the Shariah, traditions of the prophet and his companions and the interpretations of various Imams etc. to define women's rights in the modern age. But the irony of it is that while modernists have argued for the most liberal interpretations of Islam possible the conservatives have used the same sources to argue for restrictions on women's roles[30].

The advocates of reform still stand to maintain the life of Muslim women with family ties and community solidarity ensuring its values to be continued for generations. Though many countries have accepted United Nations Convention on the Elimination of All Forms of Discrimination Against Women, distinctive family laws prepared on the Shariah often contradict and collide with them and practically neutralise the possible freedom that they may have. Infact, it exposes the irony of Muslim women enjoying equality from outside and its denial inside[31]. This duality is what we could experience in the Islamic society of Keala in all the attempts at reform in recent years. In a democratic and secular system, there are limitations to the efforts of the governmental machinery to implement laws and regulations within a society seemed to be fenced by religion and its identity. Therefore, the reforms should come from within, prominently to have an effective social change. Traditional virtues become valid only when it adapt to save its cherished values and ethos transforming them relevant to the contemporary circumstances. Reforms need not provide all the time beneficial change. It could create "monsters and confusion"[32] and even for derailing of the society. What we require is a critical reform for a meaningful change aiming at a liberal society. Islamism, when it is applied to women, is found more rigid with a total rejection of western models and with the insistance of traditional values. Primarily rejection of modernity by Islamists has to be viewed as symptomatic to the hostility towards the West which had its origin after the Arab occupation of Cordova.

Any reform finally leads to a struggle over culture. The western feminists also have proved that their attempts are excessive interference on the existing western dogmas based on traditions which later transformed into a free system encouraged by individualism and capitalism. The Feminists in the West naturally oppose all kinds of restrictions longing for a free life. Islamic reformers of the later 19th and the 20th century found the West and its culture non acceptable because what they experience there is 'unIslamic' and ' irreligious'. The colonial rule, being an anathema for them, also has been looked upon as an 'anticulture' for the colonizers. This is the approach towards the West by all reformers starting from Afghani and Abduh to the militant Islamists of today. They also oppose Muslim feminists like Nawal El Sa'adawi, Fathima Mernissi, Amina Wadud, Nazira Zain-udin, Leila Ahmed, Mahnaz Afkhami, and very many in that category calling them 'un Islamic', on the ground that they are secular and liberal. The Islamist ideology is always to bring back the 'original' Islam and its traditions. In this respect the role of political Islam also can not be denied.

As Leila Ahmed observes,

> Establishment Islam's version of the Islamic message survived as the sole legitimate interpretation not because it was the only possible interpretation but because it was the interpretation of the politically dominant – those who had the power to outlaw and eradicate other readings as 'heretical'[33].

This politics of reform of women finds its best manifestation after the Islamic Revolution (1979) in Iran. The Khomeini regime enforced a "code of modesty" for women and even appointed state-sponsored women guards to execute the same properly in public places. Imbibing the spirit of such reforms in Iran, revivalist reformers like the Jama'atis in Kerala advocate the reforms in line with that of Iran which follows hard-core ideologies[34].

All the revivalists under the guise of reform aim at the establishment of religious reform centered at women. As noted, reform for them is extreme religion and a return to puritanic religion. Unlike in other countries where women have some advancement, the muted Muslim women of Kerala could be easily moulded to their requirements and reactionary ideologies further pushing them backward looking. While they appeal on revoking the western style of life in other developed Muslim countries like Turkey, Egypt and Indonesia, they need not struggle much to achieve their goal. Many Muslim women in Kerala have adopted purdah to symbolise a return to the universal Islamic cultural roots and rejection of a western imperialist tradition that in their view shows little respect for women. These young women mostly from the revivalist background and madrassah education, have also a strong perception that western fashions force women into uncomfortable and undignified outfits that turned them into sexual objects lacking propriety and dignity.

All sections of Muslim community in Kerala have an innovation of starting Quran classes for school going and adult girls to keep them exclusively in the track of Islam about which they have great concern. Such classes arranged periodically are also attended by house wives, working women etc. who later become role models for others. This programme was first initiated by the revivalist groups like the Jama'atis and the Mujihids. Now the traditional Sunni groups who formerly opposed such attempts on account of their approach to women going out, have started competitively with the fear that they may lose their grip in the community, if such programmes were not arranged. Apart from getting some awareness of the religious life, this togetherness creates an identity and a limited exposure in social life. This singularity and distinctiveness from others in the life style of a group in a pluralistic society as that of Kerala, may sometimes cause a feeling of alienation among themselves, and possibly a division in the minds of all, finally resulting to a social stratification which is most undesirable in a developing society.

A religion or culture often undergoes changes in a new situation. Kim Knott in her study on religion and identity highlights this phenomenon saying that "Ethnic identity is not a static phenomenon.. Religion is not static either.. No religion remains underaged through such occurrences [immigration]. Beliefs, practices, social organizations, and religious experiences adapt and develop as a result of the new geographical and social location"[35]. For the neo-revivalists, what they mean is, to undo. what all changes that occurred in the long passage of time in the religious ideologies, culture and life of a people, which has been already integrated in the existing situations of a region. The concepts like acculturation and synthesis have already transformed exclusive individual identities with the much accepted and unique oneness in several aspects of social life in a given space. The intervention of such people in the belief system and practices of a people is basically against the spirit of Islam, because Quran emphatically denies such interference even by the religious authorities. For Example,

> Who ever obeys the Messenger obeys God, if some pay
> no heed, we have not sent you to be their keeper[36].

This also reveals the fact that even the Prophet is not entitled to do anything other than preaching. Hence the individual is given complete freedom and no Muslim has authority over another in matters of religion. Again, in another verse, it reveals,

> If it had been God's will, they would not have done so,
> but we have not made you their guardian, nor are you their keeper[37].

This clearly reveals the freedom of thought and expression expected from all sections and groups of the revivalists while they attempt any kind of reform in the Islamic society of Kerala. Today what we could experience in the attitude of hard-core Islamists the world over is, that most of them go after the exteriors of the people like exclusion and purdah in the case of women, and wearing of a turban or a skull cap with a wild beard in the case of men.

Since women are labourers in rural areas (mainly agricultural), their role as the Islamist aspire is different, unlike their counterparts in the urban centres. In the process of urbanization they have been given the role of housewives where she naturally become the slave of the codes. In the field study and interviews in the rural areas of Malappuram, women are found still working as agricultural labourers in the field without seclusion or wearing Purdah. They are also in good percentage going as professionals and working women compared to the women of the same class in the urban areas of other districts. This is an indication of the female participation in a wider society where they could work and earn their livelihood. There are a number of reasons for such a change, including the fact that in most countries, the market economy tends to regulate supply and demand in such a way that one salary is not enough for a household to sustain a good standard of living. Other reasons might be the increase in the educational opportunities for women, which ofcourse in recent years had a substantial hike in the areas, like the one mentioned above. All these factors, in addition to the general feminist awareness, strengthened the necessity of the economic independence of women.

But the situation in other areas of the study, particularly in the case of the urban population of Calicut, Tellicherry, Cannanore and Kasaragod, is totally different. A cultural imbalance with modernism, as a result of early contact with colonialism and new western trends and awareness, made these populace of the towns highly distinctive. They were also able to acquire the new and liberal learning of the enlightened period without much religious obsession. However, this new change does not penetrate properly in the case of Muslim women of the urban centres corresponding to their men folk as a great handicap to the growth of society as a whole. The situation continued till independence.

The post independence era is also not much encouraging at least for two decades as far as Muslim women are concerned. Lack of education and economic contingency gave a lot of pressure on middle and lower class women to go as domestic servants which they could perform well within the stipulation of the seclusion desired. A very small percentage of women from these areas could go for some professions as teachers, office assistants and health workers, etc. due to the easy accessability of education from such urban centres. However, though partly educated, women of the upper class society did not attempt for such profession as they looked upon it as infradig for their family status. But in recent years, this state of affairs go to a new dimension with the gulf boom, particularly after 1970. The economic imbalance due to the women's unproductiveness and joblessness in the urban centres has thus been compensated by the inflow of huge amount of money from the gulf region. As mentioned earlier, this has a negative aspect, once again for the negligence of education, particularly of women. This often happens in segments where only money power and consumerism prevail.

Moreover, the notion among Muslims that women's duty is mainly centred around domestic affairs has to be changed. While the responsibility of women inside one's home is affirmed, her right to work outside simultaneously has to be agreed. Therefore, as per the change of economic resources and social conditions, attitudinal change towards the work pattern of women has to be given top priority.

While we observe the social change among Muslims generally and women in particular, we could see variables from first generation to second generation. Although the second generation is changing their attitude to a certain extent, the change is less marked in the case of the first, particularly when compared to other communities of the same class. These variations are noted in the education attainment, life style, family relationship, arrangement of marriage, mobility, observance of purdah and belief system. Studies carried out in both urban and rural areas also show variations significantly. While the graph of belief system, particularly in the observance of religous practices, always go high in the case of adult women, others, importantly the youth, comes comparatively low. The process of secularisation which was highly speedier in the 60s and 70s is now found much slower for the last one or two decades. This is due to several factors including incessant growth of religiosity and cultural context. The religious commitment of women increased heavily in recent years as a result of the perennial growth of madrassahs and other religious institutions. Periodical religious discourses associated with mosques and madrassahs specially meant for women, are a routine scene, now found extensively in Muslim quarters of Kerala.

Fundamentalism and Extremism

The minority feeling and the wide propaganda that "Muslims and their culture are under threat and insecurity" also work well for the embarrassment of the community and naturally, as the weaker sex the women, are the worst hit and thus strive for their own identity in whatever measures possible. This self-styled men-sponsored aloofness evolved into an alienation causing to create suspicion and a feeling of the 'otherness' in the sister communities finally resulting into a social segregation. In carrying out such a state of affairs, in Kerala situations, the role of extremists is very high in recent years. The encounter of Islamic cultural pattern with other socio-cultural patterns including western, they argue, is a reaction of Islamism to modernism[38]. But this is a narrow and committed discourse that appear most incomprehensible for others, especially in a situation where women are excluded from the process of change. The irony in the interpretation of the Islamic law by the Islamists is that, more than presenting the reality of Islam in the period of the Prophet, they stress the one framed by the orthodox law-schools that prevailed in the medieval period. In addition to this, the sectarian revivalist groups like the Mujahids and the Jama'atis also try to introduce the 'reformist' ideologies of the nineteenth and twentieth century intellectuals, who infact, have brought nothing but rigidity and exclusiveness in the socio-religious life of the people in general. Thus any debate on Muslim women and their role in society naturally lead to the role of women in Arabia in Seventh Century or their life during the political hegemony of Islam elsewhere.

Such a visionary attitude of "the past reproduced in the present"[39] by a section of reformers is highly incompatible in the contemporary socio-political situations of Muslims in Kerala. This is more evident in the issue of Taslima Nasrin, the controversial writer from Bangladesh, who pronounced that the Quran has to change, instead of saying that the interpretations of the Quran have to change. But what we could experience is, where Taslima failed, western based Muslim feminists like Nawsal-El-Sa'adwi, Fathima Mernissi, Amina Wadud, Nazira Zain-udin, Ayan Hirsi Ali and Leila Ahmed come victorious criticising Islamic jurisprudence and Shariah, perhaps more heavily than anybody[40].

Fundamentalism and extremism against women are also taking new dimensions recently on account of some external incidents. Causing a reversal of the reforms already set in, with the liberalist trends found as a result of education and employment) like that of the 'Mufta' (head cover or scarf used by Muslim girls and working women) issue staged at Alappuzha. There, it is alleged, that a IXth standard Muslim student, named Nabala is denied the wearing of the head cover by the authorities of a CBSE school, managed by the Believers' Church. This issue has been taken by the Islamists, finally leading to the transfer of the student to another institution[41]. Infact such incidents strengthen the arguments of the hard-core groups to highlight their reactionary ideologies with much criticism against liberal and secular education. Here one interesting thing is that while law supports the feminists' position, the community norms believed to have been framed under the religious laws/ shariah, perpetuate the controls and conditions against women. It is true that in all social systems, men have had privileges in society for centuries and have acquired and maintained these positions by keeping women subordinate. This is true of the Islamic society also.

Whenever the issues concerning women arise in Kerala, they carry a lot of religious and cultural factors that determines the future course of action. A most welcomable thing to counter balance the disequilibrium created by the religious institutions, several other agencies like the MES, have started schools and colleges in the backward areas. Such attempts have improved the educational status of Muslim women in a considerable way in the last 4-5 decades. Apart from the attempts from within, the governmental initiatives, particularly the left ministries, have taken incessment efforts for the upliftment of backward communities in education and empowerment. This was the same spirit behind the formation of the University of Calicut in 1968 with which Muslim women's education in the area got a hike beyond proportion, a great leap in education after independence. Muslim League, a party limited to the district, also benefited heavily by its alliance in the communist-led ministry with bargain and gain in educational facilities and reservation of employment. Virtually three decades of the Communist-led ministries have been utilised by the community very fruitfully and the credit for such a social change, that never had been for the Muslim Community earlier, goes to the situations that developed in Kerala with the new socio-political environment after 1957. Now education, unlike in the colonial situations, became so popular that the poor and the low-income groups have the opportunity of attaining it easily at their reach. The urge is apparent in the case of the education of girls, prominently exploiting the new situation in the areas where any attempt for education was not possible due to several socio-political reasons. The new awareness for reform and development became highly instrumental, for breaking the aloofness and the iron curtain put on the community for centuries.

Notes and References

1. Bina Agarwal, *A Field of One's Own, Gender and Land Rights in South Asia*, Cambridge University Press, New Delhi, 1996, pp. 51-63.
2. Fatima Mernissi, "Virginity and Patriarchy" in Aziza Al-Hibri, *Women and Islam*, Oxford, 1982, p. 189.
3. Haleh Afghar, "The Iranian Theocracy", in *Iran: A Revolution in Turmoil* (ed.), London, 1985, pp. 220-40. Following the Islamic Revolution in Iran, Several works on Islamic Revival and Islamism originated like that of Minor Reeves, *Female Warriors of Allah,* New York, 1988, Fred Hallidry and Hamza Alavi (eds.) *State and Ideology in the Middle East and Pakistan,* New York, 1988, Farah Azari (ed.) *Women in Iran: The Conflict with Fundamentalist Islam,* London, 1983.

4. Speech of Ataturk, in Bernard Lewis, *The Emergence of Modern Turkey,* Oxford, London, 1961, p. 165.
5. Chalilakath Kunhammed Haji set an example by sending his own daughters to schools against the opposition of the orthodox ulemas. See E.K. Maulavi, 'Islahi Prasthanam', *Al Ithihad*, April, 1954.
6. Leila Ahmed, *Women and Gender in Islam.* Yale University Press, 1992, p. 129.
7. S.K. Datta and Rajiv Sharma, *Pakistan from Jinnah to Jehad,* New Delhi, 2002, p. 216.
8. See Nikki. R. Keddie (ed.) *Saints and Sufis: Muslim Religious Institutions since 1500,* Berkeley, 1972, pp. 385-401.
9. Ruqaiyyah Waris Maqsood, *Islam: Teach Yourself,* Hodder Education, London, 2006, pp. 148-51.
10. Abdul A'la Maududi, *The Islamic Way of Life,* Markazi Publishers, New Delhi, 2002, pp. 16-17.
11. Ziauddin Sardar, *What do Muslims Believe*? Granta Books, London, 2006, p. 58.
12. Mazharuddin Siddiqi, *Women in Islam,* Adam Publishers, New Delhi, 2004, p. 149.
13. BBC News, 19 April, 2005 in Geraldine Terry, "Death by vigilantes" in *Women's Rights,* Palgrave Macmillan, London, 2007, p. 52.
14. See, Shaikh Zeinudin, Chapter "Divorce through writing", *Fath-ul-Mu'in,* Trans; P.K. Kunju Bava, 1978, p. 528. Moreover, Several Quranic verses and Sunnah of the Prophet nullifies such divorces categorically.
15. Quran Chapter IV, *Al-Nisa* (Women), Verse 35, Trans. M.A.S. Abdel Haleem, Oxford Classics, 2005.
16. See *Islamic Encyclopaedia (*Mal), 1993, p. 481 and Thomas Patric Hughes, *Dictionary of Islam,* 1885, p. 87.
17. Quran, Chapter XXIV, *Al-Nur* (Light), Verse 4 Trans. M.A.S. Abdul Haleem, *op. cit.*
18. "Our Women", in *Muslim*, collection of Vakkom Maulavi Foundation, 1913, Vol. III, p. 89.
19. Song written in the form of a letter, a speciality among *Mappila Muslim Women of Kerala*, usually in a mixed language mainly of Malayalam and Arabic, and rarely Sanskrit and Tamil.
20. Vakkom Maulavi, *Deepika*, Maulavi Foundation Trust, Trivandrum, 1992. (2) *Complete Works of Makthi Thangal,* Kerala Islamic Mission, Tirur, 1981, pp. 926-27 (3) E. Moidu Maulavi, *Autobiography,* National Book Stall, Kottayam, 1981, p. 123.
21. This magazine was published in 1929, K.C. Komukutty Maulavi being its editor.
22. In *Kurathipattu,* Angel Gabrael appears in camouflage as a Kurathi (lady palmist or sooth sayer) and appears before Fathima, revealing several incidents that come in her future life. This was a very common and popular practice continued as a part of folk culture and belief in Kerala mainly done by the women of the Kuravas who constitute a major section of the aboriginals of Kerala. Its companion song the *Pakshippattu* (Bird song) also is very popular among the Mappila Muslim community of Kerala. Some local events like conversion are also described in such works.

23. Haleema Beevi, *Madhyamam* Weekly, March 18, 2005, p. 36-37. See also J. Devika (Ed.) *Herself, Gender and Early Writings of Malayalee Women*, Stree, Kolkata, 2007.
24. *Nisa*, centred in Calicut was founded in 1997 under V.P. Suhara, a noted Muslim Woman activist. A journal in the same name was published, but was compelled to stop with one issue. This organisation, though not much effective, is still working for the Muslim women who become victims of unilateral divorce and temporary marriages like *Mut'a,* rampant in Calicut beach area with the contact of the incoming Arabs.
25. Stanley Lane Poole, Quoted in Leila Ahmed, *Women and Gender in Islam,* Yale University, New Haven & London, 1992, p. 152.
26. Zoya Hasan and Ritu Menon, *Educating Muslim Girls—A Comparison of Five Indian cities,* Women Unlimited, New Delhi, 2005, p. 135.
27. An interview with Dr. Fazal Gafoor (Feb. 2010), the President of the Kerala State Muslim Educational Society, Calicut. His father Dr. Abdul Gafoor was the founder President of the MES. Fathima Gafoor's biographical sketch *'Ever in Memory'* (Mal.) is revealing several aspects regarding the condition of Muslim women in Kerala and some suggestions for its improvement.
28. Suraiya Tabassum, *Waiting for the New Dawn,* Indian Social Institute, New Delhi, 2003, pp. 112-13.
29. Surah XXXIII, (Al-Ahzab) Verse 33.
30. See Nadia Hijab, *Women Power: The Arab Debate on Women at work,* Cambridge University Press, 1998. Leila Ahmed "Early Feminist Movements in the Middle East", in *Muslim Women,* ed. Freda Hussain, New York, 1992.
31. The Islamic countries ratified the UN prescription in the first phase which include: Egypt, Morocco, Tunisia, Libiya, Yemen, Iraq and Jordan.
32. Ziaudin Sardar, "Introduction", in the *Britannica Guide,* Robinson, U.K., 2009, p. XIX.
33. Leila Ahmed, *Women and Gender in Islam*, Yale University Press, New Haren and London, 1992, p. 239.
34. For details. See Afsaneh Najmabadi, "Feminism in an Islamic Republic - Years of Hardship, Years of Growth" in Y.Y. Haddad and John L. Esposito (ed.) *Islam, Gender and Social Change,* University Press, New York and Oxford, 1998, pp. 59-77.
35. Kim knott, *Identity Issues and World Religious,* Australian Association for the study of Religions, 1986, pp. 169-171.
36. Quran, Chapter IV, *Al-Nisa* (Women), Verse, 80.
37. *Ibid*, Chapter VI, *Al-An'am* (Livestock), Verse 107. Such injunctions continue in Chapters like Al-Ghashiya (The overwhelming Event) Where it says, "So (Prophet) warn them: Your only task is to give warning, you are not there to control them" (Verse 21 & 22).
38. 'Modernity' is associated with technological means, whereas 'modernism' is the ideological message of the modern age. For its better understanding see Bruce Lawrence, *Defenders of God. The Fundamentalist Revolt against the Modern Age,* Herper & Row, Sanfrancisco, 1989.
39. Jonathan Friedman observes how the construction of history is related to the

formation of identity. See Friedman, *Cultural Idenitty and Global Process,* Sage, London, 1994.

40. An article in the name of Taslima appeared in a Kannada journal in Karnataka on Purdah issue, invited much protest from the Muslims and the medias of Bijapur, Shimoga, Hasan in Karnataka. It led to direct confrontation between two sections. In the police firing two youngmen, Latheef and Sadiq, died and hundred wounded. In the article, she is alleged to have stated that "the Prophet was opposed to Burkha", to the provocations of some sections of people. Report in *Deshabhimani* (Mal.) Daily, dt. 3-3-2010.
41. Report in the *Mathrubhoomi,* (Mal.) Daily on 5th June, 2010. Even the pressures of the Department of Public Instruction and Government failed to solve the problem amicably.

5

Purdah

An Urge for Identity

Purdah recently has become a centrifugal artefact of controversy not only in the Islamic Society of the world over, but even in its outside. Though it simply means a veil, that recognises one's faith and it connotes with a wide range of seclusion, 'a means of oppression', a 'method of resistance' and an object that projects anti-colonialism—all depending on the context. This arch symbol of identity which claims to solicitize a community, presently exposes not its solidarity, but its inner weaknesses of oppression and silence. Muslim Feminists like Fathima Mernissi and Nazira Zein-al-Din refute the religious compulsion of the Veil as it is found today. As discussed in detail in the first chapter, they are totally contextual and to the spirit of the situations. Amir Ali, the author of the celebrated work, *The Spirit of Islam*, a widely read work in the Muslim World, considers it as a temporary measure instituted by Muhammed, never intended to be a permanent one which finds no place in the Quran. By *Hijab* Muslim World means the covering of the body including head and face of the Muslim women in a traditional way. To them, it is the only dress which carries as the symbol of modesty, privacy and morality. Some Islamic jurists even advocate the wearing of a face-veil ignoring the fact that women during the time of the Prophet were not practicing so. Therefore, in recent years countries like Turkey, Tunisia and Pakistan are not insisting on such "religious compulsions" as some false *fatwa* dictate.

Hijab is now characterised as a symbol of inferiority of women in Islam. But to the emerging Arab World, it symbolises a consciousness of resistance and identity, especially of the youth, against the colonial rule. Theoretically, hijab is a part of the seclusion of Muslim women from men other than the relatives, pushing them to their own living quarters. Basically it prohibits all activities of women in public spaces. But, by the end of the 20th century in the heart land of Islam, particularly in the Gulf and the Mediterranean region, the over imposed seclusion of women found a new turn, as a result of modernism and fresh opportunities for employment and life, especially with the emergence of new urban centres.

Hence in the modern Islamic societies, several movements against ulemas and their *fatwas* (religious ordinances) have come as a result of female education and awareness of gender equalities and also of social realities in almost all Arab countries and in Pakistan. There are several women's movements in Egypt, Turkey, Iran, Lebanon and in gulf states like Bahrain, Kuwait, Qatar, Trucial States and in Pakistan. For example, in 1981, in Pakistan, a new Action Forum for Women started working against the governmental discrimination on women. The forum placed for the increased role of women in the parliamentary system, implementation of a civil code, re-interpretation of Islamic law, measures to family planning etc., particularly in countries like Bahrain and Kuwait. While analysing the situations in the post-revolutionary Iran, one could observe the miserable plight of the secular feminists who are totally put under silence by the Shiite- dominant cultural climate. A state-sponsored task force in charge of inspecting and scrutinizing women in the streets in order to enforce the so-called 'code of modesty' has been introduced to question women found without hijab or for mal-veiling. Moreover, critics like Moghissi exposes the 'activism' and the achievements of Iranian women in the new rule and comments that the "Islamic regime has not opened the gates" and women are "jumping over the fences".[1]

Veil: Terminology and Theory

In the post colonial Egypt also new trends of reform have emerged as a continuation of the reform of the 19th and early 20th century, especially of the Muslim Brotherhood. Colonialism in all the Arab-Muslim societies as in the case of the Europeans, introduced new social economic systems like laissez-faire and capitalism bequeathing a new culture of a secular state with an economic interpretation of Islam. The new government asserting for a society with equal importance for material and spiritual forces considering it essential for the development of a healthy society. Here religion provides a sense of social balance in the society. Astute reformists like Zeinab al-Ghazali even advocated the discretion of women in the selection of their dress. She comments that a woman's dress at home should be determined by both women and her husband, and at the outside house it should be at the will of her husband, but within the purview of the tenets of religion.[2] Likewise, modernist tendencies in dress and life-style found some positive marks in Jordanian women after the secularist Toujan Faysal was elected to its parliament in 1993. Ideological pressures have been manifested forcefully in countries like Bahrain and Kuwait on issues like dress and modernity in 1960s and 70s expressing through protests. In 1963, in Kuwait abayas (black wraps) were burned in the course of their demonstration as symbols of their seclusion from society. What we could experience in recent years is that in almost all the Islamic countries, it is the middle and the lower classes that take the lead for getting equal footing with men and to be free from seclusion.

To most of the Muslim scholars, the issues related to women are the result of the pervasive cultural intrusion of westernization raging on Muslim countries for the last few decades. Modernisation, ofcourse, had a serious impact on women's lives and their role in the family and in the society at large. No doubt, several new factors emerged out of the technological revolution and thereby in the intellectual arena, have intensified the process of change in the socio-economic life. The new feminist demands, particularly after 1970s, have also increased as a result of their immaculate presence in the work force equal with men. The domination of women in such centres of labour is primarily conditioned by economic factors. The subordination of one sex (commonly the female), is always associated with economic domination related to their dependence leading to oppression [3]. This has certainly brought the women of the modern Islamic world to develop a dual personality in their duties of a home-maker inside and a bread winner outside. This dual role of women necessitates to wear the veil in a world of men which forbids every thing other than their labour pushing to a state of degradation. Such a situation often leads to develop a psychological defunction, particularly among the young urban working class. Therefore, as Fouad Zakaria comments, by wearing the veil, women fall at the junction between the repudiation and denunciation of the body with an ascetic appearance on one side and act as a sexual object to her husband at home on the other, taking both sexuality and chastity totally complementary[4].

Throughout the history, the veil never has been a symbol of empowerment either in the family or in the society; instead, it made her a victim of oppression and disempowerment. It symbolises the devaluation of her inherent potential related to her physique, intellect, productivity, gender and social status. But in the Islamic society women also is depicted as a model for mother and wife, ofcourse, within the parameters of the Quran and the traditions of the Prophet. More than hundred verses in the Quran are defining the multifarious role of women in family and society. The Quran emphatically states that man and woman are created out of a single soul (Surah 4:1) and have imparted equal responsibilities in all aspects of familial and social life. But under the guise of "equality" and "protection", women are humiliated and oppressed on various "divine" excuses of man-made ideologies, including the imposition of veil. The question of seeing a woman by a man with the purpose of marriage, writers like Sha'ban argues the same by quoting a tradition of the Prophet which says, "If a man gets engaged to a woman, if he can look at her lead to marrying her, let him do so". He further adds that it is not restricted to her physical looks alone, but should also consider her personality, character, mental maturity and behaviour[5]. Such an attitude towards women and their seclusion did not last long. The period after Prophet and his close colleagues (Khulafa-ul-Rashideen–the period of the four Orthodox Caliphs), gradual restrictions towards women's role could be seen as a result of several socio-political reasons. Some of the Imams who interpreted Quran and traditions also brought forth rigid stipulations with regard to the presence of women in public spaces. Even their presence in the mosque was discouraged. The orthodox theologians also complained that the major reason for the decadence of Islamic Society is due to the moral degeneration that crept into the society as a result of women's involvement in all socio-economic activities. As Mohammed Al-Ghazzali laments, "ninety percent of our veiled women do not pray at all, nor do they know of the other duties of Islam more than their names"[6]. Thus religion loses it spirit and becomes so shallow when it forfeit everything except some symbols like the veil.

It is true that the issue of the veil has become recently contentious in contemporary Islam. Even Muslims beyond the orbit of cultural Islam (a major portion of Africa Central Asia, South and South East Asia), now have a belief that it is absolutely essential for all women to veil themselves. Though Caliph Omar introduced the system on some reasons of his own, his follower Caliph Othman revoked it during the time of his Caliphate, which itself is a notation that veil is not a primordial thing. Hence, modernist-reformist writers like Ziaudin Sardar considers it only as a "perversion of the essentially egalitarian nature of Islam"[7].

The veil is often depicted as the most visible manifestation of a Muslim woman's faith. It goes by many names-*hijab, niqab, abaaya, burqa, chador, purdah* etc. It can be anything from a single scarf draped around the face and neck to a shawl and, more rarely, a full cloak or shroud that covers the head and everything, except the eyes.

The word *Hijab* has a wide spectrum of meaning, all contextual, in time and space. The term is derived from the root *hajiba* meaning to cover, veil, screen, shelter etc. Mernissi highlights various dimensions of the usage of the term veil in the Quran and the traditions of the Prophet. She further argues that "anything that separates and protects is hijab"[8]. To substantiate her argument Mernissi quotes from Ibn Hisham stating that the term hijab is found only seven times in the Quran, that too in different contexts. For example, one verse in the Chapter on Mary (mother of Jesus) reads:

> She placed a screen from them; then we sent to her Our angel,
> and he appeared before her as a man in all respects (19:17)

As referred to earlier [in Chapter One] another verse on hijab is related to the wives of the Prophet,

> When you ask his wives for something, do so from behind a screen....(33:53)

Again, in the Chapter named *Al'A'raf* (The Heights), a verse reads:

> Between them shall be a veil [barrier] and on the Heights will be men
> Who would know every one By his Marks: They will call out to the people of the Garden 'Peace be with you'—(7:46)

Verse 51 of Chapter 42 (Consultation) also says,

> It is granted to any mortal that God should speak to him except through revelation or from behind a veil or by sending a messenger....

Therefore in such a concept with a negative connotation the hijab is now claimed to be "a symbol of Muslim identity, manna for the Muslim women"[9].

Moreover the Quranic verse ordained on *Hijab* (33:53) (here, not as a dress, but only as a 'screen' or a 'piece of cloth') has come in a particular context in the life of prophet. It warns his comrades not to enter the apartment of the prophet without invitation and if ask anything to his wives, let it be behind a screen. Apart from the "imposition" of a dress code for Muslim women, this verse mainly suggests to abandon pagan customs in human relationship and demands that men and women should be held in honour according to natural and moral principles, particularly in respect to the position and dignity of women of the prophet's household. Moreover, this verse was revealed immediately after the marriage of the Prophet with Zainab Bint Jahsh amidst a small gathering who attended for a dinner in connection with the marriage in the apartment of the Prophet. Anas Ibn Malik, one of the companions of Prophet, was a witness of the event and the referred "screen" is to exclude him from the scene with an intention only providing secrecy that requires for the newly wedded couple. As Al-Tabari interprets Prophet was impatient to be alone and the veil (sitr/curtain) was to be God's answer to an ill-mannered community. Tabari himself gives much weightage to the eye-witness account of Anas Ibn Malik. While he combines the term *hijab* with *sitr*, the stress certainly is for the curtain which requires to the context[10].

It is true that Islamic scholars regarded this verse as a "descent of the hijab" and gives undue importance. Of course, it was the first of its kind which in effect made the "veil" as an instrument of seclusion and an institution of identity. A careful re-reading of this verse reveals to us that God wishes to intimate that community "certain niceties that they seemed to lack, like not entering a dwelling without asking permission"[11]. Moreover, the word *hijab* carries a multi-dimensional concept with a stress on ethics more than seclusion or separation.

This verse, supposedly on *hijab,* points to another dimension that, apart from the stress on the need of politeness on the part of the visitors at a function in a house, it seems, that the concept of *hijab* here gives some order to a very confused and complex situation providing a solution to the whole web of confusion and tension in a given situation. Again, to apply a single manifestation or a premise to a verse is against the spirit and holistic nature of the Quranic revelations. Islamic theorists like Suyuti emphatically argues that it is impossible to understand a verse without knowing the causes and situation that led to it[12]. *Hijab*, for the Sufis, is a disturbance for the soul to achieve the divine light or God or the Heaven. The mystics always search for the *Kashf* (uncovering or revealing what is hidden) opposite to *Hijab*. For some theologians, it is a punishment and charecterises it as a humiliation. Moreover, the Quranic verse Five in the Chapter *'Fussilat'*, reveals the inability of Quraysh to understand the message of the Prophet. It reads:

> Our hearts are under veils, (encased) against (the faith) you call us to;
> Our ears are heavy; there is a barrier between us and you. (41:5)

Such verses also served the incompatibility and inaccuracy of the term *Hijab* when it comes in a wider spectrum of usage.

While giving too much of stress to the wearing of *hijab* as a token of Muslim identity, or even as a 'sixth pillar" of Islam, it goes to the extent of disallowing the basic requirement of freedom that an individual possess by birth. Moreover, it is a denial of human rights to live and aspire what they could in the given socio-economic situations. It also carries the dichotomous issue of one's choice and other's compulsions. It becomes morbid and unwelcomable only when it takes the course of unnecessary impositions where it is least expected or required. Amina Wadud, the noted African-American Muslim feminist, fights against purdah, wearing hijab in her own way and style. She never considers it as a religious obligation or a mark of modesty as mandated by the Quran[13]. The much publicised 'respect and protection' of women are associated with the sexuality of women that haunts the ever growing consciousness of men who want to be dominant in all spaces of human affairs. Religious dictates are not a compilation of mere 'dos' and 'don'ts,' and if it wants to be valid for all times it must touch up on the basic human values, and if Islam is striving for the making of such a system, it certainly will confirm the proper and ideal place of Muslim women globally. Several tenets of the Quran, the traditions of Prophet and the reasonable and scientific interpretations of the early Imams are all vouch for that. Moreover, Quran emphatically states that the best garment is God-consciousness (Taqwa). In Surah Al-A'raf (The Heights) it reveals:

> Children of Adam, [mankind/people] we have given you garments to cover your nakedness and as adornment for you; the garment of God-consciousness is the best of all garments- this is one of God's signs, so that people may take heed. (7:26)

This itself is the best testimony to understand the distinct connotations of the term 'hijab' and its multifarious applications in various contexts.

In the early days of Islam, women never covered their face as a part of hijab. The eminent Islamist and author of *The Meaning of the Glorious Islam*, Mohammed Marmeduke Pickthall, considers the veil a "sheer nonsense and a burden", particularly for those women who work in the field with their brotheren and other relatives. It was observed by women of countries like Egypt, Syria, Turkey and Arabia, when they enter into urban centres, that too partially. He categorically states that purdah system is neither associated with Islam nor with Arabia[14].

Wearing of the Veil—Revisiting of a Debate?

In the early days of the Political Islam in India one important aspect to be noticed is the absence of an agricultural community. The Muslim population mainly concentrated in urban centres. This peculiarity of Indian Muslim diaspora virtually developed an urban culture in all the places where they settled. The nobles and the rich among them in the Indian cities observed purdah as those of Baghdad, Damascus and Cairo. Later those who live in the interiors also thought that to keep a religious identity and to live at par as Muslims, they should practice purdah as one of the fundamentals of Islam. Such practices of identity became more common and popular particularly in the life of the harem or zenana when the Caliphate became an instrument of political Islam, often degenerating into an oriental despotism. Moreover, in a situation of war and turmoil, women and children are the worst sufferers and they become precious captives or gifts to the victors as their first choice. Hence the kings and nobles who lived in palaces or in an enclosed city encouraged such systems to the seclusion of women who need not go to the outside world for their livelihood. That is the main reason why the ulemas and Amirs of the day never insisted the practice to the commons and the public women (including maids, singers, dancers in mehfil etc.) and those who went around as artisans and workers who are also compelled to live to the pleasures of their masters.

Seclusion of women and their oppressed life is a legacy of the feudal age when woman also were treated as a piece of land and as a private property. We know that in such an age, women, whether slave or free, were parcelled out to the feudal lord as an inanimate commodity. The critics, particularly the

Westerners, complain that Islam is still 'feudal' and 'medieval' and since it could not come out of its shell, they treat their females differently and often 'as animals'[15]. But this is only one aspect of the western approach on the Orient, which is always identified with Islam, and attributing hatred and revulsion, especially after its legitimization with the orient by Edward Said and Huntington[16]. To the west, hijab among Muslims is a symbol of 'oppression', 'coercion' and 'deception'.

The theory that purdah is an urban legacy is further ascertained in the context of Muslim women who live in the periphery as those of the Southern Malabar, especially of the Malappuram region. Here, women, including Muslims, work as agricultural labourers and as ordinary coolies without any seclusion or a veil. But the trend is now changing as a result of the revivalist Islam working in various capacities as the Jamaatis, the Mujahids and ofcourse with the existing traditionalist Sunniites. This area, compared to any other part in Kerala, has become a flourishing ground of these ideologies in recent times. The Islamic study centres in this region give more emphasis for the growth of an 'Islamic Culture' with its own identity, apart from mere religious teaching. To inculcate such a religiosity and identity of singularness, the gulf influence is not the minimum. All those who have gone to the gulf region in search of some employment and better life returned with such an ideology of Islam as found in the desert area of the Arabs. Women clad in a single purdah seemed more acceptable for those who lived there for some time, taking it an idealized (model) dress for women, later returned home importing the same to their homestead. The acceptance of such a uniform attire also gave them some confidence and a feeling of equality with *ashrafi* (high social status) Muslims, who otherwise would have been looked upon with contempt in society. The gulf boom also caused to the disappearance of landed aristocracy and the new class with the gulf professionalism thus became a driving force in the new Islamic society of Kerala.

Seclusion of women among Muslims also has been perpetuated by linking and legitimising it with shariah as a code of conduct and law to all those who practice Islam. It is true that the available Shariah is man-made, androcentric and therefore always inimical towards women. The whole content of it is not exclusively based on the Quran or the traditions of the Prophet. Instead, it contained contradictory interpretations and weak traditions often exposing their inherent debility and inadequacies as revealed in the varied jurisprudence of Imams. As the Sudanese human rights activist, Ahmed Na'im, observes, it is only a conviction as a Muslim that the public law of Shariah does not represent the law of Islam which contemporary Muslims are supposed to implement in fulfillment of their religious obligation. He also strongly believes that the application of the public law of Shariah today will be counter productive and detrimental to Muslims and to Islam itself [17]. Moreover the veil has been taken by the West as the best weapon through which Muslim society, particularly of its women, has been attacked with greater objective of branding it 'oppressive', 'anti-human' and 'undemocratic. A stereo type of the women with caricatures either veiled in public spaces or putting them behind the bars longing for the distant liberty about which they themselves are doubtful, are the routine presentation by the western press. The revivalists and the Islamists consider such attempts as a part of Islamophobia that developed in the West recently against a rival culture with a fear of its possible hegemony in future.

The western attitude on Islam and its people is quite evident from the famous lecture made by Ernest Renan at the College De France in 1862. To him,

> Islam is the complete negation of Europe. Islam is the disdain of science, the suppression of civil society, it is the appalling simplicity of the semitic spirit, restricting the human mind, closing it to all delicate ideas; to all refined sentiment, to all rational research, in order to keep it facing and eternal tautology: God is God[18].

It is a fact that both Islam and Islamic states differ in all respects with the West. That does not mean that Islam is totally anti-modern and inhuman. Such an assumption on Islam is also erroneous because, it is not with the case of one religion alone. The Church, with which the West is inalienably committed, is also often dictates against reason and science.

In places like Kerala The Islamists and the revivalists use the same weapon, probably with more sharpness to oppose the West by all means propagating that the West is always against Islam ideologically and politically. To their mind, the west nourishes modernism which does not have any compromise with religion and traditionalism. They often ask a question: Why should Islam be modernized, when it is already perfect and pure, universal and for all time? But what we require now is not a confrontation of religion with modernism, but a conciliation leading to liberalism as we aspire more. It is also to be remembered that 'purdah' is not an Arabic term; it is Persian and even the letter 'P' is not available in Arabic alphabet. 'Hijab' is the term used in Arabic which means a 'curtain' or anything that divides or separates or a device that causes for seclusion, as discussed earlier.

In fact there is no direct evidence with regard to the entry of such a veil in India or elsewhere in the early days of Islamic expansion. In India, the earliest available Muslim womens' dress could be seen in the caricatures of women in the Sultanate period, particularly of Razia Begum. Her dress never symbolises the present day purdah and in all her portraits she is presented without a face -veil. Again, her overhead dress, other than the crown, is a single piece of cloth retreating backward exposing the complete forehead, a part of the hair including the ornated frontlet. It is also to be remembered that the career of Razia was one of incessant warfare with her own brothers and misogynic nobles who never accepted a woman's accession, and for that matter, leading wars personally on horse back. The same was the case with the women of the Mughal period where we could see a host of royal women who have been engaged not only in administrative activities, but even in intellectual discourses. (The detials of whom have been given in the second chapter). The contemporary court chroniclers like Abul Fazl also make mention of the increased role of women in the Mughal court articulating a Petticoat government, or Purdah Regime (1560-64) headed by Maham Anaga, the step mother of Akbar, which intrigued and held the reigns of administration during the minority of Akbar. It was a conglomeration of a motley group of women moving freely and doing things with connivance both in the palace and in the harem without veil and without virtue[19]. The attire of Muslim women continued in the same pattern in the colonial period also following the Revolt of 1857.

As tin the case of others, the Muslim women followed the regional ethos with regard to the dress habits, but at the same time following religious instructions. Whether it is in Kerala or in Kashmir, or in Punjab or in Bengal, the women of the Islamic faith continued the local dress pattern as they were following traditionally. This cultural distinctiveness and identities still could be seen in all these regions including Kerala without much change. Meanwhile, a change in the dress habits of Mappila women could be seen only recently due to some reasons which require indepth study and examination. If this change, which is a challenge to the existing cultural ethos of the country is purely on religious ground, that would have been possible centuries earlier with the introduction of the new ideology itself. Why now and how it spreads so speedily are some of the questions to be answered in the present socio-cultural situations in Kerala where pluralism had its deep root as a legacy of the past. It is certainly not as a result of the segregation and the "increasing withdrawal from social contact due to the "deterioration of relations between the two communities" as some observed in recent years [20]. But it is true that a new trend could be seen to change over to purdah in the case of majority of Muslim women including the educated class, not as a token of the estrangement of relations with their counterparts in other communities, but as a symbol of distinction, status and identity. The uniform wearing of veil has become a practice among a major section of the community only for the last two decades. As noted earlier, it acts as a Camouflage concealing the class differences and social distinctions that Islam never agrees to pronounce conceptually, particularly in the context of the Gulf boom. Muslim women in Malabar were distinguished with their variety of ornaments and colourful dresses in a social gathering and now it almost became extinct by the extensive and somewhat compulsive use of purdah. The irony is that this is activated in a society where their menfolk commonly still stick on to the conventional Keralite or western style of dressing.

Across much of the world today, Muslim women of all ages are increasingly turning to wearing the veil. Here, we have to pose certain pertinent questions. Is this trend a sign of rising piety or a way of asserting Muslim pride? Does the veil really provide women equality and freedom from all harassment including sexual? While the first question is related to religion and its identity, the second one naturally is associated with human rights and individual dignity. All these issues are to be addressed empirically and asexually to reachout a gender-just society. While analysing the question of piety to justify veiling, Marina Lazreg, Professor of Sociology, Hunter College, University of New York, explores the adverse psychological effects of the practice of the wearer and those around her, and pays special attention to the negative impact of veiling for young girls[21]. Kerala too has developed such cases of mental abnormalities among girl students. Our observations in areas like Malappuram and Calicut, particularly in their interiors, have brought to light some instances of neuro-psychosis among school-going and college going girls who undergo treatments including counselling. Psychiatrists and neuro-physicians centred in Calicut and Malappuram reveal several cases of teenaged girls who have developed depression and neurosis due to factors generating from familial and social surroundings[22]. Though the veil does not come primarily and openly as a check to social mobility and interaction of the youngsters with opposite sex, rarely its by-products like the seclusion and social restrictions do harm the free life and mingling of them in the given social situations. An introversion and an inferiority complex could be seen in the case of such students in public schools and colleges, where such specimens are in a minority, and particularly when others go gay without veil and without taboo. But the situation in an institution run by the same community is different and there they feel more secure and safe while they live among the veiled. Those who wear the veil with social compulsions, whether it be in a work place or in an academia, are found removing it at their earliest, and any chance to remove it will be utilised accordingly whether it is in a gang of their own friends or family members.

Moreover, some pro-purdah people also believe that it is more convenient for those who do not have proper dress or ornaments to wear and a veil could cover up every thing inside. Here the veil creates an artificial unity and uniformity without any barriers of class or economic differences. The rich and the poor, the low-born and the high-born, find solace and solidarity, while they sit and enjoy together covered, in a single piece of long garment. It is more so for those who believe in an egalitarian society that Islam always aspired for. That is the main reason why the use of purdah increases very highly even in the suburbs and coastal areas of Kerala where workers and the fishermen, mostly poor, live prominently. The revivalists and the fundamentalists who consider such regions more fertile for their exercises and discourses also encourage to wear the veil in their routine religious classes which makes them more distinctive from other communities. This urge for a separate identity also creates an artificial wall between people, who are living otherwise more closer and intimate, sharing the common problems together in society.

In Kerala Muslim women are passing through an important phase of their transition in the socio-political activities as a result of the introduction of the three-tier panchayath system of administration and the allocation of 50 p.c. seat reservation for women. Political parties including Muslim League and other communal organizations are thus at a pressure to allot seats for them, ofcourse, without much willingness. It is a fact that they are facing a lot of pressures from the ulemas and the traditionalists when they (the men) are compelled to share power and responsibilities that denied to women all along.

Whenever the issue over the veil comes in Kerala, reactionaries including the revivalists complain that those who oppose it are 'irreligious' and are against Islam. Again, if it is a symbol of cultural identity, why men are exempted from such identities? And what is the additional responsibility women have to keep the so-called 'identity' than men? These are all the possible questions, but found never answered by the orthodoxy. It is also to be remembered that those who talk ill of the veil are really not opposing the religion of Islam, but only misogyny. As mentioned earlier, it is getting more popularity for the last one or two decades and that too on account of several socio-economic reasons rather than religious. We must also know that while the history of purdah in Kerala is only fifteen years old, the Islamic society (without purdah), here has a long record of at least one thousand two hundred years.

Re-veiling and Issue of Human Rights

The veiling occasionally is linked with human rights, particularly when it become a social compulsion. It depends on the mentality and acceptance of the wearer. Recently, Rayana, an engineering graduate from Kasargod, was compelled to wear the veil by some fundamentalists and Rayana and her family sought the help of the court for protection[23]. This incident is a clear indication of the violation of human rights that an individual has. Though rarely, such incidents are happening throughout the world threatening human rights in the name of religion and tradition, but only to be followed by women!! Virtualy it is not the religion conceptually that compels or insists the observance of veiling, but it is the patriarchal society that dictates things to be followed by its female members. In the Islamic society of Kerala this male dominance is comparatively stronger on account of the utilization of religion in all walks of life. Religion through its patriarchs permeates not only in the religious life of an individual but in their personal and social life without any scruples or barriers even breaking the inalienable human rights that a person possesses. Women are also partly responsible for such encroachments in their rights, because they themselves are not properly aware of these things due to several socio-economic factors from which they could not be easily free.

Some writers in Kerala have brought forth new ideas and images and the complexities on the wearing of Purdah. It is for many a symbol of resistance, associated with the negation of patriarchy. But this is an over simplification of the system, because in the present day situations, observance of Purdah connotes more, especially in the purview of human rights. Of course, a woman in Purdah brings out a feeling that she is a consumer commodity for the man, especially when the cloak wraps not only the beauty in her, but even the basic aspect of womanhood. The irony of the fact is that, instead of covering the eyes of the wicked man, the society compels the poor woman to hide herself from the sight of men. There are some who even doubt whether the use of purdah will reduce the sexual anarchy in society. Instead, they fear the possible fornication hiding any woman and cheating everybody, on the excuse of the veiling[24]. This is the negative impact of a 'noble' practice which silently destroys the very spirit of the system. In the novel *Maram* (Tree) the reputed writer N.P. Mohammed describes Amina who is absconding with her paramour by using a Purdah, making it [purdah] a villlain/instrument for mischief[25].

Both the public and the medias (including electronic) in recent years present Purdah an artefact of cheat, impersonation and incognizance, especially in the context of the much publicized 'Love Jihad', Responsible Newspapers and magazines have even serialised features on this issue in Kerala, where girls (mostly students) are persuaded to convert offering love, often with chicanery and force. Wide propaganda also has been given to this kind of a gender burglary in Kerala by some people with vested interests, in which purdah also comes as a villain, because, according to them, these are all made possible by the extensive use of the veil both by the victims and by the helpers[26]. Almost all the caricatures and photographs displayed are with conventional *burqa* with face veil showing only the eyes. Any way, even though such an issue has been died out soon, this negative image on the purdah still remains in the subconscious mind of the people at large and some of them look upon it not as a religious symbol, but one of crime and jugglary. In fact this is a miserable degradation of an artefact originally introduced with a 'noble cause' to represent modesty and humility.

Islamic world, particularly the oil-rich Arab countries like Saudi Arabia, do not give equal status and freedom to women to seek education, to get employment and even to move freely. The kings and Shaikhs are not free from the feudal lineages and their attempts to maintain their authorities could be seen in almost all the Sheikdoms of the Middle East. Now they are also facing revolts from the public supported by revolutionaries. Those western countries which have influence in these kingdoms also do not hesitate to nurture them because their oil interests and economic dreams are conveniently fulfilled by these Sheikhs than an elected democratic government. If any tendency of such modernism could be found anywhere that will be thwarted by them as in Iraq or in Afghanistan or as found recently in countries like Lybia, Egypt, Kuwait etc. The debacle to the socialist-democratic government in Afghanistan is a lesson for all because, instead of a return to democracy, a Taliban-led tribal system is pondering over the US-led puppet administration which really could not claim any root of people's rule. This is the adverse effect of the western imperialistic interference in such countries where religion and orthodoxy still pervades, probably with the nursing of the west itself, without any awareness of global change. In the excuse of resistance to Western imperialism, these countries are now returning to more rigidity and turn back to all kinds of progress and change. The issue of veiling also could be viewed in such a context of struggle and exist with an aim of making the past always alive.

The European attempt to attack the veil also has a negative impact in most of the countries where de-veiling had taken place earlier by legislations and social transformation due to education and reform. This negativism or return to veil could be seen in recent years as a protest to western culture that spreads along with imperialism. The tendency toward neo conservatism among many women is in recent years clearly displayed in the return to the hijab, the traditional dress. Peterson cites an incident in 1989 in Kuwait where a female employee was refused to shake hand a Minister when he was introduced to her[27]. This attitude continues not only in the heartland of Islam, but in all Muslim societies in Africa, Central Asia and in South East Asia. What really happened was the reforms introduced by the upper and middle class politicians and the reformists concentrated mainly in the urban centres and they could not penetrate to the interiors. While they internalised the western discourse, it was absorbed mainly by the urban 'bourgeoisie and had no impact beyond this class. The irony is that even in Turkey, Islam and the veil are recently found resurgent. There, women stage protests, lead processions and even go for hunger strikes demanding the right to veil. We should remember that these developments are found unfortunately now in Turkey, where the first legal attempts were made in modernisation through government initiative. Again, in recent years veiling as a symbol of oppression has been refuted by many Islamic theorists like Samira Fayyed, one of the leaders of the Islamic movements in Jordan. She argues that women should be given full participation and responsibility along with men in all activities including liberation movements ignoring the dress style and other trivialities.[28] Such movements and arguments to re-veiling has come as a result of the ardent opposition of the veil by Feminist writers like Nawal El Sa'adawi, Fatima Mernissi and many others. Sa'adawi in one of her lectures in Scandinevia (1980) even used the concept of 'veiling the brain'[29]. Such a conclusion she reached at by her experience in the case of a young girl who had been intelligent and brave until she put on the veil. Afterwards, it was impossible to conduct a normal discussion with her. Mernissi, as referred earlier, is trying to find out Quranic support in all her deliberations against the veil and categorically concludes that there is no religious compulsion to observe veil.

The present day Islamists staunchly oppose such movements and trend towards modernity and argue for a revival with the veil as could be seen in the Islamic societies the world over. They interpret the reveiling in the context of the Iranian Revolution and its socio-political changes, particularly in the life of women. Women have chosen the veil as the symbol of Islamization and have accepted it as the public face of their revivalist attitude. They are defensive of the veil and argue that it is an instrument of liberation and not one of oppression. They become observers and not the observed. Moreover, it liberates them from the dictates of the fashion industry and the demands of the beauty myth, and also from being the 'slaves of imperialism'[30]. In Kerala too, for the last two decades, a new trend of Islamization through dress is launched by revivalists like the Salafis, Jama'at-i-Islamis and the traditional Sunniits. As mentioned earlier, this is partly due to the influence of the Arab culture with which the Muslims of this region had incessant contacts by professional migration. Even before the entry of the so-called Purdah (here the long dress from top to toe), Muslim women in Kerala observed hijab by using a small scarf over their head in line with the regional tone.

In Kerala, varieties of the veil are used by women of various age-groups and in different tastes. Purdah even now is not commonly followed in southern and central parts of Kerala as in northern side. It is further to be noticed that the observance of purdah is more in the coastal towns like Beemapalli, Edava (Trivandrum), Kayamkulam (Quilon), Mattancheri (Cochin), Chavakkad, Triprayar, Vadanappalli (Trichur), etc. in southern and central Kerala from where gulf emigration took place. Even in the north, it is widely found in towns like Kasaragod, Kannur, Tellicherry, Mahe, Calicut etc. Those who wear the veil accept its various forms, fashions and designs. The *burqa*, as we call here, is neither uniform in size nor in its designs. Some elderly women, especially, the women of the Syed (Thangal) family use a head to feet dress using the *niqab* (face cover) exposing only the eyes with a net or without a net. Others normally use the veil with a single piece from neck to the toe and a separate headcover covering the whole hair and the ear. Some varieties of the scarf even overlap the forehead reaching upto the eyebrow. This is the most popular type of veil used in the present day Kerala without allowing a single hair to peep through. Some girl students use very rarely a type of veil which reaches a little above the ankle and partly open in the bottom, with which they could expose their inner garments like the Churidar or the Jeans. These are the selections of the fashion conscious among the youngsters. Being a thriving industry, the purdah manufacturers are highly vigilant and market conscious, and they frequently innovate the models to attract changing demands of the consumers. There are veils with exclusive body shape designs and partially transparent, which practically defeat the purpose of the purdah system.

Moreover, in Kerala, as in other Islamic societies, the issue of covering the face also has become a topic of debate. Among the four traditional Imams, it is only the Hanafi school that considers the face-veil (niqab) not obligatory. All others, Shafi, Maliki and Hambali view the face-veil obligatory. Modern Islamist theorists like Al-Albani (Syria/Jordan). Mohd. Al-Ghazzali (Egypt), and Yousuf al-Qaradawi believe that veil basically is obligatory and an inalienable identity of Muslim women. Albani, being a staunch salafi, argues that *Khimar* (covering) does not mean the covering of the face, but the covering of the head only. He also refers about a woman who came to Caliph Omar by wearing *Jilbab* (female covering). But Omar told her to remove the covering from her head since she is a slave and *Jilbab* is meant for free women. It also indicates that such a face cover is a privilege of free believing women, but not obligatory[31]. Mohammed Al-Ghazzali in his noted volume the *Prophetic Sunna* devotes a Chapter on female covering, 'The Battle of Hijab', and argues against the covering of face. He also questions the authenticity of some of the traditions (hadiths) about female face-covering. He does not consider the face as *awra* (nakedness). The writings and speeches of Ghazzali have great influence not only in the Islamic world but in all Islamic societies where it had new penetrations as in Europe and America. His style of language noted for its rhetoric instigated Islamists, who stand for the new revival of Islam not only in the outward expositions or symbols like the veiling, but for giving an intellectual and ideological basis to its present claim of world domain. Following Ghazzalli, Yousuf al-Qaradawi, made several scholastic discourses on the issue of the face-veil. He says that it is possible to look at the other sex within the limits of Islamic rules, without sexual desire. For the women, as for the men, she is also permitted to look with decency and lowering of the gaze[32]. Majority of scholars believe that the verse on *hijab*, "Prophet, tell your wives, your daughters, and women believers to make their outer garments hang low over them so as to be recognized and not insulted" (33:59) is aimed at the Prophet's wives only[33].

Any debate on the *hijab* and *niqab* the extent and the mode of covering will not end conclusively as great Islamic scholars themselves differ on such matters. In the Middle East, the 'Arab Cultural base pattern', reflecting the view of the Salafi scholars of Saudi Arabia, dominates in shaping the ideology of the veiling. In Kerala also different streams of thought take the issue of veiling to their requirement as per their lineage to the ideologues of the Arab world. In our examination and observation, what we could notice is the contradiction due to the complexities of interpretations of the different verses of the Quran and the huge corpus of hadiths (traditions). As mentioned already, there is a sharp contrast between the interpretation based on the western cultural pattern with the already existing Arab cultural pattern. This is evident from several of our discussions with women who are veiled, partially veiled and not veiled at all. They have their own explanations and arguments based on the religious texts. Our interviews and dialogues with Islamists and liberals bring out several facts behind the practice of veiling, apart from the social pressures and religious compulsions. Whether it is in the Arab world or in the west, or in any society where Islam dominates, customs and historical traditions play dominant roles in creating perceptions and attitudes, particularly when *urf* (customs) is accepted as a legal concept in the Maliki and the Hanafi schools. Historical traditions also tend to formulate a cultural background for many of the paradigms of the present day social life. A misconception has developed in recent years that veiling or re-veiling is a return to the Quran and traditions. Such a propaganda had a great influence in Islamic societies like Kerala where women are not properly educated even in religion to grasp the real meanings of the tenets. They mostly go to hear the discourses of the Islamist enthusiasts who have nothing to disclose or to propose, except some visionary ideologies.

The observance of purdah also invites a basic question whether human rights are possible in such a society. Whatever arguments that the Islamists have, the veil degenerates the individual's self and such a woman becomes inferior to men atleast in some degree with the destined submission. Though not directly, it becomes an impediment in women's progress. Veiling in a dubious way curbs girl's right to education, because pious parents believe that insistance for proper veiling in the case of adolescent girls is not either possible or effective in a mixed society. An abrupt change in such a situation may cause, as mentioned earlier, some psycho-neurotic problems in youngsters. While describing the importance and nature of human rights, Mary Robinson, Former United Nations High Commissioner for Human Rights, has this to say.

> Human rights are inscribed in the hearts of people;
> They are there long before law makers drafted their first proclamation[34].

It clearly indicates that human rights are not even the inalienable right of men, as we often say, but are the inborn rights, that nobody can deny to any human being in any space or in any time. A woman basically has the right to have a life with dignity and honour. She has even the right to live free from violence at the hands of her own husband or parents. It is true that discrimination against women violates the principles of equality of rights and respect for human dignity. The imposition of veiling of any kind on women should be viewed in such a context where their freedom and dignity are challenged. Moreover, a major share of Muslim women never knew the freedom and human rights they deserve as per our constitution and international law. Women in the Islamic society of Kerala also suffer silently all such discriminations and disabilities on account of the reason that they are women alone. Moreover, even in the case of following the religion, Quran is very liberal and it emphatically says, that "there is no compulsion in religion" (2:256). If this is the case of the religion itself, what importance has to an outer garment like purdah and for its compulsion? Again, the ban against the veil also created some problems in countries like Turkey and Iran in the initial stage, because in many countries, veil was a part of their cultural baggage and they could not remove it because they were accustomed to it for generations.

It is to be remembered that, Whether male or female dress is absolutely a personal matter and the fundamental right of a citizen. Nobody in a democratic system has the right to impose any dress of their choice over others. The excessive interplay of religion and communalism also interferes in such situations and intensify the "issues" which infact are absent among themselves. Innocent people also develop a "fear complex" and a "sense of insecurity" which ultimately make the life dreadful and uncertain. No doubt that, in Kerala, a religious strife and alienation of communities to some extent are caused as a result of making the dress as a religious symbol. Human minds are separating apart, without any hope of return, making great recess in the communal fabric of Kerala.

In Kerala, the extensive use of purdah among Muslim women increased recently as a result of the question of identity necessitated after various communal issues like the Babri Masjid and the issue of Muslim Personal Law associated with the Shah Bano case in addition to the various communal tensions and outbreaks in different parts of the country. In the ongoing analysis, what we have examined is the different strategies that the secularist-liberal discourses offered in contrast to the so called "Islamist" or fundamental thesis on the issue of the veil in the post-colonial situations, importantly after independence. The polemics often arise out of the varied interpretation of modernity, both by the Islamists and by the secularists. In Kerala, what we could experience is the ideological combine of the conservatives and the Islamist 'modernists' (revivalists) upholding cultural difference on all issues concerning the gender, purdah and family life. This is mainly on account of the feminist agenda as defined by European colonizers focusing on the veil alone in their attempt to belittle the orient and Islam. There is also one argument that while the West complain the oppression of women in Islam, they did not totally deny patriarchy as found in the western society. Neither they accept the regional ethos other than the West. Therefore, the Islamists always subsist on such a propaganda, and instead of absorbing the particularities of the region, they insist on a uniform Islamic model as a substitute to the western model. Western narrative of Islam as oppressor and the West as liberator work well, though negatively, in all Islamic societies the world over, particularly, with regard to women and the veil. Hence, under the guise of resistance to imperialism, Islamic idealogues advocate for a return journey virtually making the society stagnant and unproductive. Veiling for them, is a restoration to normalcy, and its denial invites the innovation of the West which is highly "detrimental" to the whole belief system. This is the vicious circle that develops in the dialogue on the veil, for all those, whether the West or the Islamist, who evolve strategies of domination in the present day Kerala. A famous tradition of the Prophet goes like this:

> God does not look upon your bodies and appearances,
> He looks upon your hearts and deeds.

Notes and References

1. Haideh Moghissi, *Populism and Feminism in Iran: Women's Struggle in a Male-Dominated Revolutionary Movement,* Mac Millan, London, 1994, p. 183. *See* also Mahnaz Afkhami, (ed.) *In the Eye of the Storm: Women in the Post revolutionary Iran*, London, 1994.
2. Zeinab al-Ghazali, *Al-Da'iya,* Ibn-al Hashmi (Compl.) Cairo, 1989, p. 76.
3. Alya Baffa'un, *Social Science Research and women in the Arab World,* Paris, 1984, p. 41.
4. Fouad Zakaria, "The Stand point of Contemporary Muslim Fundamentalists", in Nahid Toubia (ed.) *Women of the Arab World: The Coming Challenge,* Zed, London, 1988, p. 32.
5. Mahmud Abd al-Sami Sha'ban, *Nizam al-usrah*, Darul Ulum, Cairo, 1983, p. 341 in Y.Y. Haddad and John L. Esposito (ed.), *Islam, Gender and Social Change* Oxford, 1998. p. 16.
6. Muhammed al-Ghazali, *Our Beginnings in Wisdom* (trans.) Ismail R. Faruqi, Washington, 1953, p. 111.
7. Ziauddin Sardar, *What do Muslims Believe*? Granta Books, London, 2006, p. 79.
8. Fathima Mernissi, *The Veil and the Male Elite, A Feminist Interpretation of Women's Rights in Islam,* Basic Books, London, 1987, p. 96.
9. *Ibid.*, p. 97.

10. Al-Tabari, *Tafsir al-Quran,* Dar al-Ma'rifa, Vol. 22, Cairo, p. 26.
11. Mernissi, *op. cit.,* p. 92.
12. Al-Suyuti, *Lubab al' uqul fi asbab al-nuzul,* (Rev. edn.) Dar Ihya al-Ilm, Beirut, 1984, p. 13.
13. *See* Amina Wadud, *Inside the Gender Jihad, Women's Reform in Islam,* Oxford, 2006.
14. Marmaduke Pickthall, *Cultural side of Islam* (Mal. Trans.) Hasan, K., Minar Publications, Trivandrum, pp. 132-138. This work is a compilation of eight lectures that Pickthall made in Madras in1927. He sees Islam not mere as a religion, but a cultural force.
15. *Ibid.*, p. 139.
16. For details *See*, Edward Said, *Orientalism*, Penguin, 2003, Samuel Huntington, *The Clash of Civilizations—The Debate,* Foreign Affairs, New York, 1996.
17. Abdullahi Ahmed, An-Na'im, "Shariah and Basic Human Rights Concerns" in Charles Kurzman (ed.) *Liberal Islam*, Oxford University Press, New York, 1998, p. 238.
18. Ernest Renan, *Complete Works*, Paris, 1947, Vol. II, p. 333.
19. Vincent Smith, *Akbar, the Great Mughal*, Delhi. He also qualifies the rule as under the "monstrous regiment" of unscrupulous women.
20. Roland E. Miller, *Mappila Muslims of Kerala*, Orient Longman, Madras, 1992 (edn.), p. 251.
21. Marina Lazreg, *Questioning the Veil, Open Letters to Muslim Women,* Princeton University Press, New York, 1996. *See* also her *The Eloquence of Silence: Algerian Women in Question,* Routledge, New York, 1994.
22. Information based on the interviews and case studies from April to October, 2010 from Institute of Mental Health, Calicut, and from the Department of Psychiatry, Medical College, Calicut.
23. The incident attracted the attention of all in Kerala and the reports in newspapers from 15th to 25th September, 2010.
24. M. N. Karasseri, *A Mercy Petition for Muslim Women* (Mal.) D.C. Books, Kottayam, 2008, pp. 39-40.
25. N.P. Mohammed, *Maram* (The Tree), D.C. Books, Kottayam, 2007.
26. P.M. Binu Kumar, *Kalakaumudi* (Mal.), Oct. 11. 2009, pp. 16-26. But the concept of 'Love Jihad' has been totally rejected by the Home Minister and DGP of Kerala. To him its is often a fabricated story by some extremists from the opposite side to make communal tension and divide in the state. Here the case of two students, Sneha and Anna (both pseudonames) are described in such a way to provoke the respective communities to act or to react. Abdul Hamid, State Secretary of the Popular Front (the alleged party that instigate for the 'Love Jihad') finds it only a trickery of Sree Rama Sena as done in Mangalore. But the pity is that even constitutional institutions like the High Court of Kerala made some comments on the issue without much enquiry or proper evidence, probably putting emotions over reality.

27. J.E. Peterson, "The Political Status of Women in the Arab Gulf States", *Middle East Journal,* Winter, 1989, p. 50.
28. Samira Fayyed, "Future Opportunities and Prospects for Women in Islam" in the Seminar on Muslim-Christian dialogue at Vatican, in Rome, June 1992.
29. Anne Sofie Roald, *Women in Islam The Western Exeprience,* Routledge, London/ NewYork 2002 (edn.), p. 256.
30. Mai Yamani, *Feminism and Islam,* Ithaca Press, London, 1996.
31. See Al-Albani, *Jilbab al-mar'a l-muslima* (The Muslim Women's Dress), Amman, 1950.
32. Al-Qaradawi, *Fatwa Mu'asira* (Legal Decisions), Vol. I: 431, Kuwait, 1996.
33. The Arabic idiom *adna al-jilbab* means 'make it hang low' not 'wrap around ' as some translators have assumed.
34. Message of the High Commissioner, 4 December 1998, in Geraldine Terry *Women's Rights,* Palgrave, Macmillan, 2007, p. 24.

6

Tradition vs. Modernity

The Question of Equality and Empowerment

With all the ideological and revivalistic advancements made in the Muslim society of Kerala in the 20th century, it is the women folk of that society suffered the most in the conflict between tradition and modernity. It is true that several movements have enlivened the Muslim masses in general but consciously or unconsciously the major share of its women were either marginalized or segregated in the issue of shariah and seclusion. Though centrad around internal and puritanical reforms, such movements have never made a radical change in the status of women who forms more than 50 p.c. of the population. Instead, the neo-revivalists' schemes of reform and education further pushed them back to stay in the conventional and static cauldron. While recognizing a few 'dynamic souls' who have done some spade work to reform both the society and its women, though not with that much magnitude leading to modernization, the general aversion, and vehement opposition of the traditional ulemas and religious functionaries practically retarded the whole move on the excuse of the introduction of western education.

Any attempt at reform practically meant with a passion for the freedom of Islam and a passion for the reform of Islam. Though the literary contributions of a few writers and enthusiasts have made some positive attempts in this direction of female emancipation, that too did not go either deep into the problem of creating a liberal society or to combat the conservatives effectively.

Eventhough women make up half the population, they have endured discrimination in most societies for thousands of years. Womens' empowerment is intertwined with respect to human rights, gender equality and socio-economic development. Therefore, all social scientists consider women's equality as a prerequisite for development of any society. While empowering women, it aims to inspire them with the courage to break free from the chains of limiting belief patterns and the societal or religious conditioning that have traditionally kept suppressed and unable to express their inherent strength and power. It is a fact that the empowered woman moves through the world with a sense of confidence and grace. Her once reckless spirit is now softened by wisdom, and slowly, but firmly she speaks her truth without doubt or hesitation and the life thus she leads becomes one of her own creation. Those who examined the issues of Muslim women in India have developed some misconceptions and stereotypes to demean the religion with particular reference to ulemas in whose jargon women are 'Naqisal Aql' or 'intellectually inferior' than men. This is on account of their seclusion and marginalization from which they could not be relieved easily in the present situation. They have been internalized and have accepted all kinds of roles their men want them to be. They are told that this is what they are made to do and accept everything silently leading to a faceless and voiceless life in their social circle.

The majority of Muslim women in India are neither opinion makers nor decision makers. The most unfortunate thing is that they never realize what kind of status they have got even from Quran and the traditions of the Prophet. India's Muslims constitute 13 per cent in which their women forms more than half of it with a poor human development index, low income, illiteracy and unemployment. In a rapidly developing India, their position is so 'miserable' as the recent commission headed by Justice Sachaar has revealed[1]. It is true that they have maintained their religious and minority identity within the purview of constitutional protections. But on the otherside, they were losing great opportunities due to the resistance to innovations or modernizing influences, destined to have the lowest literary rates which only causes to insulate them from progressive forces.

Muslim women face multiple marginalization both within the community and outside. The growing wave of communal forces, particularly after the demolition of Babri Masjid in 1992 and Gujarat Carnage in 2002, has made women in the Muslim community more vulnerable. To make it worse, they bear the brunt of poverty, lack of education, inequality and lack of opportunity within their community. Both the Prophet and the Caliphs of the early period gave women all sorts of freedom and equal opportunity to involve in all human activities including warfare. Those who closely associated with the Prophet themselves were women of great potential and caliber including intellectual.

Gender Equality Quranic Concepts

It is also to be noted that the Meccan aristocracy and the rich were the first to oppose Mohammed and his religion. His reforms and new approaches towards women greatly annoyed them because it was a break from the past, particularly of the pre-Islamic age. Women, whether wives, mothers, sisters or slaves, were all bodily transferred to the next rightful heir and they can dispose them off to their whims and fancies. Women have no right to inherit anything, and after the death of the father or brother, they have no clan to anything and whatever inherited were shared by the male members of the class of the husband, usually, if not by men of her own clam rarely. A woman, whether wife or sister, was a commodity for the heirs and her future will be decided not by herself, but by the male members of the inherited clan. When a man died, his eldest son could claim the widow, and marry her, if she is not his mother. The claim will be more if she has great property accumulated from her own clan. At the time of inheritance, a wife, seemed to be nothing but a commodity, like any other movable article, to be claimed by male heirs. The new laws in Islam questioned such systems and practices and stressed the idea that any individual, whether male or female, is a subject. A Quranic verse, in the chapter on Women reads,

> Do not covet what God has given to
> some of you more than others –
> Men have the portion they have earned;
> And women the portion they have earned-
> You have rather ask God for some of His bounty (4:32)

Here both men and women are given His gifts equitably and advises to be content with what they have without jealousy to whom have more. This perhaps substantiate the right of inheritance of a woman which has revealed earlier in verse 19 of the same chapter. It reminds the believers,

> You who believe, it is not lawful for you to inherit women against their will, nor should you treat your wives harshly, hoping to take back some of the bride-gift you gave them, unless they are guilty of something clearly outrageous. Live with them in accordance with what is fair and kind.

Here Quran warns the possession of women against their will. They may be wife or slave or a dependant. It also prohibits the marriage without her proper consent or willingness. Even men who embraced Islam and having heavy wealth and booty never showed any compromise with such verses of the Quran or its egalitarian teachings. These verses are as a result of the pressures of women in Medina while they were compelled to be remarried as per the pre-Islamic custom with the intention of the possession of her property. The case of Umm Kajja and Kubaysha Bint Ma'an are examples. They in the company of other women constantly visited the Prophet and complained the problems faced them due to such practices. The new verse really curtailed license of men to keep women under their control even after she is divorced legally. Moreover, in Muslim family law, the practice called Khul, continues in one form or the other, where if a woman wanted to have a divorce, she has to pay an amount to her husband if he agrees to give her freedom[2].

Inspite of the fact that Islam always provided equality towards women in all human spheres, there are still attempts to violate it in all spaces of men's dominance. Here the mullahs and other religious functionaries take the lead. Instead of going to the light of its main thematic message, they often go to the darkest side of its ambiguity by misinterpretation. As in the case of polygamy, divorce and inheritance, this could be seen in the law of female evidence also. The Quran refers to two men or four women as witnesses in a specific situation of taking a debt or a loan, which the later interpreters argued that the worth of a woman is only half of the man. The Quran is never discriminate towards women. A verse from the Quran is highly illustrative of this. It reads,

> .... If any one kills a believer by mistake he must free one Muslim slave and pay compensation to the victim's relatives, unless they charitably forgo it; If the victim belonged to a people at war with you but is a believer, then the compensation is only to free a believing slave; If he belonged to a people with whom you have a treaty, then compensation should be handed over to his relatives, and a believing slave set free. Any one who lacks the means to do this must fast for two consecutive months by way of repentance to God. (4:92)

This verse from the Chapter on 'Women' clearly reveals that Islam discourages slavery. The gender of the victim is not specified. If the female has only half the worth, this could have been particularly spelt out. Since Islam emerged as a religion to liberate man kind from ignorance and superstition, it pronounces the value of justice and equality irrespective of sex, sect or status. Hence all noted women of the Prophetic Age and immediately after, like Beebi Khadeeja, Umm Salama, Aisha and Sukanya, enjoyed all sorts of freedom that a woman could be, without any infringement. In the life of these women and their successors, what we could feel is, that the Prophet agreed and allowed all the divinely sanctioned things to the community including women. He and his companions could not prohibit what he is not entitled to do as revealed in the Quranic Chapter, 'Repentance'. It states

> Fight those of the People of the Book
> Who do not forbid what God and His
> *Messenger have forbidden*......... (Emphasis added) (9:29)

The life style of the Prophet's period itself is a brilliant testimony of his discreet allowance for matters practiced by them within the Quranic injunction, but malice towards none. The verse above clearly means that the Prophet forbids that which God forbids. This also indicates that the Prophet could not forbid anything on his own. Hence, since the Prophet is silent or did not interfere in the freedom of women, we could presume that he was totally in agreement with the natural justice and equality that women as human beings and citizens deserve in a living society. This has been further confirmed by another verse in the chapter on 'Prohibition' (66:1), revealed in the context of an incident connected with his wives in the Prophet's home[3]. The intention of the Quran is to create a balanced and shared society. It should be reviewed with much concern of mutual responsibility between the males and the females, whether husband and wife, brother and sister, or any man and woman. 'As Syed Qutub observes, man and women are both from God's creation and He never intends to oppress any one of his creation[4]. Therefore, both the Quran and the Sunnah of the Prophet ideally vouch for the rights and privileges of women and it often warns that if any breach of that occurred, it will be dealt with severely.

With all such Quranic and divinely ordained protections, Muslim women are harassed and ill-treated in the name of some "religious laws" in most of the countries of the world, including India. The basic problem lies in the fact that women are often treated as weak, inferior and intellectually backward. With such a preconception, the males try to approach any issue concerning women, and make conclusions. This primordial lacuna, both in the reading of the religious scriptures and evaluating women are rampant in all spaces the world over, where women and their issues are discussed. Such a prejudice over women is not a legacy of the Orient or Islam alone, but is of a major chunk of the societies in the West also. The pedantic attitude of men offering equality and privileges to women so "liberally" in all socio-economic dealings virtually creates an idea of a 'donor' and a 'recipient' It is from here that emerged the disequilibrium between men and women and to the eradication of which we (both the male and the female) fight for such a long time. While biology of the female, on some occasions, marginalises them, men feel a superiority over them as the protector, leader, caretaker etc. enjoying completely the opportunities available to him. Thus whatever remains to women was "psychologically repressed and over shadowed by institutionalizing and socially legitimating male values that had the effect of creating self-fulfilling prophecies"[5].

The issues of Rayana in Kasaragod in Kerala (discussed earlier) and Irfana of U.P., are to be evaluated in this context where we could see how males dominate over religion and society and dictate things to their credit and honour. Irfana, aged 28, wife of a rickshaw puller and mother of five children, living Charthawal village in Uthar Pradesh, was raped by her father-in-law. When the case came to the body of village elders, they adjudicated that even her marriage must be dissolved because Irfana had become 'haram' (sinful) "since she had entered into a relationship with her husband's father.". They often act as judges and jury though they have no official jurisdiction other than the respect the local people give to them. (In many Indian villages almost all communities and tribes have depend on such bogus courts, and people take issues over there, rather than complaining to civil/criminal courts of the judiciary, functioning mostly in towns). In the case of the poor innocent Irfana, the so-called community leaders, pronounced the verdict claiming to be on the base of Shariah, without any further examination or going to the details of the case. The pity is that Darul Uloom, the country's Supreme Islamic Seminary in Deoband (U.P.), upheld the verdict issuing a *fatwa*. Moreover the All India Muslim Personal Law Board, a national arbiter of Islamic affairs with 41 Islamic Scholars endorsed the verdict. The victim got justice only after the case taken to a criminal court with the interference of the women's council[6]. Uzma Naheed, a close associate of Darul Uloom, after visiting all the states in India, observes that the condition of Muslim women is "miserable". This means that all the Shariah attached bodies like the Darul Uloom, All India Muslim Personal Law Board etc. realize the problems that face their women from various dimensions, but they could not break the walls of rigidity with the crowning ignorance that govern them. It is not over the true religion they depend, but only over the by-gone man-made traditions and rituals, to the requirement of their dominance.

A major share of Muslim women all over the world live in a traditional environment surrendering everything to their men folk and without the awareness of their rights and privileges. They are feared of modernity, as an instrument to the loss of their identity. The ideology of identity originated in countries like Egypt, Pakistan, Algeria and in Iran, and which later exported to other countries including South Asia, always stressed on the exclusiveness of Women and the curtailment of their rights. Unlike those of the West, Muslim women are culturally multifarious, though with a loose-knit of religion. The much publicized present day western culture, as they themselves claim, is homogeneous, especially when it is brought under the canopy of the Church which has a universal character. To find out and fight out an enemy, they have to equalize and locate a force of similar strength and potential in their march towards colonial accomplishments. To which the West consider Islam and its world as their arch enemy and fighting force. Idealogues like Huntington also anticipates a "clash" between the (Christian) west and the Islamic orient, though he is subtle about the term 'Christian'. But in all his arguments, he brings forth religion as a major factor in distinguishing civilizations. He says, "Differences among civilizations are not only real, they are basic. differentiated from each other by history, language, culture, tradition and, *most important, religion*" (emphasis mine). He further argues that more than ethnicity, religion discriminates sharply and exclusively among people. A person can be half-french and half-Arab and simultaneously even a citizen of two countries. It is more difficult to be half-Catholic and half -Muslim[7]. The western complaints against Islam that their women are oppressed get more solidification as a result of their further marginalization and seclusion with instruments like purdah. This pressure on women could be seen as a revenge and resistance to the west and its culture. Islamic intransigency compels their women to resist this opposing culture instead of fighting to have their own human rights from within. Any traditionalist debate on women will be a losing battle for them because it is found more often deductive and preconceived.

Moreover, the emergence of revivalist Islam in recent years, practically turned off all attempts at the reform of women in a liberal perspective. This travel, by turning back, is on the excuse of the western propaganda against Islam, mainly projecting issues like the denial of human rights to women and terrorism. The dilemma of the modernists is that they have to fight in two dimensions both internally and externally. Internal includes a re-reading of the dogmas with a basis on socio-political recognition. External magnitude encompasses a universal discourse based on cultural diversity and liberal modernization, but with a protective wall against the reinforcing western hegemony in the intellectual and cultural arenas. Instead of bringing everything to a forum for free debate, Islamists restrict it without allowing any possible encroachment to its structure. So long as this continues, the inequality and breach of rights will prevail. Unlike other societies, Islamic societies all over the world, now confront with another major issue of organized political involvement as found in Iran after the revolution and in Pakistan in recent times. Clerical *fatwas* legislations and periodical governmental interference on issues related to religion are all indicative of such a transformation gradually, grabbing the Muslim world[8]. The Draft of an Islamic Constitution' issued by the Al-Azhar University, Cairo (ofcourse with the pressure of the fundamentalist Muslim Brotherhood) and the Constitution of the Islamic Republic of Iran and the recent attempts of Pakistan to make it more 'Islamic' are the developments to testify this course of action, though not desirable to a major share of the people in the Islamic world including the countries of their origin.

Acceptance of any Islamic symbol including purdah is purely optional. Many Muslim Feminists wear the purdah while they oppose the same, as Siti Musdah Mulia, one of the champions of gender equality in Jakarta. She considers Islam more friendly to women. She disowns the divinity of marital law and says, "the whole marital law is men-made, none of it is a fax from heaven. The concept of equality and fraternity must not be claimed as western."[9]. Conflict with tradition and modernity begins usually as a result of male dictation and dominance over women in the socio-cultural life. In Kerala, in recent years, several issues have arisen due to such attempts of dominance in matters like divorce, social ostracism and polygamy. The incident in the Marakkara Panchayat (Malappuram District) in July 2003, is so shameful to the community that a husband has denied to stay with his wife on account of an alleged Talaq (triple talaq) that he made in one of his letters to his wife[10]. The mosque committee of the Mohalla including the Qazi and the community leaders ostracized the whole family claiming that a divorced wife could not be taken back by her 'former husband' without undergoing the ritual marriage by herself and another man. The cardinal point behind this issue is: (1) Is the *Muttalaq* valid, if it utters in one sitting? Or (2) Is it valid only if done in three different occasions in time and space? The Islamic law supports the 2nd one only, because it provides a lot of time for reconsideration and repentance leading to reunion. Moreover, several conditions have to be fulfilled before such an event. For example, the husband must be mentally normal, highly matured, and free form the fire of wrath when he pronounces the talaq. Even if it happens, divorce could not be materialized if he repents and says that it is not intentional[11]. Such cruel incidents in the name of religion are becoming so common, particularly affecting women, in different parts of Kerala. It is true that Islamic enthusiasts exploit the situation citing such incidents in other Islamic countries and Muslim dominated areas in India like UP and Bihar. While the medias, particularly visual medias like TV expose it with a negative aim and purpose, the Islamist extremists and obscurantists acquire more zeal and utilise it positively to achieve their goal as recently seen in Kasaragod (issues related to purdah, as referred to earlier) and Thodupuzha in Ernakulam district where a teacher's hand was amputated, alleging that he had blamed the Prophet[12].

Against Law and Liberty

Ofcourse the extremists get energy to provocation and to justify their action nationally and internationally. The demolition of Babri Masjid and the Liberhan Report that followed, the Gujarat carnage and some court verdicts (including Tahalka Report) etc. are often highlighted to achieve their aim of making a communal polarization leading to enmity and hatred which never could be tolerated in any civilized democratic society. The attacks on USA in 2001 and the London Bombings in 2005 are some of the serious warnings that the extremists have attempted on the West as a "test dose" as the alleged master of mind of the events, "Al Qaeda", "claimed" later. This, in one sense, is a questioning of the creditability of the much acclaimed "democracy and freedom" of the West and its monolithic culture. The disintegration of Soviet Union made their work easy and the West, primarily USA claiming as the "peace maker of the world", confirms their presence often by incursions and annexations, as happened in Vietnam, Iraq, Afghanistan and in may other countries in the Middle East. The Islamists soon realized this oil oriented neo-colonialism imposed at the excuse of democracy, freedom and modernity, and began to oppose with their rigid ideology of extremism at the expense of religion. They also highlight several incidents in countries like Switzerland voted to ban minarets for Muslim Mosques, the French resistance to scarf and the wearing of purdah by Muslim women, the Netherlands which refused to ban a film named *Fitna* to blame Islam and its culture[13]. This is apart from the

Cartoon controversy of Denmark. The blatant, criticism of Tony Blair, former British premier, Islam, and the news of insulting the Quran by American soldiers in the Guantanamo Bay by flushing it down in a toilet, created much violence and protests in Afghanistan and Pakistan[14].

Recently in states including Kerala, Shariah is being misused by the fundamentalist groups as in other parts of the world. Extremist idealogues and their supporters will not miss any chance to implement their 'Shariah based' action plan not only in the Islamic countries like Afghanistan, Pakistan or its core centres in the Middle East, but even in countries like Great Britain, France and Netherlands. Everywhere personal liberty is being questioned in the name of Shariah and by misusing Quranic tenets and traditions of the Prophet. In addition to the hard-core groups, comparatively the more 'sophisticated' revivalist sects like the Mujahids and the Jama'atis, also train the students and youth in such a way that they are the true representatives of a 'cultural Islam', stressing more for changes external than for internal. These new carriers of the resurgent Islam are really a threat for modernism and liberal Islam. These contigents with the aid of the extremists groups oppose all trends of modernity often quoting some of the incidents in France or in Britain or in Netherlands. The centres of religious discourses and even Madrassas are utililzsed for their propagandas to save the religion from the impact of the west and its culture. These revivalist sects have their own exclusive centres of learning and those who underwent their studies from such centres will be rigid and uncompromising in their approach not only in religion but even in social life.

Moreover, these sectarian groups have their own establishments and institutions as a result of the government policy of promoting religious minorities. Since all of them are meant for a particular religious group, others won't go over there naturally, making such institutions exclusively singular. Here they have no chance of mixing and interacting with others without any scope of developing a pluralistic culture. In fact this is the greatest value we get back to the "merit" of the minority/sectarian establishments built on constitutional rights. In a democratic and secular country like that of ours, it is a dangerous experience to see disproportionate rise of private institutions (educational etc.) not corresponding to the fall in the public sector. Here too the worst sufferers are the females who seldom get chances to mingle with others in an open society. Moreover religious seminaries and Madrasahs are imparting learning centred on religion alone, and the true secular and liberal education is practically denied to them. The shelled education with a walled life, till the age of 20 or 22, when most of them get married, marginalize them from the realities of a modern life. This is a clear negation of equality and human rights that others enjoy.

To overcome such hurdles and to defend women's rights, several organizations have come in different parts of the world. Baobab for Women's Human Rights in Nigeria is a good example. This is made under Muslim laws, the Sharia criminal legislation, passed in the northern Nigerian states (where Muslims are in majority) in 2000. While Shariah was imposed on women unjustly, nobody could resist it. When a woman makes a charge of rape, she has to produce four male witnesses of 'impeccable character', which could not be possible in the case of most women. The irony is that not a single woman witness is called for as witness. Again, who decides the impeccability of the witness is also a question, possibly again a male. Moreover, in states like Zanfara in Nigeria, the practice of 'policing' women's clothes by gangs of young men also made life for women horrible. They even banned women travelling along with men in public conveyances and taxis. These man-made restrictions without any base in Islamic law were imposed causing life unbearable not only for women, but for all those who live in a civilized society. There are instances of unlawful punishments like flogging and stoning to women for alleged fornication. Amina Lawal, a widow was sentenced to stonning to death for adultery even after her confession that she had a child while divorced. This verdict of the Shariah court was compelled to be repealed by the involvement of the court. Likewise the case of Briya Magazu, a 13 years old girl, charged for extramarital sex, was saved by legal challenge[15]. These incidents and several of such type in different parts of the world indicate that if the community and the court are involving in such issues and bringing them to the awareness of the public, a major share of cases of misuse of shariah could be avoided. A case of similar nature happened, in 1985, in Beemapally near Trivandrum in Kerala where a Muslim woman was alleged to have involved in adultery. Though the mosque authorities ordered for punishing her by flogging, the court interference saved the woman from such horror and harassment. Both the court and the public found on enquiry that the allegation is false and fabricated with personal grudge[16]. Moreover, the Quranic injunction, while prescribing punishment to both parties committed adultery (24:2), prescribes almost the same punishment to those who made false allegations on women with bad intentions[17]. It is also to be remembered that in Islam when prostitution does not come among the seven grave sins, false allegation on a chaste woman come in. Ofcourse these unhappy situations are on account of the ignorance of the Quranic injunctions and the role of civil law in a society. Those who are interested in money and power alone could not see matters in an egalitarian manner and more often their emotion supersede their intellect in decision making. In most cases the verdicts of such committees are in favour of men, even if they are found guilty. Sometimes, women, incapable of representing themselves, become easy victims in such situations.

For achieving equality and empowerment, an important handicap that faces the Muslim community is the unilateral divorce that takes place at an early age, especially in rural and backward areas. Girls, both educated and uneducated, are getting married very early and become mothers of one or two children before twenty. Low economic status and poor living conditions push their life into darkness and a blurred future. A survey on divorce recently made, reveals shuddering reports that in Kerala, in an average, 37 cases are taken to the court[18]. Though there is no separate account of Muslim women, that will not come below ten percent. In the case of Muslim women, it is not because that they are free from this threat, but they are not properly recorded or taken to the court of law, mainly due to unawareness, ignorance and poverty. Most of the men in that society feel that divorce is a right and it could not be questioned. They also do not know about the right of maintenance to both the mother and children after divorce. The NGOs and voluntary organizations also could not work properly among them due to social seclusion and closed nature of the family with false pride. Recently by the voluntary organizations through the present day "Kudumbasree" system, some improvements could be seen, by making them aware of their rights and also with financial and legal assistance. This is a great step forward to the upliftment of women, particularly of Muslim women in backward areas. While analyzing the reasons to the mushroom growth of orphanages in different parts of Kerala in recent years, one could realise the fact that it is due to the rampant and licencious divorce practiced by communities like Muslims, particularly in backward areas[19]. Uncared, neglected and ill attended children are taken to such orphanages providing food, shelter and education, giving a great relief to their mothers. Some of the orphanages are owned by the extremist theologians who train the students in accordance with their ideology.

If we make a close perusal of some of the terrorist activities in Kerala, we could easily connect their association, remotely in the case of some who involved in the issues. It is certain that one bereft of father or mother may develop a particular psyche with a tendency showing irresponsibility and destruction causing to be a social unfit. The mothers of such miscreants are the worst sufferers in these situations. The governmental role for rehabilitating such unfortunate widows and mothers "married living without husband" is very limited eventhough that has been taken up by the social welfare department. Therefore, since their work is very limited and highly in effective, voluntary organizations and NGOs should do something for their upliftment in society. We should also be vigilant not to allow them to be in the hands of the fundamentalists and extremists. It is up to the government to make the women aware of their rights and create self consciousness among them and to protect them from all sorts of exploitation. As A.R. Desai observes, it is only by a feminist analysis through a socialist vision, the idea of a welfare state could be possible[20].

Muslim women often are facing a grave problem from the hands of men who, instead of divorcing and freeing them, keep tied without caring and giving maintenance for her and their children. Either the community leaders or the shariah courts do not care such cases and the poor destitutes drag on their life till end. The judiciary also could not interfere because these cases are not properly identified or if any, not taken to the court. Further, she is eligible for *Fasq* (a divorce arranged by Khazi) and *Qula* (a divorce in complete agreement of the wife surrendering even the 'Mahr'). If it is not used, it is a surrender of her rights. The situation increased in Muslim society, recently as a revolt of the pressure and the change of life, created by Gulf money. The money thus acquired are not reaching to the family proper and to its enjoyment by all. Even after the passing of the new laws as that of 1986 and the reforms periodically made, the Muslims, out of ignorance, still stick to the old Shariah law of 1937.

Moreover, as Tahir Mahamood, an associate of the Indian Law Institute, observes, in Muslim Personal Law, there is no room for cultural traditions, and rituals that the people follow for generations[21]. But such an approach of making Shariah as a monolith and the only answer to various issues that may arise among Muslims living in different geographical and cultural regions of the country is not proper. In many Muslim societies there are still the practice of Hindu laws, particularly in the case of inheritance, division of property, marriage gifts etc. There are also differences among the Sunniites and Shiites. Among the Sunniites itself, slight variations in jurisprudence could be seen among the Shafiites, Hanafiites, Hambalis and Malikis. All these issues are not properly addressed in the British sponsored Shariah (1937) in India. These contradictions are also visible in the Shariah law prevalent among different Muslim communities all over the world. This conflict on the issue of property rights, particularly on the Will and Gift, still prevails among Khojas and Cutch Mamens, though they are only a microscopic minority living in the West Coast (mainly in Konkan and Maharashtra) region of India[22]. Such anomalies in Shariah law and Muslim personal Law are evident both in its content and in its application, apart from the natural drawbacks they carry. As usual, the male dominance and the ignorance with regard to the real intention of the relevant verses of the Quran and the traditions, are the reasons behind such misogynist interpretation of the various laws concerning women and the issues related to them. Both the Prophet and the early Imams and Jurists (*fuqahas*) gave ample space for further reasonable interpretations of the tenets. The present day issues are all due to the negligence, consciously or some times unconsciously, of such concessions like ijma to be followed in such contingencies which may arise while facing the realities of the modern world. Here a call like 'return to Quran' as echoed recently from some extremists corners, is quite misleading especially for those who go for a moderate path. Further the slogans like 'Save India' through Islam also have no meaning.

Here, men, dutiful of doing only right towards women, are usually found inactive or silent in situations where their involvement is highly essential. By providing equality and justice, they could be empowered to meet fresh challenges of modern society. To overshadow the legal status of women, there are attempts to impose a socio-cultural inferiority with the aid of religion and traditions. While arguing for the empowerment of women, one should make sure that they are enjoying natural justice, freedom, equal opportunity and above all, human rights.

The concept of modernism, in the eyes of the revivalists or neo-revivalists is totally different, particularly with the new interpretations of the Islamists like Mohammed Abdul Wahab, Hasanul Banna, Jamaludin Afghani, Rashid Rida and Abul A'la Mandodi. Their modernism is totally centred around the Quran and Sunna to meet the requirements of a modern society including its institutions and technology with a definite aim of restoring its strength and dynamism. To them, the adoption of modern science and technology actually meant a return to Islamic heritages, because modern European science is only an extension of the medieval classical Islamic contributions. Egyptian idealogues like Muhammed Abduh asserted that Muslims had to go for activism and resistance to European colonialism for their own welfare without a passive acceptance of foreign domination. In India, the attempts of Islamic modernism went through the hands of socio-political leaders like Sir Syed Ahmed Khan and Mohammed Iqbal. But their thrust on education, western or Islamic, led to a great leap for Muslims to get into liberal learning, especially of science. Both religion and science found a balance in the Aligarh and Jamia Millia movements with that of the Islamic seminary of Deoband, of course with the glaring contradictions in opposing degrees, but with the final victory of the liberals.

But the situation in places like Kerala is quite different. Here, colonial disturbances and resistance movements provided a new turn, especially after the event of 1921, resulting into a total retreat from modernist tendencies. The vaccum created by the revolution has become a fertile ground for the traditionalists and revivalists for the further crippling of the community. Hence, instead of absorbing modernist tendencies, religious rigidity and obscurantism found new dimensions in Kerala Muslim Society. Though such forces claimed a revivalist renaissance with the acceptance of secular education including English as a media of instruction, it never dared to go beyond the orbit of sectarian Islam like that of the Salafi, Jama'ati or the Sunniite. The restructured Madrassahs thus became practically, a buffer to the attainment of liberal education. Moreover, modernist influence, in recent years, diminished to a considerable extent on account of the perception that it has a compromise with western power and its culture along with the feeling that it is always opposed to Islam and its ethos. The periodical '*fatwas*' from seminaries like the Deoband (U.P.) and by some religious functionaries in Kerala, fully vouch for such an approach of the religious institutions in society as a whole and women in particular.

Question of Empowerment

Such a dilemma to the Muslim community likely to arise out of the pressures of the religious observations, could only be avoided by the wide acceptance of secular—liberal education and the economic empowerment. Because ignorance and economic backwardness often lead the poor masses in the community to be the victims of fake marriages, polygamy and such other practices. Some people have no other agenda than the exploitation of the weaker sections. There are several instances of such marriages with the pet name 'Arabikalyanam'(marriages with the incoming Arabs) in the coastal areas of Kerala, particularly in Calicut, in the recent past[23]. Here, parents of girls of the poor families, attracted by some money and gold, and often encouraged by some intermediaries or marriage brokers, soon become victims without realizing the harassment that follows. Some of them have been taken to unknown places where they are compelled to work in the household with the women of the same fate. There are also rare cases of some families who have become economically sound as a result of such alliances, though majority of cases are pointing negative in the graph. Surveys made in Calicut and Trivandrum speak of the intensity of the problem revealing its magnitude in an appalling degree.

In the coastal Trivandrum, particularly in the Beemapalli, Sankhu Mukham and Edava, Muslim families easily become prey to the practice of 'Malikalyanam', marriages with the men of the Mali Island near Trivandrum and the girls of the coast. Several cases of such marriages are revealed by parents living in the small huts in and around Beemapalli, Here also the exploitation begins with the interference of guides and drivers who brings men from Mali and induces poor families with girls of marriageable age. Here also the ignorance and economic backwardness causes the parents to enter into such alliances parcelling out their children to unknown frontiers of hardship, harassment and agony[24]. The pity here is that, those who shed crocodile tears for the security of minority and its women in particular, neither attend such ill doings against poor nor bring to the notice of the government or legal authorities. In this respect what we could see is the total negligence on the part of the religious organisations and NGOs with the meaningful silence of the governmental machinery. It is high time for the ulemas and social activists well-versed in Islamic theory, should educate and make the government aware of such instances, often misusing the religion. They could go with all reforms and modernity (coming even from outside), if it does not contradict with the Quran and Sunnah of the Prophet, and without apostasy and defection. Hence, it is not the religion that causes backwardness, but it is those who commercialize and politicize it for their own gain and betterment.

It is a well known fact that drastic changes have taken place in the socio-educational status of women since independence. But the condition of Muslim women continued the same without exposing the creative energies of Indian woman in all walks of life. Though leaders like Sir Syed Ahmed Khan and Poet Mohammed Iqbal in the pre-independent India have attempted to awake them from the age-old sluggishness and lethargy, it never had a substantial impact over them except in the case of some upper class women. The poor and the lowly never got the opportunity of going out of the kitchen. Our leaders in Independent India had a vision of emancipating them which actually reflected in the statement of Gandhiji to Mridula Sarabhai, a noted woman activist. " I have brought the Indian women out of the kitchen, it is up to you (the women activists) to see that they don't go back"[25]. After independence, the image of woman changed from a recipient of justice meekly to an ardent fighter for rights and justice. But in the case of Muslim women, they are still waiting in the corridors of injustice, extending their palms wide open. The much publicised economic prosperity or growth (that too in the upper class Muslims of urban centres) does not automatically shoot the graph of change in the gender front. The factors that facilitate for improvement like health, education and employment are rarely thrown open to them.

Moreover, communal polarization immediately after the partition, affected women of the community, as common in any tragedy, to a greater extent, compared to any other group or class. The post-revolt situation in Kerala (after 1921) has already been so congenial for preparing such a predicament of marginalization of communities like Muslims and more importantly of their women folk. The segregation of women, first with fear of molestation and loss of honour, and next with a revengeful urge for identity (both cultural and religious), practically pushed them to the periphery. Hence they were shut up in houses without education and social life.

> The religion based division of the country anticipated many of the questions that trouble us now across the sub continent: ethnicity, communalism, the rise of religious fundamentalism and cultural nationalism. Sharply, but poignantly, partition posed the question of "belonging" in a way that polarized choice and allegiance, aggravating old, and new, antagonisms. Subsequent contestations have revived and rephrased the questions in ever more complex ways, and how it is answered has far-reaching implication for women[29].

The Muslim retreat, began with the revolt of 1857 and intensified by the establishment of the colonial power, widely affected not only in the political arena, where they had supremacy in the past, but even in the socio-cultural life of the majority of them, irrespective of rural and urban. These factors, violence and silence, determined women's individual and collective destinies highly exposing religious and cultural singularity.

Since major share of Kerala Muslim women come within the category of middle and lower-middle classes, their economic fortunes and social status go far below, when compared to other communities belonging to the "backward classes". Here, women generally are unable to generate income as a result of several socio-cultural factors, which totally make them dependents on father, brother or husband. This economic dependency virtually makes them slaves in a patriarchal set up. But some economic variations also could be seen recently in the coastal belt and urban centres as a result of the new economic power and high standard of living they acquired by the 'gulf money'. But the majority still are among the most disadvantaged, economically impoverished and politically marginalised sections of Indian society. While others make great strides they are found crippled without even able to walk. This institutionalised inequality thrust upon their women by the dominance of a patriarchal society, knowingly or unknowingly, perpertuate social injustice, humiliation and ignominy. While explaining the genesis of the development problem among Muslims, many writers have attached great importance to the fact that there existed a delay in modernization among Muslims causing to create a rift among communities, but not among themselves.

Education and empowerment are the basic elements to the growth of any community. We have already examined the historical and socio-economic factors that made the Muslims for keeping out of secular education, without which they could not go for any employment. The uneducated and unarmed contingent could not also compete with others in the society who were really enjoying the "privileges" of the governance. This antagonism even explains the economic disparities and growth of communalism in the Indian situations[27]. The idea of 'Muslim separatist politics arose from Muslim backwardness' is a much discussed thesis. It is true that they were the principal victims of British rule. They lagged behind in education and failed to secure adequate representation in the services under the government. The origin of Muslim communalism could be traced to the backwardness of the community and to its denial of a legitimate share in power and economic opportunity. The Marxian concept of the 'loss of the old without any gain of the new' also explains the frustration and protest that develops in such classes negatively.

Though the obstacles to acquire empowerment and freedom for women are many, illiteracy and poverty are the two cardinal components that stand in the way for development. The lack of proper laws and their effective implementation also work as a major handicap to the growth of women. We know that laws do not exist in several areas of vital concern for women like sexual abuse and domestic violence. If any, they are inadequate. There is no easy solution to this complex situation where laws often act unfriendly, more often cruelly, towards women. Even the Supreme Court in an important judgement recognized that the lack of laws has an impact on the fundamental rights of women and observed that "violence against women is one obstacle to the achievement of the objectives of equality. Violence against women both violates and impairs or nullifies the enjoyment by women of their human rights and freedom"[28]. Such observations of the court reiterates that violence subjugates women and leads to inequality and that for the achievement of equality and human rights, issues of violence have to be addressed by the law. The crime reports in many states highlight the violation of women's rights, instead of ameliorating, push half of the humanity into further depths of degradation, making the goal of a human social order more distant. Condition of Muslim women and their living environment are far worse and they are the silent sufferers, not only on account of the lack of action of the civil laws, but of their own man-made religious laws. Hence to remove the fetters of inequality among them, one has to confront with all such forces, that debilitate them including the ideology of patriarchy. Without these, Muslim women's development and empowerment will remain empty promises. Moreover, the state washes off its hands, more often, in the issues of personal laws that rule over minority communities. While accepting Article 16(i) in conformity with its policy of non-interference in the affairs of minorities, it is mandatory to the state to "take appropriate measures to eliminate discrimination against women". Here, the state, while becoming sensitive to the "feelings" of the minority, virtually becomes enemies of their women. Without waiting for a consent from the fundamentalists, the state should proceed with its reforms and amendments to the betterment of the weaker and mute sections of the community, the women.

While evaluating the condition of Muslim women in Kerala after independence, one could see that they did not transform fundamentally in the socio-economic premises in which they live. Their position is still very poor, even after some education and reform implemented internally, compared to their sisters in other communities. This is more so particularly in issues related to marriageable age, higher education, polygamy, divorce and maintenance of both widows and children. When there is a sea change among the women of other communities, particularly in education, employment and empowerment, Muslim women with their age-old inhibitions and traditions became only silent and frustrated spectators adding to the burden of the family and the society at large. But this does not mean that there is no attempt for transformation anywhere. As referred to earlier, the exodus after the Revolt of 1921 and the carnage of the partition (1947) that went along, created havoc in the lives of Muslim families and the momentum of change decreased to a great extent. Though some of the urban centres in Malabar (Tellicherry, Cannanore and Calicut) showed tendencies of this change, the majority succumbed to the abyss of poverty and ignorance.

It is true, in Malabar, the colonial situations invigorated some Muslim families to go for higher and English education, particularly under the leadership of Muslim aristocrats like V.C. Mayan who taught his daughters English education at such an early period of 1930s. To teach Muslim girls in those days was a thunder bolt among the conservatives and they even characterised him as 'Kafir Mayan' (a non-believer) Amina Hashim, the eldest of Mayan's daughters was sent to the Punjab University to study Medicine. Her younger sister Aysha, acquired degree from Queen Mary's College, Madras, and become the Special Officer for Education in Malabar[29]. Another Muslim woman of great repute was T.C. Kunhachumma, a social worker, who secured an award from Arthur Hope, the Governor of Madras in 1934, for serving the victims of a storm and stampede at Tellicherry.

But with all such advances found among Muslim women, particularly in 40s and 50s of the last century, a sudden fall in their freedom and empowerment could be seen appallingly in the last five or six decades. Our analysis must go to this dimension, because the area once noted for its women's improvement, is now found in its lowest ebb It is here that one should find out reasons for its retreat, and the final marginalizatin. It is true that as women, they face with unequal treatment and discrimination from their family and society. It is not the tradition or the religion that create the lethargy, but among all other constituents, the hang over of the gulf money partially paralyses the Muslim society, importantly of their women folk who are denied to have freedom and to be educated and empowered with a gender bias. It is a fact that many seek excuses by putting matters into the furnace of cultural singularity arguing that social justice and equality could not be achieved culture-free. This also is a far-fetched contention realising only marriage, polygamy, divorce and inheritance. But one could not forget that as the ingredients of cultural autonomy, they are most important and crucial, especially economic justice. Moreover, there is remarkably different regional patterns, irrespective of religious traditions, associated with this component.

Again, in the sector of work force, the contribution of Muslim women in Kerala is less than 8 per cent when compared to others. Ofcourse, the cultural baggages with the religio-traditional pressures marginalised them without giving any opportunity to any creativity in the socio-economic life around them. Women's activities were centered in the home, and they were only expected to attend the household and child care. But some of them, particularly of lower income group, are now engaged in the income-generating activities which could be done in the confines of their home, such as weaving, sewing and embroidery and small-scale food production. But their involvement in the decision-making process is confined to domestic affairs, alone, usually involving the expenditure for home-making. The Muslim women's capability even to rule the country has been manifested effectively by the Beebees of Arakkal in Cannanore (Malabar), the only Muslim royal family reigned with the predominance of women. In the present day political scenario, which developed as a result of 50 per cent reservation for women, Muslim women, where they are in a majority, have come to the helm of affairs in the three-tier panchayat system and also in Municipalities and Corporations. While analysing South Asian Muslim women Anita. M. Weiss characterises the Muslim norms and restrictions on women as follows:

> The idealized woman stays at home, serves the men in her family, raises children, and leaves any and all involvement with the outside world to men. She neither physically intrudes into that male domain, nor even symbolically intrudes by inquiring about non-family matters. This purdah-the practical as well as figurative curtain separating the every day worlds of women and men-remains powerful symbolically[30].

Though gender relations have undergone great shifts for the last two decades in Kerala, partly by inside reform and partly by the governmental policies of reservation, no basic change in expressing their freedom and empowerment could be experienced as in other Islamic countries found recently. In countries like Pakistan, where Islamic laws have great influence over its subjects, and recently in Egypt, Libya, Yemen, Bahrain, Kuwait and Oman, protest movements and demonstrations of women are quite visible. But in a democratic country like India, where they can demonstrate without fear, such dissents are at its minimum or even nil. This does not mean that they don't have grievances, but it exposes only the trimidity and coyness in front of their 'divine' masters and patriarchs. This is because, through the ages in Kerala, Islam, gender and culture have been intertwined in all issues of the Islamic family and of its society. Although the contemporary resurgence of Islamic societies in the heartland of Islam has raised all such issues, they are least addressed in a more democratic society as that of ours. If Islam stands for equality, it should be in favour of protests and dissents to gain the same. Benazir Bhutto the former Prime Minister of Islamic Republic of Pakistan observes;

> It is the tradition of Islam that has allowed me to battle for political and human rights, and this same tradition strengthens me today. Islam denounces inequality as the greatest form of injustice. It enjoins its followers to combat oppression and tyranny. It enshrines piety as the sole criterion for judging human kind. It shuns race, colour, and gender as the basis of distinctions within society[31].

She really calls for a battle within Islam for democracy and modernization as we experience today in the whole frontiers of Islam. Being a noted Muslim woman ruler of the world, she argues for the total freedom of women and a gender-free society with socio-political commitments. When we talk of women's freedom, it carries an element of give and take, i.e. an offer or consideration to women by the male, without realising that these rights are inborn and conferred by the Quranic tenets as discussed elsewhere. Hardcore reformers like Maududi sees women as innately inferior creatures who should be wrapped up in shrouds and confined within the four walls of a house because by their inherent nature they are a moral threat to the health of society[32]. Maududi's comments are totally against the Quranic injunctions and the traditions of the Prophet. So long as a major section of Kerala women are under such influences, how could they be made free and bring them to the road of real religion? The reforms (secular) are looked upon as heresy and often equate with an attack on Islam. This is the major handicap a genuine liberal reformer faces in his attempts to bring Muslim women towards freedom and empowerment. As O. Aboo, a renowned activist writer of Tellicherry, seeing the miserable condition of the Ulema-led society, laments,

> Do not drink Honey; Do not allow to drink;
> Do not observe Din (Religion); Do not allow to observe;
> Do not die; Do not allow to die;
> Do not extinguish the fire; Do not allow to extinguish[33].

It is true that a traditional society changes very showly taking their own course without overlapping the existing parameters. But the fact is that still it is in the dimension of change, however insignificant it is. Employment and empowerment are mutually contributory. Making Muslim women aware of the demands of the day is highly imperative and a road towards freedom and justice. As women get more educated and better employed, they get more freedom and right for independent existence. This does not mean that women as an individual would be outside the orbit of her responsibilities as a wife, daughter or mother. The Quran or traditions no where discredit her, but, equips with spiritual and intellectual potentialities to make her equal to man. The tenets of the Quran and the traditions quoted elsewhere vouch for the same. A re-reading of the Quran and traditions (certainly not the so-called Shariah) is highly essential for the eradication of controversies and to bring the women to the forefront in all socio-political activities. A better understanding of the religion and a clear awareness of the situation are the prime requisites to provide them human rights and gender justice. We must also realise that, being a part of the larger socio-economic problem, the matter must be seriously dealt with. Moreover, all laws, including customs and traditions, which prevent women in playing their part individually and collectively, must be removed at the earliest. Moreover, as education is a prime factor in the process of modernization, the problem has to be studied more seriously keeping in mind that education not only prepares women with the knowledge and expertise but enables them to fight for gender justice and equality. Men should also take a strong stand to bring out their women from the age-old clutches and other hurdles that block their mobility to learn and earn power.

Notes and References

1. Justice Sachar Committee Report, Nov. 2006. It brings out the social, economic and educational status of Muslim in India.
2. Tabari, *op. cit.*, p. 113.
3. It reads: "O Prophet! Why holds thou to be forbidden that which Allah has made lawful to thee."
4. Sayed Qutb, *Fi Zilal al Quran,* (In the shade of the Quran), Vol. 2, Cairo, 1980, p. 650.
5. Alvin, J. Schmidt, *Veiled and Silenced: How Culture Shaped Sexist Theology,* Mercer University Press, Macon, 1989, p. XIII.
6. In October, 2006, after a long battle and legal procedures, the court sentenced Ali Mohammed, her father-in-law, to an 8 year imprisonment for rape and a fine of Rs. 8000. Though she was compelled to leave the village, she was relieved off the ill-fame and the harassment of the community court.
7. Samuel, P. Huntington, *The Clash of Civilizations*? Foreign Affairs, New York, 1996, p. 4-5. The observations of Huntington is highly reactionary and unacceptable. We have several countries in the Middle East and Central Asia with dual cultures of religion and ethnicity. ' Turkey, Lebanon and Palestine are the best examples. Even in Egypt, Iraq and Israel, these dualistic elements of culture and creed are highly visible. Tarikh Azeez, a close associate of Saddam Hussain, was a Christian by faith, but a typical Iraqi. Shahbas Bhatty, a minister in charge of minority affairs in Pakistan, is a Christian by faith, who has been killed by extremists for religious abuse on 3rd March 2011 and is also a true representative of Pakistani cultural trait. In South East Asia, though countries like Indonesia and Malasia, basically follow Islamic faith, they have several underlying components of Hindu-Buddhistic traditions of India. Such factors enmeshed in the history and culture of different nations highly refute the theory and conclusion of Huntington, mainly targeting the Orient, particularly Islam.
8. Mahnaz Afkhami (ed.) *Faith and Freedom*, Tauris, London, 2000, pp. 2-3. See also Ann Elizebeth Mayer, *Islam and Human Rights: Tradition and Politics,* Westview Press, 1991.
9. Extracts from "Gender Expert Musdah speaks within Reason", *Jakarta Post,* 7 October, 2004.
10. M.N. Karassery, "Priests who Excite Family" *Mathrubhoomi Weekly*, Dec. 2003.
11. The Quaran, traditions of the Prophet and various Islamic jurists rule out such artificial and unintended divorces. On the other hand, great weightage is given for reunion. Quran says "If you (believers) fear that a couple may break up, appoint one arbiter from his family and one from hers. Then, If the couple want to put things right, God will bring about a reconciliation between them (Chapter on Women, Verse 35).
12. A teacher in the Newman College, Todupuzham (Kerala), while preparing a

question paper Malayalam referred the name Mohammed (not Mohammed the Prophet as the teacher claims) in a symbolic dialogue with God to the requirement of his annotation. The extremists created a lot of fire and friction and the teacher's right hand was mercilessly amputated, an act even the prophet does not like or deserve pardon. The Christian management which runs the institution did not show any mercy towards him and they dismissed him from the college, partly acknowledging the crime "to secure the right of faith".

13. Switzerland a country with four million Muslims, even conducted a poll in whcih 57 per cent swiss people voted against allowing minarets to mosques. This has been criticised even by *NewYork Times* as "Disgraceful", in its editorial published November 30, 2009. Moreover, the issue of France is the growing numbers of Muslim migrants (naturally non-whites) from their earlier colonies also alarm them and not to tolerate a parallel culture. For details, see Asghar Ali Engineer, "Religious Diversity and Tolerance in Islam", *Islam and Modern Age,* Vol. XIII, Jan. 2010.
14. The cartoon controversy also instigated the Muslim mass not only in the Arab countries, but throughout the world. The images of the Prophet have been published in a newspaper in Denmark in September, 2005, in the name of freedom of expression. 3000 of the 187,000 Muslims living in Denmark also protested. This also led to the boycott of Danish goods in Muslim countries, causing a loss of 90 million euros in a week, and attacks on embassies in places like Beirut. (Ayaan Hirsi Ali, *The Caged Virgin - A Muslim Woman's Cry for Reason,* Free Press, London, 2006.
15. Baobab, an NGO in Nigeria, with its co-ordinator, Ayesha Imam, organized to case the 'abuse of Shariah' and to protect the 'Victims of Shariah'. It conducted several workshops on Shariah and its misuse in different parts of West Africa highlighting the variable nature of Muslim Laws in different communities living in different parts of the world. (Geraldine Terry, "Not a fax from Heaven" *Women's Rights*, Oxfam, GB, 2007, pp. 61-63.
16. Sulaikha Beevi a poor widow living with in the *Mohalla* Committee of Beemapally Mosque was harassed by the committee for adultery by which later found fake. *Mathrubhumi,* 30-6-1985. Such cases of excesses by the religious committees and leaders of the community are often disturb the life of the poor, particularly women, in the Islamic society of Kerala. Ostracism, denial of the burial of the dead in the mosque compound, interference and non allowance of marriage relations are all various methods with which the poor are singled out in society. This also happens in some cases of girls who go for higher education and raising questions on the dress code in rural areas. But it is fast disappearing.
17. In the Quran, Chapter on *Light (Surah Al Nur)* the Verse two reveals: "Strike the Adulteress and the adulterer one hundred times". Following, Verse Four reiterates the punishment for false allegation. It says, "As for those who accuse chaste women of fornication, and then fail to provide four witnesses, strike them eighty times, and reject their testimony even afterwards: They are the law breakers..." (24:4)
18. This survey has been conducted by *Mathrubhumi,* the Malayalam Daily and published it on August 1st, 2009. The filed numbers of the cases for four and a half years (From 2005 up to 2009, June) are 52, 525. It reports that Muslim cases are not completely available, because divorces through 'Talaq' are not properly recorded even in the records of the mosque.

19. As per one report the registered number of orphanages in Kerala is 1674. But a similar number are functioning in Kerala without registration. All communities, Hindus, Christians and Muslims have their orphanages where they have more numerical strength. Some of the orphanages have even the plan of converting people into their respective religions, self-defeating the very purpose of the institution. The major numbers are of Christians and Muslims. The inflow of foreign money is suspected in the case of some centres for destitutes and they are under the observation of the vigilance. See also *Mathrubhoomi,* Mal. Daily11th March, 2011.
20. A.R. Desai, "Constitution and Woman's Justice - Some Dangerous Trends" in *Woman's Justice* (Mal.) Language Institute, Trivandrum, 1989, p. 8. See also Elizabeth Wilson, *Women and the Welfare State*, Travistock Publications, London, 1977, pp. 7-8.
21. See Tahir Mahmood, *Family Law Reform in the Muslim World* (Mal. Trans.), Langugage Institute, Trivandrum, 1978, pp. 246-47.
22. See the case, Ashraf Ali Vs. Mohammed Ali 1945, Bombay, L.R. 642. Cutch Mamens are converted Muslims from higher caste Hindus of Maharashtra- Cutch area, now living mainly in Bombay, Bangalore and Ahmedabad. Khojas are a small sect among the Shiite Ismailis, now mainly found in Bombay. (For details see, A.A.A. Fayzi, *Islamic Law and Theology in India, Proposals for a Fresh Approach,* Middle East Journal, 1954, pp. 163, 183.
23. Apart from such marriages, a temporary marriage called *Mut'a* was also practiced widely in the coast of Calicut where the Arabs in early days have constant relationship. Those who come for trade could not go home in the monsoon wind at least for 3-4 months and in that interim period they enter into a marriage contract with a time span. Moreover, in such journeys of turmoil and uncertainty, their womenfolk never accompanied them. What ever may be the justifications for such a marriage of temporary nature, the children born out of the alliance later became a great problem for the family and the community at large. It is a private and verbal marriage contract between a man and an unmarried woman for a specified period, a pre-Islamic tradition, now followed by some Shiite Muslims among the *'Ithna Asha'ris* (Twelvers) in Iran. The period extends from 3 day to 3 months or even more. For details, The Sunnis reject the validity of the marriage. Caliph Omar prohibited it. For details see, John, L. Esposito, *The Oxford Dictionary of Islam*, Oxford, 2003. See also Akbar, S. Ahmed, *Discovering Islam, Making Sense of Muslim History and Society,* Routledge, NewYork, 2003, p. 58.
24. An interview with Nafeesath, aged 60, of Beemapalli, Trivandrum, was breath taking, revealing the miserable story of her daugter's marriage with a Mali man, Mohammed Naim. Her daughter, Umaifa, aged 17, was taken to Mali, after marriage where she was working as a servant to his other wives. He gave ₹ 16,000/- for the expenses of the marriage (out of which 500 was given to the broker) with some dress and gold. There were also cases of such marriages in these areas like that of Sharmila, daughter of Rahmath, who was deserted by her husband after having a child. There are also instances of treachery, for one could marry a girl for a kidney, as in the case of Tajunnisa and Husain Shihab. Herself

(a student of 9th std. in Pappanamkode School in Trivandrum) and her parents were really cheated by the guide who want only money.

25. In Bipan Chandra, Mridula Mukherjee, Aditya Mukherjee, *India After Independence:1947-2000,* Penguin, New Delhi, p. 451.
26. Ritu Menon and Kamla Bhasin, *Borders and Boundaries: Women in India's Partition,* Kali for Women, New Delhi, 2000, p. 21.
27. A.R. Desai, *Social Background of Indian Nationalism*, Bombay, 1959, p. 152.
28. The Beijing Declaration and the Platform for Action, published by United Nations, Department of Public Information, February, 1996. See also the case of Visakha Vs. State of Rajastan, 1997 (6) Sec. 241.
29. Amina Hashim, had her early education from Queen Mary's Madras and from Agra College. Earned the 'Kaisar Hind'Award from the British Crown in 1946. In 1952 Amina was a candidate of the Socialist party from Tellicherry to the election of Madras Constituent Assembly against V.R. Krishna Iyer. [Amina was also a music composer and an expert in Piano and harmonium. She made new tunes to the songs eologising Sufis in Durgahs. She was the first teacher in Piano in the Sacred Heart School, Tellicherry]. Her younger sister Aysha became the founder Principal of the Sahira Women's College, in Colombo in 1946 and a Women's College in Zambia (Africa). She was the Deputy Mayor in the Colombo Municipal Corporation in 1949. Aysha was also a noted tennis player and orator. Their youngest sister Haleema, though not highly educated, was also lover of music, particularly of Muslim Mappila Songs. The music tradition of this family still continues in Tellicherry through veterans like Peer Mohammed and T.C. Mariumma, T.C. Mariumma the present head of the family also is a expert in Mappila cuisine and a Composer of music. While having visited her for interview, she was found reading an English newspaper, that too at the age of 84. Many women politicians and social activists are in this family, like Amina Maliyekkal, the present Chair Person of Tellicherry Municipality.
30. Anita, M. Weiss, "The Show Yet Steady Path to Women's Empowerment in Pakistan" in Y.Y. Haddad and John, L. Esposito (ed.) *Islam, Gender and Social Change,* Oxford University Press, 1998, p. 125. See also Anita, *Walls within Walls: Life Histories of Working Women in the Old City of Lahore.* Boulder Colo: West view.
31. Benazir Bhutto, *Reconciliation, Islam, Democracy and the West,* Pocket Books, London, 2008, pp. 17-18.
32. Ziauddin Sardar, *Desperately Seeking Paradise: Journeys of a Sceptical Muslim.* Granta Books, London, 2004, p. 32.
33. Quoted in V.K. Kuttu, *Tellicherry - A Journey to its Muslim History,* (Mal), Tellicherry, 2010, p. 109.

7

In Retrospect

Can we aspire to have a gender-just society in the Islamic society of Kerala in the near future? Our attempt, all along, had been addressing this question and to arrive at a conclusion more wise and prudent. The opinions sought, collected and examined through the questionnaire, are only samples, though they reveal some extreme cases of battered and neglected women strengthening to postulate the final hypothesis. Scars might fade only if the wound is light, and in any case they never go away. The issues of Muslim women, as in other parts of the world, are in such a paradox. They carry with them a historical and traditional baggage as part of religion and culture and live across life-time servitude and dependage. It is true that the religious and societal pressures made the situation worse, pushing them further in a patriarchal cauldron. While analysing the miserable condition of the contemporary Muslim women in Kerala a major thrust has been given to various Quranic tenets and traditions of the Prophet to highlight what Islam has to offer to equate women with men.[1]. This is particularly keeping in mind that misogyny is only a later development and either during the days of the Prophet or his companions, women have enjoyed considerable freedom, ofcourse within the parameters of the religion. A concerted effort has been made to disprove the androcentrism basing on misinterpretation of some of the Quranic verses and fake or weak traditions of the Prophet[2].

The issues of Muslim women in Kerala all the time are discussed not on the basis of their human rights or privileges or economic development in the secular premise, but often on the bedrock of the so-called 'Shariah', which in practice turns to be anti-liberal and rarely even anti- human. In the fight between Islam and the West, often the West wins, especially on the issue of women, particularly in the context of the writings of the West-based Islamic reformers like Sa'adawi, Mernissi, Wadud and many others[3]. The western agenda of undermining the roots of the Islamic culture has become successful, importantly in the context of 9/11 in the world over, overcoming the colonial apprehensions and defeating the much debated verbosity of Islam. The problem that faces the Muslim women the world over is not that women lack political rights in paper, but they can not exercise them to the same extent as men because of cultural, social and economic barriers. The hard-line activists often link fundamentalism which virtually obstructs all kinds of reform. For example, one could easily detect the danger behind a statement made by Maulana Hifz-ur-Rahman, a hard-core cleric in Pakistan. He says;

If we allow women to participate in elections, this village will become like Lahore, or Karachi or Europe—full of obscenity and vulgarity[4].

In Afghanistan, the women's representation is looked upon as an encroachment of men's rights and "eating the rights of men"[5]. In places like Kerala, there are at least two basic streams of change, working both inside and outside, the insiders include reformers from within. While a contingent of west-based feminists try to transform the theological premise of the issue, the revivalist reformers argue for a change from within which dangerously take them to the shell of obscurantism. Unfortunately in Kerala or even in India no such radical movements or initiative are visible as in Egypt or in Morocco. Here the attempts of revivalist reformers, instead of a change for better, virtually defeat the very purpose of women's reform and empowerment. This certainly will take to a reverse of all the efforts for the liberal and humanistic interpretation of both religion and tradition.

Moreover, the fundamentalists, in all their discourses, to uplift women, bring the western cultural context as the major threat to Islam importantly in this era of globalization. They place reformed Islam as a counter to the forces of modernity of the west. The Islamists in Kerala, as in other parts of the world, deal with women's issues essentially reactive and trap them with the struggle over culture[6]. But if we make a close perusal of the revised religion as brought forth by the neo-Islamic modernists, it itself has to be considered as a by-product emerged after intrution of western modernism in all the Islamic states. Though puritan in outlook, organizations like Muslim Brotherhood and even major seminaries like Al-Azhar have imbibed the spirit of western ideology and education in the formation and re-orientation of their curriculum to the tune of the present-day requirements. It is also to be noticed that the leadership of the recent revolts and upheavals found rampant in the Arab world is initiated and led mainly by the products of such universities in Lybia, Egypt, Syria, Yemen and Jordan. The emerging middle class of these countries with deep dislike of orthodoxy and tyranny take up the charge of the revolts for democracy and a liberal constitution. It is also a fact that in such a situation of revolt and reform, the fundamentalists too take their own toll with hidden agendas as are seen in the disturbed Arab world of today. The irony here is that while one tries to destroy the old, the other tries to restore the old social order and reconstruct the Islamic rule and its cultural traditions. Though the secularists and liberals have their definite aim and direction, the hidden forces of the religionists act with more vigour, without a wise contemplation and vision of the future. In the conflict between fundamentalism and liberalism, it is always the moderates and the progressives who suffer the most and lose their hope.

Those who stand for the implementation of Shariah law basically misunderstand the status of Shariah. Because Quran refers to Shariah as a path alone, not as a ready made system of law waiting to be put in practice. They virtually reduce the Islamic law to a handful of symbolic elements as wearing of a veil or growing of a beard, etc. In order to get a clear picture of the position of women in Islam one must start by drawing a clear distinction between custom and religion. People so often confuse the two, that in so many cases custom is even trying to gain an upper hand over the religion.

No wonder that the diversified nature of the Islamic society of Kerala with its inherent social inequality and intergroup disparity, move in unison in the case of women and knowingly or unknowingly marginalised them. To the segregation and suppression of women, all the sectarian Islamic groups like the Salafis, Jama'atis and the puritine Sunniites are equally responsible because all of them dogmatically interfere in the educational, religious and cultural life of the women. In a pluralistic society as that of Kerala, why Muslim women alone have such problems and why they are segregated from others? This is a pertinent question that could be answered variedly in the context of the new development in Kerala. It actually begins with the fake 'religious modernism' that offered to them through madrassahs and religious discourses. The followers of other religions like Hinduism or Christianity could not deliver such anachronic customs and practices to their women in the name of religion in India. For instance *Sathi*, an aristocratic practice found earlier in the Hindu society, could never be enforced in the present day. The patriarchy among the Ulemas and community leaders classified the women alone as a separate division distinctively from the males and enforces rules and regulations as found in the *Shariah* over them very strictly while the men are given complete freedom from such entanglements. With all the secular education and economic fortunes for a few, a major share of them is still battered and marginalised, particularly in the rural set up and in the regions like Malappuram and Kasaragod where the Muslim community has a considerable majority.

Even after the introduction of the revivalist ideologies, the expected metamorphosis did not have come in the life of Muslim women in Malabar. Instead of applying reason and liberalism, they still propagate rigidity and puritanism qualifying them as the only road to the 'straight path'. This social milieu has heavily damaged the existing cultural ethos of fusion and synthesis. Their attempt to present Islam in a totalitarian attire,[7] virtually minimised its merit and universalism inviting much criticism. Here, the epithet the 'West' or 'Western' is used or misused every where when the question of secular and liberal education takes its heed. It is mostly the women who are cheated and exploited in the name of Shariah as dictated by some fictitious ulemas making it "a prescription for totalitarianism"[8].

The poor women in the rural areas of Kerala are not capable enough to get modern education because it is beyond their reach. Poverty and ignorance reign all and this situation drags the majority to go for the religious education alone and their ignorance and illiteracy make them further 'unfit' in society. To many, modern education is a luxury because they are not entitled to earn it since their role is different as a wife or a home maker. One can run away from modernisation, but one can't hide from it. As the feedback suggests, some rays of hope could be seen rarely in some spaces where liberal and secular education have penetrated. If every woman is at liberty to have human rights (inalienable) first, she could be totally free from all social, religious and economic encumbrances and pressures. If so, she should have freedom for a choice-based education, employment, marriage with her consent, and discretion to choose her dress modalities including facilities for economic activities. Such a woman could be an asset in a family as a wife and mother and earning member which might ultimately create a healthy society. The greatest tragedy of the Muslim girls, particularly in backward areas, is the denial of their rights to education and employment. The women education is generally considered as a key to reduce poverty and to enhance confidence, self-reliance and strength. Studies on low and middle income families have brought forth the fact that after giving secondary school education for girls, a reduction in infant mortality, maternal death and even the birth of unnecessary children.

It is a fact that, women in the Islamic society of Kerala are compelled to carry the age-old customs and traditions as "divinely" proposed and implemented by the fake ulemas who hold nothing other than the male-authored texts and man-made Shariah. Here, the Quranic tenets and traditions are selected and interpreted in such a way that it could serve only the purpose of highlighting their own ideology in a patriarchal and feudal society.

Lack of awareness and education make them a tool in the hands of others and majority of them did not even know the new trends and resurgence coming up in other parts of the world[9]. These factors clearly reveal that in Islamic countries (with government based on Islam and Shariah), political activism could be easily possible, because there their demand for democracy (against militancy, autocracy and tyranny) project first and secondly for gender equality, freedom and liberalism. In countries like India, both are not issues for a revolt. Whereas in countries like Pakistan, Turkey, Egypt, Jordan and Syria, the idiom for westernization (including dress) and political radicalization emerged with the new awareness among the urban (middle and lower middle class) women by the last quarter of the 20th century.

This breaking of barriers of tradition also has been paralysed and partly balanced by the activism of Islamic forces wherever they have hold but with a new religious idiom of change. But in region like Kerala, it is the second phase of that development and change (based on Islam), took more root than the true liberal, assertive, politically aware phase as now seen in the Islamic countries. This means that women, here, did not have the first phase of change more effectively and the new transformation is only a reassertion of the conservative and traditional ideologies of the past. Thus the religious conservatism finds a fertile ground in a class still in transition without having political pressures as in Islamic countries. In some measure this explains the gap between the two generations of women, one passive, the other, though active, but conservative and traditional, who always dominate the other, and act as the representative of the new emerging generation of Islam.

But those women, though attached to traditionalism and exposed as a replica of the resurgent Muslim women, never is a representative or part of the rural poor who are still repressed and marginalized. The aspirations for education, employment and empowerment, are reposed in the policy matters and measures of the government.

While the governmental machinery always stands for social liberation and the upliftment of the weak and the backward, others try to push them further regressive with the slogan of the past. This is quite evident from a simple issue rose in recent years.

When the Supreme Court made a verdict to have a civil registration in local bodies to all the marriages conducted traditionally by the Qazis and Christian priests, all of them protested in the name of marriage as a 'religious function' and presented a petition before the government. In fact such a verdict virtually upholds the freedom, protection and prestige of womanhood[10]. The protesters feel that such interferences of the court or of the state are encroachments on the 'religious privileges' and have to be 'suppressed' at any cost. On the contrary, it is the duty of the state that its citizens are properly protected from all violations of law and natural justice. Social issues and challenges of women in the Islamic society of Kerala are mainly due to the negation of freedom that imposed over them by the ulema-oriented society. In fact they suffer from several psychological and attitudinal problems mostly thrust upon them as a residue of the past. Any debate on the liberation of Muslim women depends on the attitude of the ulemas and religious leaders who still have no vision of a developed and advanced society with a class of free women. Their outdated compulsions are easily targeted against women than men as an instrument of identity. These restraints on women are framed on vital issues like divorce, inheritance and property, though Islamic law had its own solutions to combat these.

Freedom of Muslim women, as in any part of the world, has to be visualised with a pragmatic perspective and with a conceptual frame work of growth and development. In determining the work force in a community, women's share also has to be evaluated. The role of Muslim women in the Kerala context is not at all appreciable in the economic productivity of society. Instead, this lagging behind causes to hinder the common socio-economic development effecting the total growth rate of the country. A qualitative change in this direction could not be possible without a total social transformation of that community. The economic independence of Muslim women is still a dream to be true. Moreover the nature of the work force is totally different in urban and rural areas. In rural and backward areas, where the veil could not be imposed severely, the involvement of Muslim women, particularly in agricultural field and construction sector, is appreciable. This certainly enhance the economic stability of the family and her freedom and confidence as an individual. This handicap found in the urban elite is now balanced by the inflow of the gulf money, eventhough it wraps and pushes them to the corridors of seclusion, atleast in the case of some.

Moreover, the issues related to Muslim women of Kerala are to be linked with the questions of human rights because most of them reveal the total denial of such rights and in rare cases, it borders on to violence and oppression. The denial of rights in most cases is in the name of Shariah and tradition. Domestic violence is a clear testimony of the negation of human rights which could be questioned legally. But in the case of Muslim women, including educated, who are supposed to be the "slaves" of shariah, suffer everything silently to the cause of honour and religion. It is here, both voluntary organisations for women's protection and the government should take actions against the infringement of laws by a handful of them. We have several examples of innocent women thus saved on account of legal involvement[11].

It is high time to form a 'legal cell' exclusively for such neglected women who suffer due to ignorance, hollow- honour, shariah-phobia and above all, with poor living conditions. A revised curriculum with more stress on women's rights as per true Islam and the country's secular law, is also highly recommendable to avoid excesses on women who are mute and voiceless. Religious functionaries who deliberately go disarray by making fake *fatwas* have to be punished severely under the law of the land making them responsible for all the damages incurred, and by imposing financial obligations. These will certainly lead to a re-reading of the Quran and traditions with a realistic approach which the fundamentalists always want to oppose.

Most of the Mappila Muslim families in Kerala have developed into micro-level families freeing themselves from the erstwhile joint families as a result of the newly acquired socio-economic fortunes. The employment opportunities, though limited and less lucrative, still provide the women some what a social security and a familial dignity. The housewife can pull along her family with confidence, minimising the dictation of her husband. While analysing the South

Asian societies, economists like Amartyasen observes, that women in the global south are important agents of change, promoting social transformations, individually and collectively. He also attributes positive trends in such societies like falling in fertility rates, improved child survival rates, and women's increased ability to make decisions for themselves[12].

The fundamentalists, on the contrary, project the reverse of it quoting instances of the elopement of some school/college going girls or harassment of women in work places to substantiate their argument for complete seclusion or the walled life of the females. Ofcourse, violence is a violation of human rights greatly affecting their confidence and self-esteem. But to overcome global issues like poverty and violence, women's participation and involvement are highly mandatory. Moreover, the rural Kerala is still living on agriculture, and its economy largely depending on the sweat of the poor. Those who oppose women who go out for some job, may have to lose their comfort or atleast a meal which the rural poor count much. Therefore reluctancy in sanctioning freedom to women is also linked with the selfishness of men who go for their own ease and contentment.

There are still large number of men who do not agree to woman going out to work or being educated. Their argument is that, if a woman, leaves her house to engage in such activities, she will lose her femininety, and probably her chastity and honour. But even in Islamic countries like Egypt, the poor women workers of the factories and peasants in the agricultural fields participated vigorously and effectively in the National Revolution of 1919. They went out onto the rural roads, side by side with the men, cut the telephone wires and disrupted the railway lines in order to paralyse the movements of the British troops. It was from the remarks of these toiling masses of women that the female martyrs of the 1919 national revolution came. These industrial workers and peasants were the first women to rebel in the early 20th century Egypt[13]. In a tiny Arab state like Bahrain also could be seen an *intifada* (uprising) with heavy women participation. The protesters were from the less favoured strata of society, demanding to the end of the colonial (British) rule, against the importation of foreign labourers, for more employment opportunities for the natives and for democracy and social justice. In the petition submitted, the women signatories were 25 per cent, that too from the lower-middle class of rural areas. The core issues that the nation and women protested are economic, social and political inequalities as they manifest themselves. As subalterns within an oppressed social system, women need to be alert to fight out for agendas of their own[14].

The above are only some sample notanda to substantiate the argument that Muslim women, the world over, have great initiative for reform and revolt even at the beginning of the 20th century, itself. Though late, similar incidents could be seen in Kuwait, Republic of Yemen, Jordan and in many other countries in West Asia and countries like Philippines, and Pakistan in South Asia[15]. It must also bear in mind that these stirring gestures are not from any other heretical country, but from the heartlands of Islam with conservatism and tradition of continuity for centuries. The issues of Muslim women, the world over, are of the same nature and that should be tackled tactfully with a concerted effort by a joint venture of the elected governments and Islamic intellectuals, without making the issues further worse.

Again, the quality and the content of the curriculum provided by the private agencies, Madrassahs and other NGOs, are to be examined and monitored periodically to make sure that they comply with state syllabi. A board of control may also be constituted with civil, judicial officers or advocates and seasoned ulemas, to watch over the hindrance of rights and privileges and to avoid the possible fear which may arise in minorities. It is also true that some Muslim organizations formed for serving the community educationally and socially, never go into the depth of the problem of their womenfolk who are still behind the 'curtain' or in the back door as recently revealed through the report of Justice Rajinder Sachar. The services of such agencies are concentrated mainly in the urban elite, and the poor and the backward are still in the periphery or in the corridor, waiting for a dawn. Those who secured institutions in the minority address and claim, are not even ready to give a berth to the unfortunate, impoverished and voiceless in their society. Ironically, instead, what one could experience is that they have no hesitation to spend crores by way of legal battle to avoid the genuine claim and shares of the poor of their own society. Hence, the present day situation of Muslim women is mainly an enigma of their own creation which could be solved only by their own initiative. As H.A.R. Gibb observes, spread of modernism is a warning that reformulation can not be indefinitely shelved[16].

A pertinent question often arises is that what is the additional responsibility of Kerala Muslim women to hold and embrace than what their sisters in religion in other parts of the world have, particularly in the context of their speedier rejection. The present day movements found globally are highly suggestive of this blatant truth. Moreover, when burning issues confront Muslim women, why should they cling on to Shariah law which virtually distracts Muslims from their pressing needs. In the Shariite Arab world, the imperialists have their own agenda (of political and economic) to their survival and resource exploitation. Recent threats and developments in these countries reveal the hollowness of the state managed by the oil politics and to the richness of the petro-dollar that pervades the Middle East and the West pointing to a dismal future for all.

Recent incidents in West Asia and in other Islamic countries of the world also reveal a fact that their challenge is against a rule which is either tyrannical or authoritarian and Islamic by faith and name. The final phase or the fate of the revolts is not much discussed as happened in Morocco, Egypt, Pakistan or Jordan. But the situation in a liberal democratic country like India is totally different. More often issues related to religion are not touched upon by the elected governments or even by the judiciary. This has been manifestsed in fullest extreme in the issues of Shah Bano (1985) and Muslim Women (Protection of Rights on Divorce) Act, 1986. Any action of the government will be questioned in the garb of "minority" and all such attempts are in the list of failures. Moreover, the initiative of a secular government will be labelled and defeated once for all as "unIslamic" by the obscurantists with the oft-repeated slogans like 'Islam in Danger'. Amidst such delicate issues, the liberal reformers and secularists should fight and get a space for those who go for a social change. A great shift in the condition of women in the traditional Muslim societies is inevitable. The Islamists are urged by their own ideals to reform the traditional society and to reduce the gap between historical reality and ideal Islam. This is more urgent in respect to the reform of women.

An innovation that could help the reform and resurgence of Muslim women in Kerala is the mutual trust and a dialogue between the intellectuals and the Islamists of all streams and sects for finding out a final solution to this growing problem involving human rights. A re-reading of the tenets and traditions concerning women and their freedom is highly imperative for all those who are concerned, and sitting around a table, consisting of experts in religion, jurists and intellectuals and social scientists is the need of the hour. The misuse and misreading of the Shariah should be stopped at any cost with the sanction of the Ulemas to avoid further contradictions and that should be treated as a prerogative for any reform concerning Muslim women. Nothing could be a resistant to the inalienable human rights of any individual.

A docile attitude towards women, instead of giving gender justice, and empowerment, will certainly push them further back, compared to others of the parallel communities, and make them unfit to face the challenges of modernity. Of course, a problem that we do share with moderates and liberals generally is the difficulty of defining the borderlands between Islamist commitment and extremism, particularly in the light of gender analysis. It becomes more rigid and extreme when the question of freedom of women comes. The growing influence of this group with perceived bias towards women and their issues is a sensitive but common topic of debate in the present day situations. Moreover, Muslim women, have to be made aware of the misuse of the Shariah by the so called leaders and ulemas exploiting their ignorance. The urgent need to uplift the condition of Muslim women is a joint effort on the part of the community and the government including local bodies. To save and reform their women, the Islamic society itself should go for a radical structural change accepting the realities and challenges of the modern world. The constitutional rights of a citizen of a democratic country could not be abrogated by the injuctions of Shariah or by the Ulemas. Such a situation will add to a retrogressive situation in the growth of individualism and social progress. In Kerala such a socio political milieu is existing particularly in the case of Muslim women and that hinders her social mobility and progress.

Notes and References

1. *See* Chapter I, particularly verses 33:35, 4:1, 33:32-33 and notes 9 and 10.
2. Fathima Mernissi, "A Feminist Interpretation of Women's Rights in Islam" in Charles Kurzman (ed.) *Liberal Islam*, Oxford, 1998, pp. 112-126; particularly the *hadiths* stated by Abu Huraira, a companion of the Prophet.
3. For more details see, Nawal El Sa'adawi, *The Hidden Face of Eve,* Fathima Mernissi, *The Veil and the Male Elite; Beyond the Veil* etc; and Amina Wadud, *Inside the Gender Jihad.*
4. Walsh D. "The place where women risk their lives to run for office", *Guardian,* 13 August, 2005.
5. Tom Coghlan, "Election Hopes of Afghan Women," Online, BBC News, 14th August, 2005.
6. Leila Ahmed, *Women and Gender in Islam,* Yale University Press, London 1992, p. 236.
7. M.S. Agwani, *Religion and Politics in West Asia*, New Delhi, 1992, p. 86.
8. Ziauddin Sardar, *Desparately Seeking Paradise: Journeys of a Sceptical Muslim,* London, 2004, p. 36.
9. The recent developments in the Islamic countries like Libya, Lebanon, Egypt, Morocco including the gulf countries have now become a threat even to their governments. Some of the rulers like Hosni Mubarak have been unseated by the mass movement.
10. *Mathrubhoomi Daily* (Mal.) June, 14, 2007. Muslim Jama'at committees along with some representatives of churches jointly met the Chief minister of Kerala and expressed their deep concern and anxiety on the Verdict of the court and requested that the government should not take any action to implement the same. This also is a clear indication of a joint venture of religionists to gain their aim usually living in different poles.
11. The Ostracism to a Muslim family in Kadampuzha (Malappuram) in connection with a *Muttalaq* (tripple divorce) in which one poor couple Aboobacker and Aysha involved, in July 2003, but miserably failed with the proper intervention of the court. The same was the case with the alleged adultery on one Sulaikha Beevi of Beemapalli (Trivandrum) in 1985, who also won the case through court.
12. Amartya Sen, *Development as Freedom,* Oxford University Press, Oxford, 1999.
13. Nawal El Saadawi, *The Hidden Face of the Eve-Women in the Arab World.* Zed Books, London and New York, 2007, pp. 260-262. She salutes hundreds of unknown women martys while referring some of them like Shafika Mohammed (Killed by the British on 14 March, 1919), Hamida Khalil, Sayeda Hasan, Fahima Riad and Aisha Omar. *See* also Abdel Rahman, El Rafii, *Fi Aakab El Sawra El Masria,* Vol. I, Cairo, 1959.

14. Mallon, Florencia, "The Promise and Dilemma of Subaltern Studies: Perspectives From Latin American History", *AHR Forum*, Dec: 1994. See also May Seikaly, "Women and Social Change in Bahrain", *International Journal of Middle Eastern Studies* (26, 1994) Seikaly has done a statistical study on the role of Bahraini women in the protest movements and reform in their country.
15. Y.Y. Haddad and John, L. Esposito (ed.), *Islam, Gender and Social Change,* Oxford University Press, 1998. See also Benazir Bhutto, *Daughter of Destiny,* Simon and Schuster, NewYork, 1989. Benazir's last work *Reconciliation* also reveals her legitimate quest for a space in politics, not as a woman, but as a citizen free of gender. The recent political developments in Islamic countries like Lybia, Egypt, Bahrain and Syria are also suggestive of the fact that, the expected total change is not yet a reality.
16. H.A.R. Gibb, *Modern Trends in Islam,* Chicago University Press, 1947, pp. 108-123. *See* also, Gibb (ed.) *Whither Islam? A Survey of Modern Movements in the Muslim World,* London, 1932.

Appendix-I

Questionnaire

The Questionnaire contains questions on:

(1) General and Religious (2) Personal based on Society and Culture; Different Format prepared to (1) Urban and Rural residents (2) Different classes and Economic status (3) Educated and Illiterate and (4) Different age groups.

1) Why does Islam separate men and women?
2) What was the role of women in early Islam?
3) Are women second-class citizens in Islam?
4) Can you justify the wearing of the Veil?
5) Why are women not allowed to seek employment?
6) Can Muslim men have more than one wife?
7) How does Islam treat divorce?
8) Can you tolerate domestic violence as a woman?
9) Is abortion allowed in Islam?
10) What does Islam say about birth control?
11) Can a woman lead a congregational prayer in Islam?
12) Can a women be a leader in politics?
13) Will Islam allow a woman to be a ruler by election?
14) Is Islam medieval and against change?
15) Do you consider the Quran and Sunnah as the only answer to all issues in the Islamic Society?
16) Do Muslim women require a gender Jihad?
17) Is Shariah still relevant concerning women in the modern social life?
18) What kind of hijab (dress) you prefer to wear?
19) Are you in favour of representative power by reservation or assertive power by open competition?
20) Do you agree to have co-education?
21) Do you consider education of girls equivalent to boys?
22) What is the ideal marriageable age for girls?
23) Comment on the role of women in decision making?
24) Have your husband ever discussed with you the number of children you would like to have?
25) Do you vote every time?

Appendix-II

Notes on Imams Interpreters and Reformers

Muhammed Ismail Al-Bukhari (d. 870) author of *Sahih al-Bukhari,* one of six works of Hadith widely accepted as authentic along with *Sahih Muslim*. Most authoritative for Sunni Muslims. Approximately 7, 275 traditions in nine books, compiled and arranged thematically after careful testing of genuineness of traditions.

Muslim al-Hajjaj (d. 875) author of Sahih Muslim, one of the six collections of Hadith Authoritative along with Bukhari, to Sunni Muslims. Consists of forty two books, arranged topic wise.

Mohammed Ibn Idris Shafi (d. 819): Jurist theologian and founder of the Shafi School of Islamic Law. Born in Gaza and died in Egypt Expert on Quran and Sunnah. Authorised the practice of *Ijma* (Consensus) and rejected *istishan* (juristic preference) as a source of law.

Abu Hanifa (d. 767): Founder of Hanafi School of Law. Bornat Kufa (Iraq). Applied reason and logic in jurisprudence. His law noted for liberality and personal freedom. It is the most popular with largest following in the Islamic World, nearly one-third.

Ahmed Ibn Hambal (d. 855): Native of Baghdad, propounder of Hambali School of Law. Favoured the literal interpretation of the Quran beyond mere interpretatin of scholars. Stood for strict rule of Islamic law. His collection of the tradition is the *Musnad*. Anticipated a politico-religious alliance. His school became the basis of the Salafi movement started by Mohammed Abdul Wahab (18th C.) and the ideology of the Islamic State of Saudi Arabia.

Malik Ibn Anas (d. 795): Founder of the Maliki School of law. Born and lived in Medina, Malik compiled a collection of traditions of the Prophet, called *Al-Muwatta,* a treatise for Sunniites. Stressed both personal opinion and analogy in legal matters. Accepted consensus, ijma, when Quran and traditions are found silent.

Al-Tabari (d. 923): Early Muslim historian and compiler of traditions of Prophet. Wrote a commentry on Quran. His monumental work, *The History of Rulers and Kings,* outlined the individual interests in rule rather than ideological or institutional, an important innovation in the methodology of history. He stressed that history could only be transmitted, not deduced or inferred.

Abu Hamid al-Ghazali (d. 1111): Born in Khurzan, studied at Baghdad, Ghazali is a combination of a jurist and a mystic. His master piece, *Ihya Ulum al-Din* (Revival of religious Sciences) is renowned for its integration of theology, ethics and mysticism, Other works are *Tahafut al Falsafah* (Destruction of the philosophers), an effort to debunk philosophy, *Al Munqid min al-Dalal* (Delivery from error) etc.

Rabiah al-Ada wiyah (d. 801): A female mystic from Basra. Viewed Sufism in another direction stressing the doctrine of selfless love. Emphasized ascetic detachment, renunciation of the world supreme and absolute love of God. Preached that people should worship God out of love, rather than the fear of hell and the promise of the paradise. A model among the mystics.

Ibn Taymiyyah (d. 1328): Highlighted the supremacy of Quran and Sunnah and condemned the practice of Saint worship. He favoured independent reasoning (ijthihad) and tied Islam to politics and state formation. Influenced later thinkers like Abdul Wahab, Hasanul-Banna and Syed Qutb.

Mohammed Ibn Abd al-Wahab (d. 1791): Hambali jurist, and ideologue of the Wahhabi movement. Being a conservative theologian, advocated a return to Quran and traditions. Denounced practices of shrine cults, saint worship and any intermediary between God and man. Opposed *taqlid* (addherance to traditon). Reached into an alliance with King Ibn Saud, resulting into the formation of the rule of the Saudis in Arabia.

Hasan al-Banna (d. 1949): Founder of Muslim Brotherhood in 1928 in Egypt, later transforming into a political movement. Proclaimed Islam as a comprehensive system of life and Quran as the only acceptable constitution and law. Rejected secularism and Arab nationalism, because, to him, Muslims irrespective of ethnicity and nationhood, forms a single unit. Advocated for an Islamic society under an Islamic law. Assassinated by the Egyptian police in 1949.

Mohammed Abduh (d. 1905): Egyptian theologian journalist, reformer and the architect of Islamic modernism. Educated at Al Azhar University, and a disciple of Jamaludin Afghani and supported Pan Islamism, He applied reason to revelation. His popular work was *Risalat al Tawhid* (theology of unity).

Rashid Rida (d. 1935): Syrian revivalist, later lived in Egypt and a disciple of Mohammed Adhuh. Published journal *Al Manar*, to articulate and discriminate ideas of Mohammed Adbuh and others. Believed Quran and Sunnah unchangeable, but insisted to acquire modern education. An advocate of the revival of the Caliphate.

Sayyed Qutb (d. 1966): Egyptian Islamic thinker and activist. To him, Islam is a timeless body of ideas forming a comprehensive way of life. Justified violence against governmenet if it goes violent. A critic of the west and their culture and their support to zionists against Palestine.

Jamaludin Afghani (d. 1897): An activist born and raised in Iran, but with an Afghan blood strain. Strong advocate of Pan Islamism. Widely travelled in India and Africa. Emphasized Muslim soldarity against Christian West and opposed western imperialism. A political activist who utilized Islam for change and reform.

Mirza Ghulan Ahmed (d. 1908): Founder of Ahmedi Movement in Punjab (India) in 1889. Claimed to be the Mahdi of Muslims, the Messiah of Christians and the avatar Krishna for Hindus. Denied Mohammed as the last prophet. The movement is labelled non-Muslim and fiercely opposed by Muslims.

Abul A'la Maududi (d. 1979): Indo Pakistan Revivalist and the founder of Jama'ate - Islami (1941). Advocated rule of Islam as dictated by God and opposed to secularism. Author of more than 150 works, propagating reform and revolution.

Qardawi, Yousuf (b. 1926): Egyptian Islamic activist and ideologue. Calls for Muslim unity and the formation of a universal Caliphate. Calls the youth to the rejection of western ideologies. Opposes recognition of Israel and Zionism. Condemns vilolence and rejects both religious and secular extremism.

Glossary

Allah	:	literally 'God', who has no gender and can not be imagined by human mind.
Caliph	:	Successor, Ruler of Islam
Din	:	Religion including the notions of culture, civilization and tradition.
Fatwa	:	Religious Decree
Fiqh	:	Islamic jurisprudence
Fitna	:	Civil war
Fasq	:	Divorce initiated by wife.
Hadith	:	Sayings and doings of Prophet, traditions.
Hijab	:	Curtain, Veil
Hijra	:	Prophet's emigration to Madina; Beginning of Islamic Calender.
Idda	:	Women's waiting period after divorce
Ijma	:	Consensus
Ijthihad	:	Independent judgement
Islam	:	Peace, submission to God.
Insan	:	human being (without gender)
Jahiliyya	:	Age of ignorance
Kuda (Mal)	:	Umbrella, also used as veil by Muslim and Brahmin women (Marakkuda)
Jihad	:	Striving against evil; religious war
Jilbab	:	Female's covering in various forms
Kuppayam (Mal.)	:	Jacket with full sleeves
Malappattu (Mal)	:	Songs in Arabi-Malayalam in praise of Saints, e.g. Mohiyudeen mala.

Mujahid	:	One who fights for the sake of God.
Mahr	:	Dowry
Mundu (Mal)	:	Lower garment (for South Indians)
Nafs	:	Soul
Niqab	:	face veil
Qazi	:	Islamic judge
Qiyas	:	analogical reasoning
Qul'a	:	A divorce in complete agreement with wife
Pattu (Mal)	:	Songs
People of the Book	:	Jews, Christians and Muslims (followers of Abraham)
Sabeena	:	Arabi-Malayalam Song
Sahih	:	Authentic
Shariah	:	Law based on Quran and Sunna; usually path
Sufi	:	Mystic
Sunnah	:	Custom of the Prophet
Surah	:	Chapter of the Quran
Tangal (Mal)	:	Descendant of the Prophet; Syed
Talaq	:	Male divorce
Tauhid	:	Unity of God
Tattam (Mal)	:	Old form of a scarf or head cover used by Malayali Muslim women
Ulema	:	Religion scholars
Zina	:	Fornication, adultery.

Select Bibliography

Primary Sources

Abdul Khader Badaoni, *Muntakhab-ut-Tawarikh* (Trans.).

Abul Fazl, *Ain-i-Akbari.*

Al-Ghazali, Abu Hamid, *Ihya Uloomiddin,* Cairo edn.

Al-Suyuti, *Lubab al'uqul fi asbab al-nuzul,* (Rev. edn.) Dar Ihya al-ilm, Beirut, 1984.

Al-Qaradawi, *Fatwa Mu'asira* [Legal Decisions], Kuwait, 1996.

Asqalani, *Fath al-bari,* (Trans.), Maktaba al-Misr (1928 edn.)

Bukhari, *Sahih al-Bukhari,* Collections of Hadith.

P.K. Haleema, *Chandira Sundari Mala* (Arabi - Malayalam), Ponnani, 1922.

Pulikkottil Hyder, *Letter Song of Mariyakkutty* (Arabi - Malayalam), Tirurangadi, 1924.

Ibn Majah, *Sunan, Kitab al-Adab.*

Ibn Khaldun, *The Muqaddimah* (An Introduction to History), FranzRosenthal (Trans.), Princeton, 1969.

W. Logan, *Malabar Manual,* Reprint, Delhi, 2009.

Nizamudin Ahmed, *Tabaqat-i-Akbari* (Trans.)

Mohammed Abduh, *Tafsir al-Manar,* Dar-al-Fikr, Cairo.

Muslim, *Sahih Muslim,* Collections of Hadith.

The Holy Qur'an, Translation and Commentary, Presidency of IslamicResearches, IFTA, Mecca.

Qur'an (Trans.), MAS Abdel Haleem, Oxford University Press, 2005.

Justice Rajinder Sachaar, *Commission Report,* Govt. of India, 2006.

Shaikh Zeinudin, *Fath-ul-Mu'in,* (Trans.), 1978.

Syed Qutb, *Fi Zilal al-Qur'an* [In the Shade of Qur'an], Vol. 2, Cairo, 1980.

Tirmidi, *Sahih, Abwab ar-Rada.*

Arabi-Malayalam Folk Songs Consulted

Kathupattukal, Letter Songs.
Kurathipattu, Soothsayer Song - Imaginary song in conversational, style between Angel Gabrael and Fathima, the daughter of the Prophet.
Pakshipattu, Bird Song - Based on Islamic Myths.
Sabeena pattukal, On Mystics and Prophets.
Mala Pattukal, Mainly on Women characters in Islamic History.
Kissa Pattukal, Based on Stories from Islamic History.
Pata Pattukal, War Songs.

Secondary Sources

Abu Shiqa, *Tahir al mara'a fi asr al-risalah,* Kuwait, 1990.
Abul A'la Maududi, *The Islamic Way of Life,* Markazi Publishers, New Delhi, 2002.
Al-Albani, Nasir-ad Din, *Jilbab al-mar'a l-muslima,* [The Muslim Women's Dress], Dar IbnHazm, Amman, 1994 edn.
Ahmed Kharat, *The Status of Women in Islam,* Egypt, 1975.
Akbar S. Ahmed, *Islam Under Siege,* Blackwell, U.K. 2003.
_______ *Discovering Islam, Making Sense of Mulsim Historyand Society,* Routledge, London, 2003.
Albert Hourani, *A History of the Arab Peoples,* Faber and Faber, London, 2002.
Amartya Sen, *The Argumentative Indian,* Penguin, London, 2006.
_______ *Development As Freedom*, Oxford University Press, New Delhi, 1999.
Amina Wadud, *Inside the Gender Jihad, Women's Reform in Islam.* Oxford, 2006.
Anis Ahmed, *Women and Social Justice in Islam*, Naushaba, New Delhi, 1994.
Anis Kidwai, *Azad ki Chaon Mein,* [In the shadow of Freedom] National Book Trust, Delhi, 1990.
Alya Baffa'un, *Social Science Research and women in the Arab World,* Paris, 1984.
Alvin J. Schmidt, *Veiled and Silenced: How Culture Shaped Sexist Theology,* Mercer University Press, Macon, 1989.
Ann Elizebeth Mayer, *Islam and Human Rights: Tradition and Politics,* Westview Press, London, 1991.
Anne Sofie Roald, *Women in Islam—The Western Experience,* Routledge, London, 2002.
Archana Chaturvedi (ed.), *Muslim Women and Development,* Commonwealth, New Delhi, 2004.
Asghar Ali Engineer, *Lifting the Veil,* Sangam Books, Hyderabad, 1996.
Ayan Hirsi Ali, *The Caged Virgin - A Muslim Woman's Cry for Reason,* The Free Press, U.K., 2006.
Aziza Al-Hibri, *Women and Islam,* Oxford, 1982.
Benazir Bhutto, *Reconciliation, Islam, Democracy and the West,* Pocket Books, London, 2008.
Beniprasad, *History of Jahangir,* Allahabad, 1940.
Bernard Lewis, *The Emergence of Modern Turkey,* Oxford, London, 1961.

Bina Agarwal, *A Field of One's Own, Gender and Land Rights in South Asia*, Cambridge University Press, New Delhi, 1996.

Bipan Chandra, Mridula Mukherjee, *India After Independence: 1947-2000,* Penguin, Aditya Mukherjee, New Delhi.

Charles Kurzman (ed)., *Liberal Islam,* Oxford University Press, 1998.

S.K. Datta and Rajeev Sharma, *Pakistan from Jinnah to Jehad,* New Delhi, 2002.

A.R. Desai, *Social Background of Indian Nationalism,* Bombay, 1959.

J.' Devika (ed.), *Herself, Gender and Early Writings of Malayalee Women*, Stree, Kolkata, 2007.

Edward Said, *Culture and Imperialism,* Vintage Books, London, 1994.

_______, *Orientalism,* Vintage Books, (Reprint), 2003.

Elizabeth Wilson,, *Women and the Welfare State*, Travistock Publications, London, 1977.

Fathima Ghafoor, *Ever in Memory,* (Mal.), Calicut, 1988.

Fathima Mernissi, *Beyond the Veil,* Schenkman, New York, 1975.

_______ *The Veil and the Male Elite, A Feminist Interpretation of Women's Rights in Islam,* Basic Book, New York, 1991.

Friedman, *Cultural Idenitty and Global Process,* Sage, London, 1994.

Frederick Engels, *The Origin of the Family; Private property and the state,* Eleanor Leacock (ed.) New York, 1972.

Fred Hallidry and *State and Ideology in the Middle East and Pakistan,* Hamza Alavi (eds.) New York, 1988.

Farah Azari (ed.), *Women in Iran: The Conflict with Fundamentalist Islam,* London, 1983.

Fazl-ur-Rahman, *Islam and Modernity: Transformation of an Intellectual Tradition,* Chicago University Press, 1982.

_______, *Major Themes of the Quran,* Minneapolis, Bibliotheca Islamica, 1980.

Geraldine Terry, *Women's Rights,* Pluto Press, London, 2007.

Gerda Lerner, T*he Creation of Patriarchy,* Oxford University Press, New York, 1986.

Haideh Moghissi, *Populism and Feminism in Iran: Women's Struggle in a Male-Dominated Revolutionary Movement,* Mac Millan, London, 1994.

Haleh Afghar (ed.), *Iran: A Revolution in Turmoil*, London, 1985.

Y.Y. Haddad and, *Islam, Gender and Social change,* Oxford John L. Espasito (ed.) University Press, 1988,

John, L. Esposito, *The Oxford Dictionary of Islam,* London, 2004,

_______, *What Everyone Needs to Know About Islam,* Oxford University Press, New York, 2002.

John, L. Esposito and Dalia Mogahed, *Who Speaks for Islam?* Gallup Press, New York, 2007.

Julia Leslie (ed.), *Roles and Rituals of Hindu Women*, Motilal Banarasi Das, Delhi, 1992.

M.N. Karasseri, *A Mercy Petition for Muslim Women* (Mal.), D.C. Books, Kottayam, 2008.

Kim Knott, *Identity Issues and World Religions,* Australian Association for the study of Religions, 1986, pp. 169-171.

C.K. Kareem (ed.), *Kerala Muslim Directory,* Cochin, 1991.

Kamalipour, Y, *The U.S. Media and the Middle East: Image and Perception,* Connecticut, Prayger Publishers, 1995.

V.K. Kuttu, *Tellicherry—A Journey to its Muslim History,* (Mal), Tellicherry, 2010.

Leila Ahmed, *Women and Gender in Islam*, Yale University Press, NewHaven and London, 1992.

Mahnaz Afkhami (ed.), *Faith and Freedom, Women's Human Rights in the Muslim World,* IB Tauris, London, 2000.

Mahnaz Afkhami and Erika Friedl (ed), *In the Eye of the Storm: Women in Post Revolutionary Iran,* London 1994.

Maulana Wahiduddin Khan *Women,* Good Word Books, New Delhi, 2002.

Muhammed Saqi Mustaid Khan, *Ma'assir-i-Alamgiri,* (Eng. Trans.) J.N. Sarkar, 1958.

Mushirul Hasan (ed.), *India's Partition: Process, Strategy and Mobilization*, Oxford University Press, Delhi, 1993.

_______, *Legacy of a Divided Nation: India's Muslims Since Independance,* Oxford University Press, Delhi, 1997.

_______, *Will Secular India Survive?*(ed.), Imprint One, Delhi, 2004.

Marmaduke Pickthall, *Cultural side of Islam* (Mal. Trans.) Hasan, K., Minar Publications, Trivandrum, 1972.

Marina Lazreg, *Questioning the Veil, Open Letters to Muslim Women,* Princeton University Press, New York, 1996.

_______, *The Eloquence of Silence: Algerian Women in Question,* Routeledge, New York, 1994.

N.P. Mohammed, *Maram* (The Tree), D.C. Books, Kottayam, 2007.

Maria Mies, *Women: The Last Colony,* Kali for Women, New Delhi, 1988.

K.T. Muhammed, *This is Earth*, (Mal.), Calicut, 1959.

K.K. Muhammed, Abdul Karim (Compl.), *Complete Works of Makthi Thangal* (Mal.), Kerala Islamic Mission, Tirur, 1981.

Mazharuddin Siddiqi, *Women in Islam* Adam Publishers, New Delhi, 2004.

E. Moidu Maulavi, *Autobiography,*(Mal.), National Book Stall, Kottayam, 1981.

Mai Yamani, *Feminism and Islam,* Ithaca Press, London, 1996.

Nawal El Saadavi, *The Hidden Face f Eve, Women in the Arab World,* Zed Books, London, 2007.

Nikki, R. Keddie (ed.) *Saints and Sufis: Muslim Religious Institutions Since 1500,* Berkeley, 1972.

Nahid Toubia (ed.), *Women of the Arab World: The Coming Challenge,* Zed, London, 1988.

K.N. Panikkar, *Against Lord and State*, Oxford University Press, 1989.

Percival Spear, *A History of India,* Vol. II, Penguin, 1970.

Promilla Kapur, *Empowering the Indian Woman*, Publication Division, New Delhi, 2001.

Partha Chattergee, *The Nation and its Fragments: Colonial and Post Colonial Histories,* Princeton University Press, 1993.

Ritu Menon and Kamla Bhasin, *Borders and Boundaries, Women in India's Partition,* Kali for Women, New Delhi, 2000.

Robertson Smith, *Kinship and Marriage in Early Arabia,* Boston, 1903.

Ruqaiyya Waris Maqsood, *Islam,* Hodder Education, London, 2006.

Roland E. Miller, *Mappila Muslims of Kerala*, Orient Longman, Madras, 1992.

Samuel P. Huntington, *Clash of Civilizations and the Remaking World Order*, Simon & Schuster, New York, 1996.

Shamshad Husain, *Between Minority and Gender Status* (Mal.), Language Institute, Trivandrum, 2009.

Shaikh Mohammed Ghazali, *Sunna Between Fiqh and Hadith,* Cairo, 1990.

Sheikh Ghita, *History and Principles of Shiism,* 1985.

Sheikh Mohammed Abdullah, *Mushahadat Va Ta'asurat,* Aligarh, 1969.

Shivanath Shastri, *History of the Brahma Samaj,* Vol. I.

Tahir Mahmood, *Family Law Reform in the Muslim World* (Mal. Trans.), Langugage Institute, Trivandrum, 1978.

______, *Personal Law in Crisis,* Delhi, 1986.

Vanita Ruth, *Love's Rite: Same-Sex Marriage in India and the West,* 2005.

Vakkom Abdul Khader Maulavi *Thoughtful Movements in Islam,* (Mal.), Bharatha Chandrika Publishing House, Perumbavoor, 1954.

Vincent Smith, *Akbar, the Great Mughal*, Delhi, 1958 (edn.)

William Dalrymple, *The Last Mughal—The Fall of a Dynasty,* Bloomsburg, London, 2007.

Zakia, A. Siddiqui and *Muslim Women, Problems and Prospects,* MD Anwar Jahan Zuberi (ed.) Publications, New Delhi, 1993.

Ziauddin Sardar, *What Do Muslims Believe?*, Granta Books, London, 2006.

______, *Desperately Seeking Paradise: Journeys of a Sceptical Muslim*. Granta Books, London, 2004.

Zoya Hasan and Ritu Menon, *Educating Muslim Girls—A Comparison of Five Indian Cities,* Women Unlimited, New Delhi, 2005.

Zoya Hasan and Ritu Menon *Unequal Citizens—A Study of Muslim Women in India,* Oxford University Press, New Delhi, 2006.

Index